The Reluctant Cook

Angela Coles

Whittet/Windward

First published 1980

Text ©1980 by Angela Coles
Illustrations ©1980 by Whittet Books Ltd

Whittet Books Ltd, The Oil Mills, Weybridge, Surrey

Design by Richard Adams

Illustrations by Robert McAulay

British Library Cataloguing in Publication Data

Coles, Angela
    The reluctant cook.
    1. Cookery
    I. Title
    641.5   TX717

    ISBN 0-905483-18-9

Acknowledgements

I would like to thank the following people for their
help, support, inspiration and recipes: Anna Gruetzner,
David Robson, Marie Stone, Gina and Jeremy Newson,
Janet Wagstaff, Sue Coles, Anita and Jo Falinski,
Patti Seidman, Sally Bradberry, Craig and Ann Sams,
Jonathon Green, Susie Ford, Lynn Allison,
Lindsay Bareham, Sarah Ball, Lis Leigh, David Winter,
Patricia Ault, Eileen Gorman, Carole Jameson,
Ro Fitzgerald, Ron Sutherland, Angela Phillips,
Scarlett MacGwire, Francis Fuchs and my mother.

Printed and bound in Great Britain
at The Pitman Press, Bath

Measures

It's a good idea to buy a set of measuring spoons.

1 level tablespoon of —

pearl barley	=	1 oz.	(25 g.)
cornflour	=	¼ oz.	(8 g.)
fat	=	½ oz.	(15 g.)
flour	=	¼ oz.	(8 g.)
chopped nuts	=	¾ oz.	(20 g.)
sugar	=	½ oz.	(15 g.)

Weights

The metric conversions given throughout the book are not exact equivalents, but follow these scales:

½ oz.	=	15 g.
1 oz.	=	25 g.
2 oz.	=	55 g.
3 oz.	=	85 g.
4 oz.	=	115 g.
5 oz.	=	140 g.
6 oz.	=	170 g.
7 oz.	=	200 g.
8 oz.	=	225 g.
10 oz.	=	285 g.
14 oz.	=	400 g.
1 lb.	=	450 g.
2 lb.	=	1 kilo
¼ pint	=	145 ml.
½ pint	=	290 ml.
¾ pint	=	430 ml.
1 pint	=	575 ml.
1½ pints	=	1 litre

Abbreviations

g.	=	gram
ml.	=	millilitre
oz.	=	ounce
lb.	=	pound
tsp.	=	teaspoonful
tbs.	=	tablespoonful

Equipment

Not all of these are essential, but they will make your life a lot easier:

fish slice
perforated spoon
palette knife
rubber spatula
swivel-bladed potato-peeler
small wooden spoon
large wooden spoon
tin opener
grater
lemon squeezer
small vegetable knife (stainless steel or carbon steel)
large chopping knife (stainless steel or carbon steel)
kitchen scissors
pastry brush
baster
substantial chopping board
rolling pin
corkscrew
peppermill
balloon whisk
measuring jug
measuring spoons
wire mesh strainer
colander
shallow ovenproof dish
shallow baking tray
roasting tin
small and large ceramic/cast-iron casserole
straight sided porcelain soufflé dish
1½ pint pie dish
meat thermometer
ladle
kebab skewers
graduated mixing bowls
garlic crusher
chip pan
graduated saucepans
small heavy bottomed frying pan
large heavy bottomed frying pan — preferably with lid
poacher
quiche tin with removable bottom
Mouli legumes food mill
electric blender
storage jars
kitchen towels

Chapter 1

Choosing Ingredients

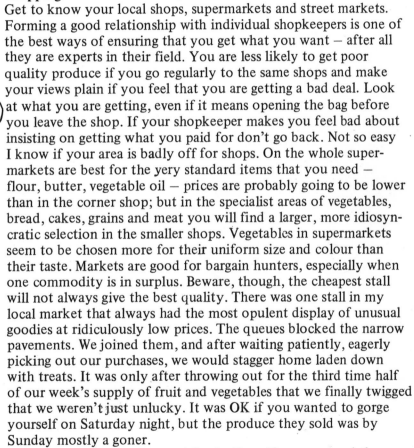

Shopping

Get to know your local shops, supermarkets and street markets. Forming a good relationship with individual shopkeepers is one of the best ways of ensuring that you get what you want — after all they are experts in their field. You are less likely to get poor quality produce if you go regularly to the same shops and make your views plain if you feel that you are getting a bad deal. Look at what you are getting, even if it means opening the bag before you leave the shop. If your shopkeeper makes you feel bad about insisting on getting what you paid for don't go back. Not so easy I know if your area is badly off for shops. On the whole supermarkets are best for the very standard items that you need — flour, butter, vegetable oil — prices are probably going to be lower than in the corner shop; but in the specialist areas of vegetables, bread, cakes, grains and meat you will find a larger, more idiosyncratic selection in the smaller shops. Vegetables in supermarkets seem to be chosen more for their uniform size and colour than their taste. Markets are good for bargain hunters, especially when one commodity is in surplus. Beware, though, the cheapest stall will not always give the best quality. There was one stall in my local market that always had the most opulent display of unusual goodies at ridiculously low prices. The queues blocked the narrow pavements. We joined them, and after waiting patiently, eagerly picking out our purchases, we would stagger home laden down with treats. It was only after throwing out for the third time half of our week's supply of fruit and vegetables that we finally twigged that we weren't just unlucky. It was OK if you wanted to gorge yourself on Saturday night, but the produce they sold was by Sunday mostly a goner.

Avoid refined or processed foods. Even if you can read the small print on the side of the packet, it doesn't really reassure you. What are those mysterious 'preservatives', 'colourings' and 'flavourings', and what are they doing to you? Use wholemeal bread, pasta and brown rice wherever you can. They are more nutritious and taste better than their refined relations. In this book, salt and pepper means 'sea' or 'crystal' salt and freshly ground black pepper.

You may prefer to substitute 'polyunsaturated fats' — e.g. soya oil, safflower oil and vegetable oils — for expensive and cholesterol-high olive oil and butter.

Eggs

An egg that is not bad is not necessarily a fresh egg. Eggshells are virtually airtight containers and, providing they are not damaged, the egg inside will stay palatable long after it has parted from its parent. Egg cartons are labelled with a week number, and your grocer will tell you which week you are in. Don't buy a carton without first examining the contents for cracks and breakages. You can tell an unfresh egg, when cooked, by a little hollow in the white when it is shelled. The white slowly evaporates as the egg ages. There is nothing wrong with it, you'd be overpowered by an unmistakable stench if there were. Free-range eggs are more expensive than battery ones but their flavour is better and some people heartily dislike the idea of eating the product of caged, anxious birds.

The colour of an eggshell is purely cosmetic; whether brown or white it bears no relation to either the flavour or nutritional value.

Meat

A good butcher is the best ally that you can have when choosing meat. Tell him what you intend to do with the meat that you buy, the sort of cooking time the recipe recommends and what you want to pay. S/he may have a suggestion for a different cut or type of meat from the one that you originally intended to buy, depending on what is in stock and what the quality is like. There is no point in asking your butcher if the meat you are buying is tender. He is hardly likely to say, 'No, I'm sorry, it's really tough.' Anyway, it's not an appropriate question unless you are buying expensive cuts of meat.

Choose a butcher where there is a wide selection of expensive and cheap cuts. The cheaper cuts tend to be just as good value for money but need more skill in cooking. You can ask the butcher to cut the meat as you wish to use it; with more complicated operations like boning a breast of lamb it's best to choose a quiet time or give a little notice, but most butchers will cut stewing meat into cubes or grind pork or beef for you on the spot.

Choose meat that looks bright and moist; it should not appear dry, dark and dull. The cheaper cuts in some butchers are often displayed in still frozen chunks; unless you know your butcher well I would be inclined to avoid these pieces. The grainy, frosty appearance of frozen meat tends to disguise quite how much fat is running through the meat. The amount of fat in between the

long bunches of muscle in meat is one of the elements that deter-
mines the price. Fatty, gristly meat is often unappetizing and tough
if insufficiently cooked, but fat does serve a very valuable purpose
in some methods of cooking. For instance you would not dream
of cutting the fat off a pork joint or a lamb chop, because the
fat will help to moisten the meat as it is cooking and, in the case
of pork, the crackling is a treat in itself. But on the other hand
if you don't cut away the fat surrounding stewing meat you will
have rubbery, tasteless, greying blobs floating amongst the meat
and vegetables. One of the most disturbing things about meat is
the fine layers of fat running invisibly between the lean cords of
muscle. Animal foods — and particularly animal fats — have been
pinpointed as one of the major causes of ill health in western
societies; there are good indications that we should eat less meat
rather than treating it as the most important element in our
diet, and that we should choose the meat of wild, hardy, better
exercised wild animals like venison, duck, rabbit and fish too.

The tastiest and the toughest meat comes from the muscles
like the leg muscles that do the most work.

Frozen poultry

A great deal of poultry has been frozen or is still frozen when you
buy it. Ask the butcher if it has been frozen because it is absolutely
essential that it should be completely defrosted when it goes in
the oven. The bacteria like salmonella which cause food poisoning
can be woken up during cooking and are not killed until the meat
is heated to 190°F. Before serving chicken, always pierce with a
knife point through to the bone to be sure that the flesh furthest
away from the heat source is not pink or bloody. Continue cooking
if it is.

Fish

Sadly it is not always possible to buy fish straight from the sea or
stream and fish is inedible if it is not fresh. There are good simple
rules for what to look for when choosing fish.
(i)   Eyes: the eyes on fresh fish are bright and plump. If eyes are
      sunken or opaque they should be avoided.
(ii) Fresh fish don't smell fishy! They smell faintly of the sea, like
      a walk along the beach.
(iii) Fresh fish have red gills.
(iv) Stale fish look very limp with dull dry or slimy yellow scales.
(v)   Fresh fish bounce back when you prod them, stale fish will
      keep the mark of your finger. Yuc. And you will probably
      carry the pong around with you all day.

Mussels
(i)   Don't gather them around the sea shore unless you know the

area very very well. In many places the sewage effluent in the water makes them dangerous to eat.

(ii)   Eat the day that you buy them — this applies to all live shell-fish.

(iii) Discard any that are cracked or broken.

(iv)   Discard any that do not close up when you give them a sharp tap.

Fishmongers are an invaluable source of recipes for fish. They will also clean, gut and fillet fish and remove heads if you ask them.

Fruit

There are some fruits where it is a matter of personal taste whether you buy them hard or soft but there are some general rules.

(i)   Don't buy fruit that is bruised. The best side is usually turned in an appetizing display towards the public while the bruises are hidden at the back. Examine the contents of the bag.

(ii)   Do not buy apples and pears that have dull wrinkled skin. Although with apples if they are very cheap and small it is sometimes worth taking the risk — they can be sweet.

(iii) Citrus fruit with loose skin that gives to the fingers may conceal shrunken and dry fruit.

(iv)   Lemons are tricky. You can sometimes choose the one that looks large, fat and plump only to find that a thick layer of white pith is surrounding a minute ball of pale, juiceless flesh. Difficult to spot these but go instead for the smaller, rounder, smoother skinned variety. After a while you learn to spot them; somehow the skin just looks thinner.

(v)   Soft fruit: should look plump, juicy and shiny, with no dark, soft patches. Be careful about buying fruit in punnets; try and look underneath the top layer since it sometimes conceals mouldy and squashed fruit.

(vi)   Melons should give around the ends when you press them gently with your thumbs. They also have a faint fragrance and the seeds will occasionally rattle when you shake them.

(vii) Pineapples are ready to be eaten when the leaves at the top come off easily when pulled.

Dried fruit is a good standby for any store cupboard. Eat it as it is — although not too much at a time, it does tend to expand in your stomach — or soak it for fruit puddings, chop it into salads, skewer it with meat on kebabs. You may find that it is slightly cheaper to buy loose in health-food shops rather than in packets.

Vegetables

(i)   Green vegetables should be bright and crisp with no signs of limpness; watch out for brown and yellow leaves.

(ii)   Don't buy potatoes with green patches on the skin — they have been left exposed to light for too long. Potatoes should be stored in the dark or in a paper, not polythene, bag.

(iii) Carrots are best for flavour when they are relatively small, thin and sharply tapering. The fatter, larger varieties seem to be more watery and blander in flavour (this is true of a lot of vegetables).

(iv) Leeks should be fat and clean looking. It is sometimes better to buy those that have already been trimmed than those with an abundance of coarse green leaves that may not be tender enough to use even in soups or stews.

(v) Check the Mediterranean vegetables — peppers, aubergines, courgettes — for wrinkled skin or soft spots.

(vi) Large, flat, field-type mushrooms tend to have a stronger flavour than the small white button ones. They're cheaper too.

The best, cheapest vegetables and fruit are those bought in season.

Herbs, seasonings and spices

Herbs always have most flavour when used fresh, but unless you have a good greengrocer your choice is liable to be limited to parsley and sometimes not even that. I recently spent a Saturday morning in a street market in a small Hampshire town with at least twenty vegetable stalls and couldn't find a single sprig of parsley except for the green plastic stuff in the fishmonger's window. If you can grow them in a window box or corner of the garden, do. But if you can't, the dried variety will have to do. (But avoid dried parsley, which usually has no flavour and is not worth buying). You can really get ripped off buying dried herbs. The amount that you get for the price that you pay for those tiny and ornate glass jars is utterly daft: you are buying the container. The herbs will probably amount to less than a couple of pence worth. The more unusual ones will have been hanging around the shop for some time and will probably have lost their flavour anyway. Buy herbs loose in health-food shops and store them in jam-jars in the fridge. Given the opportunity, buy fresh herbs in bunches and dry them hanging up in the kitchen. Parsley, thyme, coriander and sage can all be kept fresh for a couple of weeks in an airtight jar in the fridge. Don't wash them before you put them in the jar.

If you are lucky enough to live in an area with a Chinese or Indian grocer you should be able to buy spices like mustard seed, black pepper, fennel seed, cumin seed, caraway seed, cardamom and star anise in 1oz. (25g.) or 2oz. (55g.) bags or even loose. As with herbs, they will be far less expensive than those ubiquitous little jars. Keep a stock of dried red chillis — fresh green ones are sometimes on sale in the greengrocers — paprika (two sorts, with and without chilli added), dry English mustard and maybe a bottle of

Worcestershire sauce. Large and very cheap bottles of soy sauce are a good buy in Chinese supermarkets. Look through the ingredients on the label and choose one without sugar.

Spices keep for a long time, so if you see an unusual one buy it and keep to use later.

Oil

You will need two main sorts of oil in the kitchen — a good quality salad oil and a fairly plain cooking oil. You can, of course, use the one variety for both purposes. In Italian shops there is a light flavourful oil called 'Olivette' which is a mixture of olive oil and vegetable oil which can be used for most things. Olive oil, although it is expensive, is one of the great delights of the kitchen. Flavours differ according to the country of origin and the pressing. Some of the strongly flavoured dark-green olive oils can only be bought in their countries of origin — Spain, Italy and Greece. There they can be very cheap; I find I bring bottles of the stuff back for presents and then develop a disinclination to give them away. Without holidays to keep you supplied, buy olive oil in gallon cans from Italian delicatessens; it will be much more economical than buying small bottles. Olive oil is not used in Chinese cooking, the flavour is too strong. Find out which vegetable cooking oil you prefer by buying small bottles; I find that many of the super-market cheap oils have an unpleasantly obtrusive flavour. Try corn oil, safflower oil, sunflower oil, sesame oil or soya oil. For special salads there is the delicate and expensive walnut oil.

Vinegars

Again, you will need two sorts of vinegar — a dark malt vinegar and a finer quality salad vinegar. Salad vinegars can be made from red or white wine, or cider; and can be flavoured with herbs or chilli. Non-brewed condiment — or chip-shop vinegar — is not vinegar.

Grains

It is always better for your health, and once you get used to them for flavour too, to eat whole unrefined grains. The grains most of us eat regularly are in bread, rice and pasta; although I love crispy white bread I regard it more as a treat than a staple. There are eight main types of grain — whole rice, barley, rye, oats, wheat, buckwheat or kasha, millet, maize and popcorn. Combined with a pulse — beans, peas and lentils — they provide an excellent source of protein. Usually cheaper in bulk in health-food stores.

Pulses

The pulses are the dozens of delicious types of peas, beans and lentils. They can be fresh or dried. The dried varieties keep for quite a long time, but cooking time increases with age. After you've had them in your cupboard for about six months you may find they are almost impossible to cook really soft.

Some nutritionists advise soaking beans for at least 48 hours and discarding the cooking water.

Sugar
'Pure, white and deadly'. Sugar does you absolutely no good at all. It can and does do a lot of harm. Apart from making you fat and rotting your teeth, it has such an overwhelming flavour that it ruins your palate too. But I do get the occasional craving for it, like all other wicked, forbidden things so there are recipes in the book that include sugar; if you wish, substitute raw brown sugar or honey. There isn't a great deal of difference in their effect, but they do taste better.

Note
Use plain flour for all recipes.

Unless stated otherwise, the recipes are for 4 people; if they're very abstemious, perhaps 6.

Chapter 2

Quick, Easy Recipes

As you get to love and enjoy cooking you will gradually acquire a huge repertoire of skills; almost by instinct you will use the various methods of cooking and preparing food; you will get a practised eye for judging quality and quantity and an instinct for what certain noises and smells mean. But there are plenty of straightforward meals that you can make with absolutely no expertise or experience. Elaborate preparation doesn't necessarily mean that food tastes better.

In this section all you have to do is take a bit of this and that, stick them together and the dish is ready. Most of the operations are common sense; the only two terms of any complexity are 'melting' and 'sautéing'. When you 'melt' vegetables in oil or butter, you do not literally reduce them to a liquid. All you do is: heat the oil or butter in a frying pan until a small piece of whatever you are going to cook sizzles pleasantly, not fiercely, when dropped in to it. Don't wait until the butter is going brown, that's too late. Throw in the vegetables and stir them until they acquire a floppy, translucent quality. Master this technique and a whole range of dishes opens up to you.

Sautéing literally means to make something 'jump' in hot oil or butter in order to soften it before adding liquid. In many ways it is very like 'melting' but sautéing is a stage in a process; the idea is that you are softening the food before adding the liquid. The oil can get to a higher temperature than the liquid (which would evaporate) and it will therefore caramelize the sugars in the vegetables. This gives a richer, sweeter flavour to the dish. Heat a mixture of oil and butter as before and, when they sizzle, add the vegetables and keep turning. Don't go and make a long telephone call and leave something to sauté; when you come back it will be burned.

The other thing you should understand is 'simmering': it means to cook in liquid just below boiling point. Boiling liquid bubbles actively; simmering liquid gives an occasioanl bubble, but mostly just quakes.

SALADS

It's a very good idea to eat raw vegetables at least once a day. Cooking, however carefully, diminishes the food value of vegetables. Vitamin C is particularly vulnerable to heat. So a salad once a day is obviously the easiest, most appetising way to do this. Of course salads aren't just made up of the especially grown salad greens — make them up from what you have in the kitchen. Don't include too many different ingredients though or you will create an undistinguished mush where one flavour will be swamped by another. Use one piquant element, onions or a chopped fresh herb or garlic, a teaspoon of strong mustard or a little chopped fresh chilli in the dressing. Most salad vegetables are comparatively easy to prepare. There are a few fancy ways of cutting radishes and tomatoes but they do very little either for the taste or the appearance of the food. The appearance of a salad depends upon the quality and freshness of the produce you use and this is all to do with discriminating buying. Limp lettuce and yellowing watercress will never inspire anyone to enjoy eating them; and don't use up all the leftover vegetables in the bottom of the fridge.

You may want to serve two or three different salads together — maybe including meat or fish — as a complete meal.

Dressings

Vinaigrette
Mix together 4 tablespoons of oil, 2 tablespoons of vinegar, a generous pinch of sea salt, freshly ground black pepper, a small pinch of brown sugar and a generous teaspoon of dry English mustard or whole grain French mustard. Beat with a fork, whisk or shake in a screw top jar, any extra can be stored in the fridge. Don't include chopped garlic or herbs if you are going to store it — they will go soggy and unpleasant. For salads, fresh herbs are almost obligatory, since dried herbs just get stuck in your teeth; chop them directly into the salad.

Choose a wine or cider vinegar or one of the branded makes that include a sprig of herbs in the bottle. Tarragon is good and chilli is delicious for a spicy salad. The flavour of malt vinegar is too harsh. Lemon juice can be substituted for vinegar for a lighter dressing. Try the different varieties of olive oil. Some have very strong almost crude flavours and are not suitable for more delicate salads, some are almost bland. Buying a gallon from an Italian or Spanish delicatessen will work out cheaper. Safflower, soya and sunflower oils are good too and walnut oil is delectable. Sesame oil has a pleasant aroma and taste of sesame seeds. Chopped herbs — mint, pasrley, chives, thyme, sage, fennel and celery leaves — and crushed garlic, chopped olives and capers are all possible additions.

A yogurt or single-cream dressing suits some salads. Thin the cream with a little milk. Home-made mayonnaise is in Chapter 3,

but if you aren't yet up to that, commercial brands are very good. Experiment with buying the smaller size jars to find out which one you prefer.
prefer.

You can add chopped herbs — mint, sage, parsley, chives — chopped capers, olives, garlic, crumbled hard-boiled egg, lemon juice or grated lemon peel for more flavour.

Fruit
Diced or sliced fresh fruit can be used in small quantities in salad. Try oranges, pears, apples, fresh pineapple, small seedless grapes apricots and dried fruit. The juice of citrus fruits — oranges, lemons, limes and grapefruit — can be substituted for vinegar in vinaigrette dressings or used alone flavoured with herbs.

Nuts
Add whole or halved hazels, almonds, walnuts, cashews or peanuts to salads or crush them with garlic in a pestle and morter and add to a vinaigrette. If you roast the nuts under the grill till they're brown they taste better.

Some of these salads are whole meals in themselves; others will make a meal served with cold meat, fish, cheese or hard-boiled eggs, crusty bread or potatoes baked in their jackets. One word about lettuce: only wash it if it needs it, the heart rarely does. Pat it dry immediately in a tea-towel or your dressing will get watered down. Don't cut lettuce, tear it into pieces.

Avocado salad

Peel and slice 1 or 2 medium-sized avocados and toss with a garlicy vinaigrette dressing and lettuce, chopped spring onion, watercress and a stick of chopped celery. If you are not going to serve avocado salads immediately squeeze a little lemon on to the flesh or it will turn brown.

Variations
Add peeled shrimps or prawns/quartered hard-boiled eggs/cubes of strong Cheddar cheese/mint leaves.

Guacamole

Mash the flesh of three ripe avocados with a small pot of plain yogurt and the juice of half a lemon (or put them all in a blender). Add 3 or 4 small chopped tomatoes, a small grated Spanish onion, 1 or 2 chopped cloves of garlic, salt, freshly ground black pepper and 2 or 3 dashes of Tabasco to taste. Serve with hot crusty bread or Greek pitta bread or cos lettuce leaves.

BEAN SALADS

Green bean salads

Choose only beans that are in absolutely perfect condition. You can use any kind of green bean. French ('bobby') beans and runner beans should be a pale apple green colour with no shrivelled or wrinkled bits or dark green patches. Break off the ends of bobby beans and either snap in two or keep whole. With runner beans skim the edges with a sharp knife or potato peeler to remove the strings. Cut in diagonal strips about ½" wide. Steam or boil the beans in enough water to cover them by about 1". Salt. Drain off the water when they are cooked but still quite firm.

Toss in a garlicky vinaigrette dressing with either:

sliced tomato and sweet Spanish onion
anchovies, parsley and onions
lightly cooked mangetout peas
sliced hard-boiled egg

DRIED BEAN SALADS

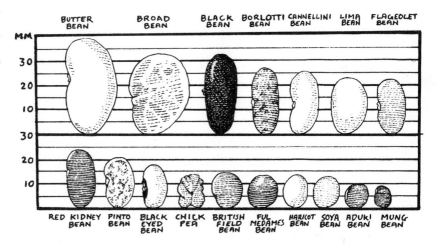

There are dozens of different varieties of dried bean. They are very simple to cook, although if you are going to soak them the night before (which is a good idea) this obviously requires a little forethought. There are excellent pre-cooked canned varieties which are a terrific standby for hot and cold dishes. Together with a whole cereal like barley, wheat or brown rice they are a rich and healthy source of protein.

Cooking dried beans
Wash thoroughly in cold running water. Remove all broken or discoloured beans and make sure there are no stones lurking amongst them. Soak in plenty of cold water. Throw out any beans that do not sink to the bottom of the pan. Soaking overnight is ideal but a couple of hours is sufficient. Cook the beans in the water in which they were soaked or you will lose valuable nutrients. Bring the pan to the boil and then turn down to a gently

bubbling simmer. Do *not* add any salt to the cooking water or the beans will never soften. A tiny pinch of a very smelly Indian condiment called *hing* (asafoetida) will help to alleviate some of the more dire gastric reverberations of eating beans, but the most effective safeguard is proper slow cooking. Most dried beans need around 2 hours at the least. When cooked they should be soft and mushy all the way through. The only fast way to cook dried beans is in a pressure cooker. If you want to use the rich, delicious cooking liquid, as in Ful Medames, boil the beans furiously for the last 10 to 20 minutes to reduce the amount. Stir occasionally or the bottom of the pan will catch. Substitute stock for water for more flavour. Quantities given are for dried beans, but do remember to cook them. Little red aduki beans do not need soaking and take only 45 minutes to cook.

Tuna, onion & kidney bean salad

Mix together flaked tuna fish, 1 tin or 6oz. (170g.) kidney beans (these are the red ones) or white haricot beans (the white ones which, in tomato sauce, come in tins as 'baked beans') and half a finely sliced Spanish onion. Toss in a garlicky vinaigrette with chopped parsley. Try substituting cooked bacon or salami for tuna.

Bean & boiled egg salad

Beat together in a salad bowl the juice of half a lemon, 4 tablespoons of olive oil, a crushed clove of garlic, salt, pepper and a teaspoon of grainy mustard. Add 10 to 15 sliced black olives, 1 tin or 6oz. (170g.) of red kidney beans, borlotti (pink with brown spots) beans or aduki beans (little, round red ones) and 2 or 3 sliced hard-boiled eggs.

Ful Medames

You can buy *ful* or *foul* beans in some delicatessens or health-food shops but the tinned variety are very good.

1 tin or 6 oz. (170 g.) of ful beans (cooked)
½ sliced Spanish onion
2 chopped tomatoes
small pinch of ground cumin
a strong flavoured olive oil
salt, pepper and chopped garlic to taste
5 - 6 tbs. juice from cooked beans

Combine all the ingredients together. Serve with quarters of lemon, hard-boiled eggs and pitta bread.

Chick pea salad

Steam ½ lb. (225 g.) of sliced courgettes until they are cooked but still firm. They should not taste at all bitter. Crush a clove of garlic; mix into a small pot of plain yogurt. Chop a handful of mint leaves. Mix all together with 1 tin of drained chick peas or 6 oz. (170 g.) of dried chick peas (cooked).

Houmous

Houmous is a classic Greek dish. It is made from ground chick peas, tahini and garlic. Tahini is a paste made of ground sesame seeds and oil. You can buy it ready-made in Greek shops and health-food stores. The quickest way to 'make' houmous is to buy one of the Greek tinned varieties and serve it with chopped garlic, a little olive oil, a slice of lemon and a sprinkle of paprika or cayenne. It's a different dish to freshly made houmous but OK. The second quickest way is to use tinned chick peas instead of cooking them yourself. But the real way to do it is easy.

10 oz. (285 g.) of chick peas
2 or 3 crushed cloves of garlic to taste
a jar of tahini
salt and pepper
olive oil

Soak the chick peas overnight. Cook for about 2/2½ hours at a gently bubbling boil until they are soft and buttery tasting. The longer you can allow for cooking the easier it will make the next stage — the mashing. The water will probably bubble up into a dirty scum a couple of times in the first hour. Skim it off with a spoon and throw it away. Mash the cooked chick peas or liquidize. You (and your blender) will find this easier if you add a little of the cooking water. Season with garlic, salt and freshly ground black pepper. It's a good idea to mash some of the chick peas to a fine cream and some much coarser — the texture is more satisfying. Blend in the tahini to your taste. Some people like as much as half the amount of chick peas, I prefer very little. Serve with a little olive oil poured over the top, a sprinkling of chopped parsley and paprika, olives, pickled green pepper or chillis and hot Greek bread.

Hot chick pea salad

Use the recipe for Pasta Alla Piquante (p. 39) and substitute chick peas for pasta. For a milder version omit the chillis and you will have a rich tomato sauce.

Jeremy's bean & barley salad

6 oz. (170 g.) red kidney beans
2 oz. (55 g.) pearl barley
half a small green pepper in thin slivers
1 clove of crushed garlic
olive oil, white wine vinegar
salt, freshly ground black pepper
raisins

The quickest way to make this salad is in a pressure cooker, but of course you can make it in a saucepan too. Soak the beans and barely overnight. Cook them together until they are beginning to break up. Allow to cool. Drain off the liquid — if there is only a little thick liquid left you can leave it in the salad. Add slice green pepper, 3 tablespoons of olive oil, 1 tablespoon of vinegar, salt, pepper, garlic and about 20 raisins. Let the salad stand for half an hour before serving. This can be served as a hot dish omitting the vinegar.

Chicory or endive salad

Slice the chicory across into 1″ (2.5cm.) slices. Toss in a salad bowl with some single cream and 1 tablespoon of olive oil and ground black pepper. A small pot of cream will coat 5 to 6 heads of chicory. One large head would be sufficient for two people for a side salad. Add sliced ham or cold roast beef and serve as a main course.

Celeriac salad

1 x 8 oz. (225 g.) celeriac root
1 tsp. grainy mustard
salt and pepper
squeeze of lemon
1 small clove of garlic

Wash celeriac and peel off knobbly skin with potato peeler. Slice into very fine matchsticks. Squeeze with lemon. Peel and chop garlic and mix into mayonnaise. Mix in the mustard and pour over the celeriac. Season and chill for half an hour before serving.

Celeriac & carrot salad

1 celeriac root
½ lb. (225 g.) carrots
juice of half a lemon
finely chopped parsley

Cut the carrots into matchsticks (see chopping vegetables p. 27). Peel the celeriac and cut also into matchsticks. Add lemon juice and parsley and serve.

CUCUMBER SALADS

The French way

I spent my adolescent summer holidays staying with a rather aristocratic French family on school exchange visits. They protested heartily that the delicious meals that their cook Marie produced were merely simple country fare. To me they were an endless source of astonished delight. One of my absolutely favourite starters was a cool juicy cucumber salad. I've tried over and over again to reproduce it and never quite succeeded but this is as near as I've come.

Peel a large fat cucumber and slice it fairly thinly. Put it in a large deep salad bowl with a generous amount of vinaigrette dressing made with grainy mustard and red wine vinegar. Chop chives or parsley over it and leave to stand in the fridge for half an hour before serving. Serve with crusty French bread and unsalted butter.

Dorrit Forti's recipe

Slice a cucumber paper thin with a potato peeler or a mandolin. Salt very heavily and leave to stand for a couple of hours. The salt will draw a lot of liquid out of the cucumber. Drain it off. Squeeze out the cucumber, and dress with a light vinaigrette made with a white wine vinegar and a few dill seeds.

The Indian way (*raita*)

This is a traditional Indian accompaniment to hot food; it will cool enraged palates far faster than drinking water. It is very refreshing with any hot food and equally good as a summer salad. Peel half a cucumber and cut into little chunks. Mix with a pot of plain yogurt with salt, freshly ground black pepper and a few cumin seeds. If you can buy fresh green coriander from an Indian or Arab greengrocers scatter a few chopped leaves on top before serving.

This salad can also be made with chunks of cold cooked potato or sliced onion.

OTHER SALADS

Chinese cabbage & chicken salad

1 small head of Chinese cabbage (which is a crisp, delicate vegetable like a lettuce but with large, stalky leaves)
4 - 6 oz. (115 - 170 g.) of chicken, in small chunks
4 spring onions sliced lengthways
a few cashew nuts (optional)

Slice the cabbage leaves across in fine strips. Toss in a salad bowl with the onions, chicken and nuts and dress with a vinaigrette containing a generous teaspoon of grainy mustard.

Cheese & pears

Layer slices of strong Cheddar cheese with slices of unpeeled firm pear. Squeeze a little lemon juice on the pears to stop them turning brown. Scatter with finely chopped mint leaves.

Fish & fennel salad

1 smoked mackerel/whiting/trout
sliced head of fennel
1 lemon
mayonnaise

Flake the fish with a fork into bite-size pieces. Slice the fennel lengthways into long thin strips. Dress with mayonnaise, the leaves of the fennel chopped finely and grated lemon rind. Serve with slices of lemon and brown bread and butter.

Jerusalem artichoke & watercress salad

½ lb. (225 g.) scrubbed scraped Jerusalem artichokes
bunch of cleaned washed watercress
1 lemon

Wash the artichokes thoroughly; you'll probably need to scrub them with a stiff vegetable brush. Cook them with a little salt in a pan of gently bubbling water. They take about 20 minutes. Allow to cool and slice. Toss in a salad bowl with the watercress and the juice of half a lemon, salt and pepper. The lemon will stop the artichokes turning brown.

Variations
Add half a small carton of sour cream and/or half a pint of peeled shrimps or prawns.

Greek salad

Eaten on a Greek island in the midday sun, this can be a meal in itself; in cold England you may have it as a side dish.

crispy lettuce leaves
sliced cucumber
quartered tomatoes
radishes
finely sliced white onion
cooked white beans or black-eyed peas (optional)
Greek feta cheese
olives

Make a bed of lettuce at the bottom of the salad bowl or plate. Pile the beans mixed with the onion in the centre and arrange the other vegetables around the beans. Scatter crumbled feta and olives over the salad and sprinkle with a small pinch of dried oregano. Serve with lemon wedges, oil, vinegar and pickled peppers. Try cold boiled potatoes with melted butter and parsley with it instead of Greek bread.

POTATO SALADS

Potato salads are best made with sweet new potatoes, but if you're a real potato freak almost any sort will do. The orangey-red skinned Cyprus ones are particularly good.

Potato & egg salad

Potatoes respond best to butter dressing; failing that, an unobtrusive amount of mayonnaise is OK. Scrub 1 lb. (450 g.) potatoes. Do not remove the skins. A lot of the Vitamin C and most of the flavour in a potato is in its skin. Put in a saucepan with lots of cold water and a good pinch of salt. Bring to the boil and leave to simmer until the potatoes give easily when prodded with a knife. Do not overcook or they will break up in the water. Drain. Keep the water as a basis for vegetable stock. While the potatoes are cooking hard boil 3 or 4 eggs. Slice the eggs and mix roughly into the chopped-up potato with at least 1 oz. (25 g.) of butter or 4 - 6 tbs. mayonnaise. Season with salt, pepper, dry English mustard (½ teaspoon) and either chopped chives or the green part of a spring onion.

Variations
Use chopped mint instead of chives/add cold, cooked sliced runner beans or broad beans and olive oil/add cooked bacon bits/ add peas and mint/tuna/anchovy.

TOMATO SALADS

(Should only be made with firm, crisp tomatoes)

Tita's tomato salad

Cut 1 lb. (450 g.) of large Italian or Spanish tomatoes in thick slices on to a flat serving dish. Dress with a generous amount of strongly flavoured Spanish, Greek or Italian olive oil and a sprinkling of coarse sea salt and crushed garlic. This is tomato salad at its most robust.

Tomato salad with onions & parsley

Cut 1 lb. (450 g.) of small, firm, sweet tomatoes into quarters. Mix in a salad bowl with finely sliced white onion, chopped parsley and a garlicky vinaigrette. Grind an extra twist of black pepper over the dish before serving.

Variations
Use fresh basil instead of parsley/cleaned raw spinach/red kidney beans and mint.

Egg, tomato & mozzarella salad

Cut rings of tomato, mozzarella and hard-boiled egg and lay them in sequence around a flat serving dish. Dress with garlicy vinaigrette and leave to stand for half an hour in the fridge before serving. Serve with crusty wholemeal bread.

Tomato, red pepper & orange salad

4 firm tomatoes
1 medium-sized red pepper
1 large juicy orange
1 medium Spanish or white onion — finely sliced in rings
  vinaigrette made with olive oil, red wine vinegar and chopped
    parsley or fresh basil

Peel the orange. Make sure all the white pith is completely re-moved. Cut out the stem of the pepper and pare away all the whiteish flesh and seeds from the inside. Cut the tomatoes, red pepper, onion and orange into rounds. Layer in a deep salad bowl starting with a bed of oranges. Season each layer sparingly with salt, pepper and fresh herbs. Pour the vinaigrette around the edge of the bowl so that it soaks through all the layers. Chill for half an hour before serving.

Tomato, watercress & alfalfa salad

Toss together
1 bunch of cleaned watercress
alfalfa sprouts (a handful)
4 - 5 tomatoes
vinaigrette dressing

Alfalfa sprouts are a rich source of vitamins and protein. You can buy them in some health-food stores or sprout them at home yourself. They have a sharp, fresh, crunchy texture.

Taboulee

Taboulee is a Lebanese salad made with tomatoes, onions, parsley, mint and cracked wheat *(bulgour).*

6 oz. (170 g.) dry bulgour
4 finely chopped tomatoes
1 small finely chopped onion
1 large bunch finely chopped parsley
1 large bunch finely chopped mint
juice of ½ a lemon
olive oil, salt and pepper
crushed clove of garlic

Soak the wheat in cold water until it is chewy but not crunchy — about 1 hour. Drain through a fine sieve and push out excess water with knuckles or a small saucer. Mix with all the other ingredients. The amount of olive oil, lemon and crushed garlic is a matter of personal taste but the finished salad should have quite a sharp, refreshing flavour. Eat with pitta or cos lettuce leaves.

SPINACH SALADS

Use spinach in salads instead of lettuce or endive. The small tender centre leaves are sweet and crisp, the outer leaves have a slightly stronger flavour. Spinach needs two or three washes. Pick out all the discoloured leaves and stems and swish it around in a bowl of cold water. The sand and grit will drop to the bottom. Pick out the leaves in handfuls and drop into a colander. Repeat until the leaves are clean. Don't pour the leaves and water through the colander or you will be back where you started. Shake off the water and leave to crisp and dry in the fridge or on a windowsill.

Anna's walnut & spinach salad (for 2)

¼ lb. (115 g.) of washed spinach leaves
4 - 5 mushrooms sliced umbrella style
4 - 5 shelled chopped walnuts
½ clove of finely chopped garlic
salt and pepper
3 tablespoons olive oil or walnut oil

Crush the walnuts, garlic, salt and pepper in the bottom of the salad bowl with the olive oil. Toss in the other ingredients. Make sure the spinach leaves are well coated with dressing. They can be left whole or torn into bite-size pieces.

Variations
Add crispy cooked bacon bits/tuna and hard-boiled eggs/anchovy fillets/sliced tomato/alfalfa sprouts/croutons (fried bits of bread) and crumbled blue cheese.

YOGURT SALADS

(see *raita,* p. 21; Sugar Daddy, p. 34).

Beetroot, mint & yogurt

1 large cooked beetroot (buy them ready cooked or pickled)
1 small carton of plain yogurt
4 - 5 sprigs of fresh mint

There's no need to take a knife to the skin of a freshly cooked beetroot and they're the only ones worth eating. Except for the skin around the wrinkled root end it should just push off with a gentle pressure from the fingertips. Cut into bite-sized chunky cubes and mix with yogurt and mint. Season with salt and pepper.

Tzatziki

½ lb. (225 g.) cooked, chopped spinach
1 small pot of plain yogurt
1 small crushed clove of garlic (optional)
squeeze of lemon
salt and pepper

Chop the spinach into the yogurt. Season with garlic, lemon juice, salt and pepper. Serve with hot Greek bread.

Variations
Substitute leeks for spinach.

Mushrooms with yogurt & lemon juice

6 oz. - ½ lb. (110 - 225 g.) of sliced mushrooms
4 - 6 tbs. plain yogurt
juice of ½ a lemon
salt and pepper

Coat the mushrooms with lemon juice and yogurt. Add salt and pepper. Leave to stand for 20 minutes before serving.

Leek salad

1 lb. (450 g.) of small young leeks
vinaigrette
chopped parsley

Slice off the hairy root end of the leeks and the coarsest of the green end. The inside leaves of leeks are tender and succulent almost right to the end. I cut away the covering tougher leaves by sharpening the end like a pencil, this leaves the juicy inside exposed. Cut lengthwise and rinse under cold running water. Leeks are grown in sand and if it is not all washed out eating them can be an unpleasantly gritty experience. Cook in boiling salted water until tender — about 15-20 minutes. Drain and allow to cool. Dress with vinaigrette, chopped parsley or crumbled hard-boiled egg.

Salade Niçoise

Toss gently together
salad greens — lettuce, spinach, watercress
quartered hard-boiled eggs
tuna fish
anchovies
black olives
chopped tomato, spring onions, cucumber
parsley
garlicy vinaigrette

A whole meal served with boiled new potatoes, potatoes in their jackets or crusty bread.

VEGETABLES

Preparation
Washing and chopping: always wash vegetables in cold water. Warm water will make them go limp. Root vegetables and potatoes usually need to be scrubbed if you are not going to peel them. Buy a small vegetable scrubbing brush. Don't use the washing-up brush unless you're fond of the taste of detergent. Cut away eyes, discoloured and bruised parts of root vegetables and any mushy bits from soft vegetables like tomatoes, green peppers, aubergines, courgettes, etc. Cut away any green patches on potatoes. This is particularly important if anyone who is pregnant is eating with you, since the green bits may be poisonous. Some knobbly bumps on root vegetables are the result of illicit activity by creepy crawlies. Check for little burrowing holes and make sure you're not getting a surprise helping of protein. I prefer to use as much of the vegetable as possible. I never peel root vegetables unless I can help it, since

27

he skin is often full of flavour and provides roughage. But it has to be admitted that roast potatoes do taste rather different if you don't peel them and they certainly don't look 'right', although they are still delicious.

This is not the traditional way of preparing root vegetables, although the French method of boiling potatoes in their skins has become much more widely accepted in this country and you only have to taste them once more to understand why. The ferny tops of carrots can be added to salads and so can beet leaves; or cook them like cabbage in salted boiling water and serve with butter.

Wash green vegetables very carefully in cold running water to wash out the sand and debris that works its way between the leaves. Spinach and leeks in particular are susceptible, and can have a horrible gritty texture if they are insufficiently washed. Remove yellowing or brown leaves from green vegetables. I assume nobody needs to be told to remove the slimy bits.

Cutting vegetables into matchsticks

Cooking vegetables

Boiling: the English are frequently accused, not altogether unjustly, of boiling everything that comes within their grasp. The reason for the complaint is that often 'boiling' means 'overcooking' vegetables. There are few things uglier (and smellier) than a jaded, grey, watery Brussels sprout, few things less palatable than a carrot reduced to a tasteless pulp by sloshing about for too long in too much hot water. Like our bodies, vegetables are made up of a high percentage of water and this 'leaks' out during the cooking. It is the steam from the vapourizing juices that cooks the inside of a potato baked in its jacket; the drops of rinsing water on spinach are sufficient to stop the leaves from burning in the pan until enough moisture is released for it to cook in its own juices. It is always

28

better to cook a vegetable in its own juices rather than to add water which washes the vitamins and minerals away. Keep the cooking water as a base for vegetable stocks or soups.

Root vegetables go into cold water. Green vegetables go into boiling water. Add a generous pinch of salt, bring back to the boil and turn down to bubble gently. The point of adding salt is that it raises the boiling point of water, so the cooking is faster. Cook in the minimum amount of water. Green vegetables should only just be covered; root vegetables will need a little more.

Cut vegetables up into similar sized bits so they cook at the same speed.

Steaming vegetables is much better than boiling but it takes longer. It is better because you don't lose anything into the cooking water, and also it's less easy to overcook. Green vegetables like broccoli, sprouts and cauliflower take about 15 minutes; carrots, parsnips, swedes and turnips may take half an hour. Keep an eye on the water in the saucepan underneath, do not let it bubble through the steamer, but on the other hand do not let it boil dry. A steamer can be placed over a pan of rice, pasta or potatoes.

Chinese bamboo steamers are very cheap. Buy them in Chinese supermarkets or kitchen shops. There are also metal steamers available shaped like large perforated buttercups that open up to fit any saucepan.

Cooking times: root vegetables should be cooked until a knife point slides effortlessly right through to their centre. Don't keep doing this or you'll end up with diced vegetables. Do not twist the knife or use a fork which will break up the vegetables. If you have not peeled them, a sure sign that they are in danger of overcooking is the skin splitting and peeling back.

Broccoli, artichokes and cauliflower should also be tested with the point of a knife in the thickest part of the stem. Stand broccoli, cauliflower and asparagus with their stems in water and the tender flowers above it. The steam will cook the tops. Always cook covered to prevent the steam escaping.

You get a very clear visual clue from green vegetables when they are cooked. They turn a much brighter intenser colour and loose leaf vegetables become floppy and translucent. Fish a bit out and have a nibble. The flavour should be sweeter and milder than the raw vegetable. Firm but with no trace of rawness. Test Brussels sprouts through the cross at the base by sticking a knife through. It is very, very easy to overcook green vegetables. Watch carefully while they are cooking. Five minutes too long, and they'll taste awful.

Things to do after boiling
— Drain and serve with knobs of butter and finely chopped parsley.
— Purée with a food mill or blender with butter and/or milk (for creamy root vegetables and potatoes).
— Mash, dot with butter and brown under the grill (root vegetables).
— Cover with thin white sauce and scatter with toasted breadcrumbs. Brown under the grill.
— Cover with cheese sauce and grated cheese. Brown under the grill.
— Sauté in hot butter with garlic and/or parsley.
— Sauté Brussels sprouts with hot butter and flaked almonds.
— Purée turnips with an equal amount of cooked white rice, and butter.
— Leave to cool and serve as a salad with vinaigrette or mayonnaise.

Planning ahead
Peeled, washed root vegetables can stand overnight in cold water but do not add salt or they will go slimy. Green vegetables will keep fresh in a polythene bag in the fridge. Parsley will keep fresh and green for up to three weeks in a screw top jar in the fridge but not if it is at all damp.

Making chips

You need a proper chip pan with a basket to make chips.

1 lb. (450 g.) potatoes
1½ pints (860 ml.) cooking oil
salt

Peel the potatoes and cut into even chip shapes. Pat dry in a tea-towel and sprinkle with salt. Heat the oil until a blue haze rises from it. Put the chips into the basket and lower into the oil. They should bubble furiously. If they stop bubbling it is because the cold chips have lowered the temperature of the oil. Turn the heat up immediately. Raise the basket from time to time and shake the chips to be sure that they are not resting against each other. Drain and serve when they turn golden brown. If you want to half prepare them you can cook them until pale gold before your guests arrive, remove from oil and then finish them off before serving. If the fat is not hot enough the chips will be soggy. If the chips are wet they will make the hot fat spit.

Baking
Potatoes, parsnips, sweet potatoes and Jerusalem artichokes can all be baked in their jackets.
(i)   Scrub and remove 'eyes' and discoloured bits.
(ii)   Dry with a clean tea-towel or sprinkle with salt — for a

frosted look when baked. Rubbing with oil will make the skin crisper.

(iii) Prick with a fork or the skin may burst in the oven.

(iv) Bake in the oven. How long you bake them for depends on the temperature. At a high temperature, gas mark 9 (475°F) the time will be very short, 45 minutes at the most; if you have other things in the oven at a lower temperature you will have to bake for much longer. Test to see if they are cooked by gently squeezing with an oven cloth. The skin should give little resistance. If it gives just a little and then feels hard, the outer layer only is cooked. In a very hot oven turn over halfway through the cooking or they will burn on one side.

Variations

Baking potatoes wrapped in aluminium foil shortens the cooking time but the result is more of a steamed potato than a baked one. The skin is much softer.

Baked new potatoes

There are two ways of baking small new potatoes. Either as above but for only 30 minutes *or* in an ovenproof dish dotted with butter and sprinkled with yellow mustard seed at gas mark 7 (425°F) for 1-1¼ hours. Turn a couple of times during the cooking.

Roasting

Potatoes, onions, carrots, sweet potatoes and parsnips.

(i) Scrub away all dirt and cut away any blemishes or peel finely. Peel onions.

(ii) Cut large vegetables in halves or quarters. Leave onions whole.

(iii) Boil potatoes for 5-10 minutes and drain. This speeds up the roasting time.

(iv) Place — preferably without touching one another — in a greased shallow baking dish and dot generously with knobs of butter, margarine or beef dripping, or oil. Cook at gas mark 7 (425°F) for 45 minutes. Turn halfway through the cooking. Onions do not need turning and they can take slightly longer to cook. Sweet potatoes and parsnips will cook in 35 minutes.

Vegetables can also be cooked around a joint of roasting meat.

Cheese potatoes

Cut the potatoes in two when they are cooked. Remove the white fluffy insides and mash with a little grated mature Cheddar. Pile back into the skins. Close the potatoes and bake for another 5-6 minutes. You could also add finely chopped spring onion or chives, cooked crispy scraps of bacon, chopped capers, sour cream and butter. (Bake 1 large potato per person.)

Pommes Dauphinois

Possibly the best way to eat potatoes.

1 lb. (450g.) of potatoes
1 lb. (450g.) of onions
8-10oz. (225-285g.) of Cheddar cheese
3 or 4 tbs. of single cream or top of the milk
salt and pepper
2-3 oz. (55-85g.) of butter

Wash the potatoes and remove any discoloured bits. Cut across into thin rounds. Peel the onion and slice in circles. Grate the cheese. Butter a shallow baking dish. Cover the base with a single layer of potatoes, put a layer of onions on top and then a layer of cheese. Season each layer with a little salt and pepper and a couple of dabs of butter. Carry on with the layers, ending with one of potatoes and cheese and maybe a little grated onion. Dot with butter and dribble the cream over the top so that it seeps through the cracks. Bake covered for 10 minutes at gas mark 7 (425°F) and then turn the oven down to gas mark 5 (375°F) for 45 minutes to 1 hour. Uncover for the last 15 minutes to brown the cheese. This dish is delectable hot or cold. Serve as a main course with crispy fried bacon and a green salad or as a vegetable dish with almost any meat. The potatoes can often take an infuriatingly long time to cook. If you want a short cut boil them for 5 minutes before layering in the baking dish. This will cut the cooking time by 15 to 20 minutes.

Braising vegetables
Braising in the oven is a slow way of cooking vegetables in the oven in their own juice with a little stock and butter.

Method
(i)   Trim and wash vegetables.
(ii) Butter a shallow ovenproof dish.
(iii) Fill with vegetables, 3 tbs. of chicken, beef or vegetable stock and 2 oz. (55 g.) of butter. Season with a little black pepper.
(iv) Bake covered for 1½ hours at gas mark 3 (340°F).
(v)   If there is a lot of liquid in the dish at the end of the cooking, drain if off into a saucepan and boil furiously — this is called 'reducing' — until only half the original amount remains.

Suitable vegetables: endive (chicory); celery (trim leaves and roots but leave the head whole if the dish is deep enough — if not slice the head in half lengthways); fennel; leeks. Add tiny whole peeled shallots or pickling onions if you wish. Mix together turnip, celeriac and parsnip cut into 'chip' size pieces. Drop them into boiling water for 5 minutes before draining and baking — use the vegetable water instead of stock.

Variations
— Wrap fennel, leeks, celery and endive in ham before cooking.
— After cooking cover with a thick layer of grated cheese and brown under the grill.
— Substitute red wine or cider for stock.
— Use lettuce and peas in layers — lettuce leaves at the top and bottom of a buttered dish and garden peas in the middle. If the lettuce is still wet from being washed, use only half the stock.
— Add tiny whole, peeled shallots (little onions) or pickling onions if you wish.

Suzie's swedes

1 swede (6 to 8 oz. per person) (170 - 225 g.)
chopped parsley
butter

Peel the swede and cut into chunks. Bring to the boil in a saucepan of salted water. Turn the heat down until the water is bubbling gently. Test with a fork. It is cooked when it breaks up easily — about 20 minutes. Drain. Mash with a potato masher, fork or electric beater until no lumps remain. Stir in butter and chopped parsley.

Crudités

Crudités are a substantial starter to a meal. The basic ingredients are lots of very fresh vegetables and salads cut into sticks and dipped into garlic or lemon mayonnaise. Try quartered tomatoes, curcumbers, carrots, celery, watercress, apple, pear, radishes, celeriac, fennel, batavia or another crisp leaved lettuce, beetroot, green and red peppers, cauliflower flowerets, chicory, cos lettuce, spring onions, raw mushrooms and sprigs of fresh herbs. Serve with quartered hard-boiled eggs, capers and olives. The recipes for mayonnaise are on page 130. Aioli (garlic mayonnaise) is wonderful with crudités. Other dips to try are houmous, Sugar Daddy, potato and sweet potato, sour cream of chopped chives and cheese and herbs.

Sugar Daddy

This is sometimes called *moutaboul* and is a sweet nutty mixture of toasted aubergine, garlic and yogurt. Cut a large aubergine into slices. Do not peel. Brush with oil and either place under the grill or in a medium oven gas mark 5 (375°F). When the aubergine is toasted dark brown turn it over and toast the other side. It's better if it blackens because the burnt bits give it flavour — particularly burnt skin. Mash the aubergine into the contents of a small pot of yogurt with a crushed clove of garlic and the juice of half a lemon. Season with salt and pepper. Serve with crudités or hot pitta.

Potato & sweet potato

Bake a potato and a sweet potato in their jackets in the oven. The sweet potato should go on a lower shelf as it cooks quicker. (In case you hadn't already discovered — the top of an oven gets hotter.) At maximum heat they will take about 45 minutes to cook or they can go in the oven with anything else that is cooking for longer. If the oven is very hot turn the potatoes halfway through the cooking or they will burn on the top. Mash or liquidize when cooked with their skins and a clove or garlic, 4 or 5 table-spoons of olive oil and some finely chopped parsley.

Cheese & herbs

½ lb. (225 g.) cottage cheese or cream cheese
finely chopped fresh herbs
small crushed clove of garlic (optional)

Mix all the herbs and garlic together into a fine cream. This is a much cheaper and more appetizing version of the ready-made herb cheeses you can buy.

SOUPS

Leek & potato soup

3 - 4 leeks
3 - 4 medium-sized potatoes
1 medium-sized onion
1½ pints (860ml.) of chicken or vegetable or herb stock
1½ oz. (40g.) of butter
salt and pepper

Cut off the coarsest outer leaves of the leeks and the hairy root ends. Chop across into ½" circles. Wash very thoroughly in cold water to remove any sand. Drain. Scrub the potatoes and cut away any discoloured parts. Cut into small chunks. Slice the onion. Melt the butter in a large saucepan until it is bubbling. Throw in the vegetables and keep turning them over with a wooden spoon until the onions are transparent and the leeks are floppy. Do not let the vegetables brown — this is a pale soup. Add the hot stock, stirring all the time. If you are using a packet stock, taste before adding any more salt. Season with a generous grind of black pepper. Bring to the boil and then turn down to simmer until the potatoes are tender (about 30 minutes). You can thicken the soup by mashing the potatoes against the side of the pan with the back of a wooden spoon and stirring them back into the mixture when cooked.

Variations
(i)   With cream. Add a small carton of single cream to the soup when it is ready. Bring gently back to the boil and then re-move from the heat. Check seasoning — sometimes the cream makes it a little bland. Sprinkle with chopped chives.
(ii) Vichyssoise. Liquidize the soup or pass through a sieve after adding the cream. Serve chilled with chopped chives or mint.

Gazpacho

A spicy, cold Spanish vegetable soup that takes minutes to make if you have a liquidizer and quite a lot longer if you haven't.

1 cucumber
2 green peppers
1 - 1½ lb. (450 - 675g.) of sharp red tomatoes. The large
    Mediterranean ones are ideal, bland ones will not do. You can
    also use tinned tomatoes.
1 Spanish onion
1 - 2 chopped cloves or garlic
salt and pepper
5 or 6 tbs. of olive oil

Chop everything into small cubes. Put aside a small quantity of cucumber, green pepper, tomatoes and onion. Liquidize every-thing else or pass through a fine vegetable mill. Add olive oil, salt and pepper to taste. Serve chilled with the extra chopped vege-tables.

PASTA

Pasta is one of the things, along with Basmati rice and Italian salami, that I'd be content to eat every day of my life. It is bliss-fully easy and can be very quick to prepare. It is not in my opinion best served as the ubiquitous and heavy 'spag bol'; a thick coating of minced meat and tinned tomato does nothing to enhance the delicate flavour of pasta, particularly fresh pasta. Fresh pasta can be bought in some Italian grocers in fine, flat strands called tagliarini; its broader relative is tagliatelle, and broader still, 2″ - 3″ wide, is lasagne. Apart from the usual creamy white sort which seems to taste strangely different according to which one of the dozens of shapes — curls, shells, linguine, macaroni, vermicelli, spaghette, spaghettini — you are eating, there is green spinach-flavoured pasta and even pinkish tomato-flavoured pasta. Serve separately or mixed together. Some shops also sell the little meat-

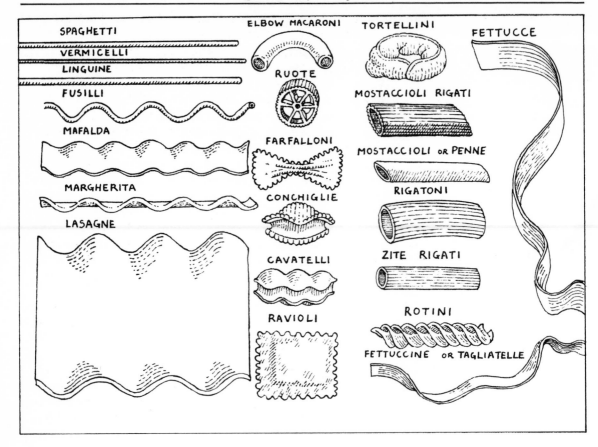

SPAGHETTI

VERMICELLI

LINGUINE

FUSILLI

MAFALDA

MARGHERITA

LASAGNE

ELBOW MACARONI

RUOTE

FARFALLONI

CONCHIGLIE

CAVATELLI

RAVIOLI

TORTELLINI

MOSTACCIOLI RIGATI

MOSTACCIOLI or PENNE

RIGATONI

ZITE RIGATI

ROTINI

FETTUCCINE or TAGLIATELLE

FETTUCCE

stuffed pillows called ravioli and vacuum packs of agnelloti stuffed with cheese and meat. They are a good, fast standby to keep in the back of the fridge if you can resist the temptation to eat them. Of the dry pastas, which take a bit longer to cook, the Italian imported varieties seem to have a much more distinctive flavour than the supermarket brands. Fratelli de Cecco is my favourite. Wholemeal pasta is more expensive but much more nutritious.

Cooking pasta

The most important thing to remember is to use lots of water. Dry pasta absorbs a lot and will stick together and to the pan if you don't use enough. How much you put in the pan per person depends very much on whether you are serving it for a first or second course and of course your appetite. A pound (450 g.) is around the right amount for four good eaters as a main course. It doesn't matter if you cook too much, it can go in a salad the next day and with crisp strips of bacon mixed in it's lovely hot or cold for breakfast.

Bring a large pan of water — 5 litres/10 pints of water — to the boil. Add a generous teaspoon of salt and a tablespoon of oil to prevent sticking and scatter the pasta in if it's small shapes or bend it in against the bottom of the pan if it's a spaghetti type. Briskly whisk the past around with a fork to make sure none of the strands have stuck together. If they do they don't cook, but remain hard and raw. Cook at a gentle bubbling boil without a lid. The cooking time varies according to shape and freshness. Fresh soft pasta will only need 3 to 5 minutes, unless it is lasagne which needs 10 to 15 minutes. Dry pastas usually have times on the packet, but allow anything up to 20 minutes. Test as it cooks; some people prefer it 'al dente', when the pasta still has a slight resistance when you bite it but not a crunchy raw core. Some people like it very soft. Drain in a colander and serve with lots of butter or olive oil. The simplest dressing is butter and Parmesan cheese with a clove of finely chopped garlic and a sprinkling of chopped parsley. You will never buy those tiny tubs of ready grated Parmesan again once you've grated it yourself straight on to your plate from a chunk of fresh Parmesan. Buy it from Italian shops and delicatessens.

Lasagne and cannelloni are used principally as stuffed pasta; recipes for them follow in Chapter 3. The following recipes can be used for any of the other kinds of pasta.

Pesto
Pesto is a mixture of finely ground or chopped fresh basil leaves, olive oil or melted butter, crushed garlic, salt, ground black pepper and pine kernels. The Italian imported ready-made sort that you buy in jars is very good and has pine kernels ground in too. Fresh basil is available in some greengrocers in the summer months or you can grow your own from seed. In the winter don't substitute dried basil, use the ready-made pesto which keeps very well in the fridge.

a handful of basil leaves
1 - 2 cloves of garlic according to taste
sea salt
ground black pepper
olive oil or melted butter
1 oz. (25 g.) ground pine kernels (optional)

Finely chop or liquidize all the ingredients together and slowly add enough oil or butter to give the mixture the consistency of a runny mayonnaise. Toss with the hot pasta. Serve with Parmesan.

This recipe can be infinitely varied with other fresh herbs — sage, parsley, mint, thyme, chives, fennel leaves — chopped together or singly and any old bits of grated cheese. Finely chopped or pounded anchovy is good too and a little chopped fresh green or red chilli. Alternatively use finely chopped raw spinach instead of basil.

Mushrooms

Mushrooms seems to have a real affinity with the noodle types of pasta. Slice them across through the stems so they look like little umbrellas and 'melt' about 3 oz. (85 g.) per person in a generous amount of butter or oil in a thick bottomed saucepan with a lid. Let the butter or oil bubble gently first then throw in the mushrooms and put a lid on. Turn the heat down as low as it will go and cook 5 - 10 minutes. Pour the whole lot over the pasta. Quartered hard-boiled eggs are an optional extra.

Tuna

Drain the oil off a tin of tuna and break the fish up into its natural flakes with a fork and toss with the pasta. Serve with chopped parsley and lemon wedges. You could also add a few capers or black olives and a little crushed garlic, otherwise this dish might be a bit bland.

Alla carbonara

1 rasher of bacon or slice of smoked ham per person
1 small onion
chopped garlic
chopped parsley
freshly ground black pepper
salt
2 oz. (55 g.) of grated Parmesan
1 or 2 eggs

Cut the meat into matchstick-size strips with a pair of scissors. If it is bacon, fry until crispy in its own fat. Put the bacon in the frying pan over a low heat; gradually, if it is fatty bacon, the fat will start to melt and it will cook in its own juice. For more expensive, very lean bacon you may need a knob of butter to stop it sticking. When it is crispy throw in the chopped onion and garlic. Toss until the onion goes transparent and silky. The pasta should have been cooking at the same time. In a large warmed serving bowl break 1 or 2 eggs (1 is sufficient for 2 people). Beat them up with a balloon whisk until there are no nasty slimy bits running through the yolk. Dump in the drained pasta and toss with two forks. The pasta has to have just come out of its cooking water for this recipe because it is the heat of the pasta that cooks the eggs. Throw in the other ingredients and serve. Serving pasta — particularly spaghetti — is probably more difficult than cooking. Long slippery loops hang between saucepan and plate. You can also stir in 2 or 3 tablespoons of single cream if you wish but this is verging on Cholesterol City. If you use ham for this recipe it doesn't need cooking.

Pasta servers are a help.

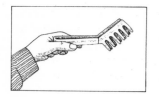

Tomato sauce (Napolitana)

1 large Spanish onion
1 - 1½ lb. (450 - 675 g.) of hard, red, sharp tomatoes or a 14 oz.
*   (400g.) tin of tomatoes (Italian are best)*
3 tbs. of olive oil or 1 oz. (25 g.) of butter
1 - 2 chopped cloves of garlic
salt and pepper
1 pinch of dried basil or oregano or 6 - 7 leaves of fresh basil

Peel and slice the onion in rings. Heat the oil or butter until a piece of onion sizzles in a deep heavy bottomed saucepan when you drop it in. Melt the onions and the peeled and crushed garlic in the oil until they are transparent. While the onions are cooking chop the tomatoes into little chunks. If you're using tinned tomatoes, use the juice. Add with the herbs and seasoning to the onions. Bring them to the boil and then turn down to a medium heat to simmer gently. Fresh tomatoes will need 30 to 40 minutes to cook, tinned need a minimum of 20 minutes. The longer you cook this sauce the better the flavour. If you are using fresh tomatoes they may dry out while cooking, so you may need to add more water.

Alla piquante

When my friend Jo Falinski makes this recipe he makes two sauces, one for the faint-hearted of sensitive palate who don't want the roofs of their mouths lifted off, and one for red-hot lovers.

1 small onion peeled and finely sliced
olive oil or butter
2 or 3 hard, red, sharp tomatoes or a small tin of Italian tomatoes
dried red chillis chopped (a quarter pound [115 g.] of these in a
*   screw topped jar will last a very long time)*
1 or 2 peeled and chopped cloves of garlic
salt
black pepper
2 tbs. of olive oil or 1 oz. (25 g.) of butter

Heat the oil or butter in a frying pan. Melt the onions until they go transparent. Add the garlic and chopped chilli. This is something that you will have to experiment with; start by using a ¼ chilli and taste the sauce before it is almost cooked to see if you need more. There's not much you can do about it if you need less except to serve a small spoonful of sauce with the pasta and put the rest in the fridge. Add the tomatoes and simmer on a low heat until they are completely broken up. It takes around 20 minutes but with all tomato sauces the longer you cook them the better the flavour becomes. Serve with care and Parmesan.

Chicken livers

2 - 3 oz. (55 - 85 g.) of chicken livers per person
peeled and chopped small onion
clove of peeled and crushed garlic
12 - 15 whole sage leaves (fresh or dried in the bunch
   (optional)
2 tbs.of olive oil or 1½ oz. (40 g.) of butter

First of all you have to do something incredibly vile but vitally necessary. Sort through the chicken livers to make sure that the bile gland — which looks pretty much as it sounds, small, green and nasty — has not been left in. If it's left in during the cooking you will have to throw the whole lot out and go and get fish and chips.

Let the butter gently bubble and then cook the onions in it until they go opaque. If you are using oil test it with a bit of onion. It should sizzle pleasantly, if it fizzes and spits the oil is too hot. Stir in the chicken livers and the rest of the ingredients and keep stirring gently until they go crumbly and a pale pinky brown all the way through. Don't have the heat up too high or they will go leathery.

Vegetable pasta sauce

Take a small handful of any seasonable vegetable: peas, green beans, shredded green or red cabbage, carrot cut into matchsticks, chopped apple, spring onions, celery cut into matchsticks, fennel, quartered tomatoes, sliced courgette, onion, watercress, sliced red or green pepper, mushrooms, flowerets of cauliflower or broccoli, for instance. Avoid aubergine because it soaks up a lot of oil and has to be cooked much longer.

garlic
any fresh herb
butter or oil (2 oz. [55 g.] or 2 tbs.)

Melt the butter or oil in the pan, throw in the vegetables as it bubbles and continue to stir and toss until the vegetables are soft-ish but still retain some firmness when bitten. If you are using tomatoes, mushrooms or frozen peas don't add them until the other vegetables are nearly ready. They are so juicy that if you add them too soon the other vegetables will stop sautéing and start stewing. All the vegetables should be cut into approximately same-size chunks. You can just toss the vegetables with the pasta when they are cooked and serve or cover it all with a layer of grated cheese and brown under the grill. You could add tuna or sliced bacon or chopped hard-boiled eggs to this dish; or raisins; or cashew nuts. Nuts always taste better if you brown them under the grill before using.

Anchovy & broccoli

1 lb. (450 g.) of rigatoni/shell/corkscrew pasta
1 lb. (450 g.) broccoli cut into flowerets
1 tin of anchovies
1 large peeled and sliced Spanish onion
2 or 3 peeled and chopped shallots (optional)
garlic to taste
olive oil

Steam or boil the broccoli until tender, then chop. Heat the oil until a piece of onion will fry gently in it. Throw in the onions, chopped anchovies and garlic and continue stirring and tossing until the onion is tender. Add chopped broccoli. Toss together with the pasta.

PASTA SALADS

A pasta salad can be the heart of a meal or served as a side dish. The spagetti-type pastas are not really suitable for salads — it's better to use macaroni, shells or corkscrews. They should not be too soft, so don't overcook. These are some suggestions but you can bung in pretty well anything you fancy. You will need one piquant element, for instance olives, or the mix will be too bland. Dressings made with vinegar do not seem to blend well with the flavour of pasta.

Pasta with egg & anchovy

¼ lb. (115 g.) cooked cold pasta
2 crumbled hard-boiled eggs
10 black olives with the stones removed
4 - 6 anchovies cut into small pieces
a small handful of finely chopped parsley
1 small pot of plain yogurt
juice of half a lemon

Crumble the hard-boiled eggs either by passing through a parsley mincer or rubbing through a sieve. Mix all the ingredients together and season with salt and freshly ground black pepper. Tuna could be substituted for the anchovies or added as well.

Pasta with peas, ham & cheese

¼ lb. (115 g.) cold cooked pasta
¼ ln. (115 g.) of cold cooked peas
2 slices of ham cut in strips (or diced cooked chicken)
2/3 oz. (55 - 85 g.) of cream or herby cheese
olive oil
chopped mint

Mash the cheese into 2 or 3 tablespoons of olive oil. Toss all the ingredients together.

Pasta with bacon & eggs

¼ lb. (115 g.) of cold cooked pasta
3 or 4 rashers of cooked bacon
2 crumbled hard-boiled eggs
10/12 chopped capers
1 tsp. of grainy mustard

Cut the bacon into small pieces. Mix all the ingredients together. Sprinkle with a few drops of Tabasco if you like things hot.

Pasta with spinach

¼ lb. (115 g.) of cold cooked pasta
1 lb. (450 g.) of spinach
olive oil/garlic to taste

Wash the spinach at least three times and pick out any mushy or discoloured bits. Throw out any woody stems. Put all the spinach on a very low heat — as low as you can get it without it going out — in a large pan. The water from the washing and ½ oz. (15 g.) of butter will cook the spinach. Cover the pan and keep turning the spinach. It takes about 10 minutes to cook. Drain off any excess liquid (spinach is *very* full of water). If using frozen, thaw it and drain. When it has cooled down chop it fairly small (lots more water will come out then) and mix it with the pasta with olive oil, crushed garlic, salt and black pepper to taste. This salad would be good with sliced pink onion, anchovies, watercress or Greek feta cheese; also crumbled crispy fried bacon; or sauted mushrooms.

Cold Buttered Pasta is delicious.

RICE

The best white long-grain rice for flavour is Basmati Indian rice, which has a wonderful smell when cooking and an equally delicate flavour. Buy it in Indian grocers, but be sure to sort through the grains first to make sure there are no small stones and twigs left from the sorting. Use Italian risotto rice for Mediterranean dishes. The grains are long and plump and have a very distinctive flavour. It can be bought in Italian delicatessens. The best brown rice is organically grown. It is slightly more expensive than the non-organic types.

Branded rice sold in cardboard packets is expensive: the quantity is almost always less than 1 lb. (450 g.) while the price will often be higher than that for 1 lb. (450 g.) of non-packet rice. The quality is usually quite good but the taste tends to be bland.

Long-grain is the kind to use in savoury dishes, and short-grain is for puddings.

Cooking rice

Despite the sticky gluey masses that you may have produced or been served in the past, rice is easy to cook particularly if you use this strictly heretical method. The secret with *white rice* is to use lots of boiling salted water, at least a litre per person. Scatter 3 - 4 oz. (85 - 115 g.) of rice per person into the water, bring back to the boil. cover and turn down to simmer. After about 15 minutes fish out a few grains and taste. It is cooked when it is firm and tender with no crunchy core inside. Drain through a wire sieve and serve with lots of butter. Use ½ teaspoon of turmeric in the cooking water for yellow rice or a few strands of saffron for special occasions. Saffron has sweet fragrant taste and colours the rice pale orange.

Brown rice

Brown rice should be cooked in the minimum of water. It is much more nutritious than white rice and it would be foolish to throw out half its food value with the water. For 1 cup of rice use 2 cups of cold water. Bring the rice and water to the boil together with a little salt. Turn down the heat until the water is hardly simmering. Cover. It will take about 45 minutes to cook and should completely absorb the water. This is the tricky bit — if you cook too long it begins to dry out and burn. Better to use more water and, if necessary, drain the rice.

Rice & peas (for 4)

¾ lb. (345 g.) white or brown rice
½ lb. (225 g.) bag of frozen peas/1½ lb. (675 g.) fresh peas
6 oz. (170 g.) mushrooms (optional)
2 oz. (55 g.) butter
handful of chopped mint

Cook the rice with a pinch of salt. Add the peas to the rice for the last 10 minutes of cooking. Fresh peas may need 12-13 minutes; it depends how young and tender they are. If you are using brown rice, add an extra cup of water with the peas. While the peas and rice are cooking cut the mushrooms in fine slices and sauté in a little of the hot melted butter. Drain the rice and peas and tip into the frying pan with the mushrooms. With a wooden spoon over a low heat gently mix all the ingredients together for a couple of minutes. Turn off the heat and stir in the chopped mint (parsley would do or fresh green coriander). Serve on a warmed flat serving dish with the remaining butter dotted over the top. If you are not using mushrooms simply mix together the chopped herbs, butter and rice and serve. This may seem a very generous amount of butter, regulate it to your taste but I find that the more butter that you mix with white rice the better it tastes.

You can serve this dish with grilled or casseroled meat or fish; as a main course on its own or with Parmesan cheese, flaked tuna and capers.

Rice & tomato sauce

¼ lb. (115 g.) of rice per person
tomato sauce (see Pasta — Napolitana p. 39)
Parmesan cheese
2 -3 sausages per person (optional)

Make the tomato sauce and grill the sausages as the rice is cooking. You can use any kind of sausages but the fat spicy Italian ones from Italian delicatessens are particularly tasty. You can either serve the three ingredients separately with a bed of rice and helpings of sauce and sausages or mix the sauce into the rice before serving with chunks of sausage. Sprinkle Parmesan cheese over the whole lot.

Egg & onion rice

¼ lb. (115 g.) rice per person
1 egg per person
½ oz. (15 g.) of butter per person
1 bunch of spring onions

As the rice is cooking wash the spring onions, cut off the hairy root and only the very tips of the green leaves. Cut across in fine circles. Gently sauté in frothing butter melted in a frying pan. Beat the eggs. When the rice is cooked, drain and tip into the frying pan with the onions and stir together. Remove the pan from the heat and pour the egg(s) into the rice beating with a fork. The heat from the rice will cook the egg.

You could make a more elaborate version of this dish by adding shrimps or peeled prawns to the rice. Serve with lemon wedges.

Rice with broccoli, walnuts & cheese

¼ lb. (115 g.) rice per person
4 - 6 oz. (115 - 170 g.) broccoli/cauliflower per person
1 oz. (25 g.) coarsely chopped walnut pieces each
1 tsp. of sesame seeds
3 oz. (85 g.) grated hard cheese
½ oz. (15 g.) butter

Cook the rice in a large saucepan and steam the broccoli above it either in a steamer or a fine mesh sieve. Chop the walnuts as the rice is cooking. Mix the walnuts into the chopped rice, pile onto a flat serving dish with the broccoli on top. Sprinkle with cheese and sesame seeds. Dot with butter and brown under the grill until the cheese melts, and the sesame seeds are popping. Serve with crispy grilled bacon/quartered hard-boiled eggs.

Popcorn

Popcorn is easy to make and very nutritious. It is fun too. You will need a very large saucepan with a lid.

4 oz. (115 g.) popping corn
1 oz. (25 g.) oil/butter

Heat the oil or butter in the pan. When it is hot throw in the corn and cover. After a while you will hear the corn beginning to explode; keep shaking the pan to move the unpopped corn to the bottom of the pan. Don't leave it for too long without shaking or the corn will burn. When the popping stops, the corn is ready. There are usually a few unpopped kernels left in the bottom of the pan.

Coatings
Butter and sugar
When the corn starts popping, quickly open the lid and shake in 2 or 3 tablespoons of brown or white sugar. Keep shaking the pan while the corn is popping to distribute the sugar evenly.

Salt and butter
Toss the hot popped corn with butter and a shaking of sea salt.

Marmite topping
Melt 3 tablespoons of Marmite or other yeast spread in a saucepan with an equal quantity of butter. Pour over the popped corn. Scatter with finely chopped onion (optional).

FISH

(See Choosing Fish Chapter 1). A good fishmonger can be an invaluable source of recipes.

Prawns with brown bread & butter

Serve a generous half pint of prawns per person with brown bread and butter and wedges of lemon. Use whole prawns, with their heads and tails intact, not frozen ones. All they need by way of preparation is a quick rinse under the cold tap. Pat dry with paper kitchen towel.

Grilled fish fillets or cutlets

Brush the fish with a generous amount of melted butter. Grill flesh side up under a hot grill until the flesh is white and opaque all the way to the skin. This should take 10 to 15 minutes. Cutlets can be turned over halfway through the cooking time. If they are thick they may need an extra 2 or 3 minutes a side. Try sprinkling the fish with basil or marjoram before cooking. Fresh is best, dried is OK.

Suitable fish
Plaice, sole, halibut, flounder, cod. Small whole fish can be grilled too, but slash the skin diagonally two or three times before brushing with butter or olive oil. Cook for 5 to 10 minutes on each side.

Scallops on skewers

Cut the flesh of 1 or 2 scallops per person into 2″ cubes. Thread on to skewers with rolled up rashers of streaky bacon. Grill for 8-10 minutes turning all the time and brushing with melted butter and the juices from the grill pan.

Stuffed mackerel

Get the fishmonger to remove the backbone of the fish and cut off its head. Split the belly with a sharp knife and rinse the inside. Fill the inside with stuffing. Butter a sheet of aluminium foil and seal the fish inside. Bake as gas mark 4 (350°F) for 25 minutes.

Stuffings
Mix together with breadcrumbs any combination of: chopped lemon peel, capers, anchovies, parsley, fennel leaves, salt, pepper, butter, chopped black olives, finely chopped onion or fresh chopped peeled ginger (be very sparing), fine oatmeal, chopped nuts. Moisten with a little milk and press together. The mixture should be fairly dry, the butter holds the other ingredients together. Use this for any whole fish, good quality chops and chicken.

Kedgeree

cooked brown or white rice (see p. 43)
1 hard-boiled egg per person
½ - 1 tsp. of curry paste or powder
1 fillet of smoked fish (if using haddock which is good gently
*   simmer in ¼ pint [145 ml.] milk in a frying pan for 10*
*   minutes before flaking)*
chopped parsley/fresh green coriander
butter (1 oz.) (25 g.)
lemon wedges
salt and pepper

While the rice is cooking flake the fish into small chunks and boil the eggs and cut into quarters. While the rice is still hot mix in the curry paste and butter and then gently fold in the fish, eggs and parsley, taking care not to break up the eggs. Season with salt and pepper and serve with the lemon wedges.

Smoked fish

You can buy smoked fish in fishmongers and delicatessens. It is ideal with summer salads or as a starter or can be transformed into a very professional looking pâté with this recipe of Ro Fitzgerald's from the Bristol Arts Centre restaurant. She uses smoked mackerel, but other smoked fish would be equally good.

5 oz. (140 g.) of smoked mackerel
juice of ½ large lemon
3 oz. (85 g.) of softened butter (To soften, take out of the fridge
*   and place in a warm corner — airing cupboard, radiator, sunny*
*   windowsill — for around an hour before needed. Or melt on a low*
*   flame; don't let it brown.)*
1 dessertspoonful of chopped parsley
pinch of black pepper
pinch of ground mace
2 teaspoons of tomato purée
1 clove of peeled, crushed garlic

Remove the dark skin and bones from the mackerel. Blend together all the ingredients in a liquidizer or rub through a fine wire sieve with a wooden spoon (hard work this). The mixture should be as smooth as possible. Pour into a lightly oiled dish. Chill. It will set quite hard. Serve with brown bread or toast.

MEAT

(See Choosing Meat, Chapter 1)
Only the more expensive cuts of meat are really amenable to quick, simple cooking although there are exceptions, chicken for example, and liver. The less expensive cuts, stewing meat and mince need longer, more inventive cooking and they are dealt with in Chapter 3.

Steak tartare

For this simplest of meat dishes you will need 6 - 7 oz. (170 - 200 g.) of very good quality lean steak per person. Unless you buy it from a butcher whom you trust implicitly don't buy ready ground beef — it is often very fatty. Choose the steaks and ask the butcher to grind them especially for you.

Season the meat with salt and pepper and shape it gently into a flat mound on the plate. Make a depression in the centre and into it crack an egg. Surround the meat with garnishes of capers, anchovies, raw sliced onion, tomato, cucumber, pickled cucumber, watercress and mustard. Serve with Worcester Sauce. Not a dish to serve before canvassing your guests first; lots of people recoil in horror from the idea of eating raw meat (and raw eggs).

Hamburgers

Home-made hamburgers are delicious, easy to make and bear very little resemblance to those pallid lumps of boiled flannel masquerading under the name in a lot of hamburger bars. You will need good ground steak as for Steak Tartare, between 6 to 8 oz. (170 - 225 g.) per person. Divide the meat into even portions of 4 to 6 oz. (114 - 170 g.) each and carefully press into shape (they should be about 1″ thick. There is no need to add any binding agent, as the meat should stick together with a little gentle pressure. Heat 1-2 tablespoons of oil for each hamburger in a heavy bottomed frying pan until it is very hot — a blueish haze will start rising above the oil. It needs to be hot to sear the outside of the meat and seal in the juices. Place the hamburgers in the pan. The oil should fizzle quite aggressively. If it is not hot enough it will seep into the meat and, quite apart from being greasy and unpleasant, the hamburgers will fall apart. Cooking times depend very much on whether you like the meat rare on the inside or not. Three minutes on each side is about the minimum to seal the outside and heat the meat through; at 6 or 7 minutes the insides will still be pinkish and at 10 minutes they will be very well cooked indeed. Disintegration is the problem with hamburgers, so don't keep turning them over. Serve either in round bread rolls or as a main course with vegetables. There are lots of commercially produced chutneys and pickles designed to go with hamburgers, but I find most of them rather sweet. Less synthetic alternatives are Worcester sauce, Tabasco, one of the fiery West Indian or Chinese red chilli sauces, lemon slices, parsley, a choice of mustards, tomato and raw onion chopped together and seasoned with salt and pepper, raw sliced onion with yogurt and paprika, anchovies, capers or garlic mashed into softened butter, sour cream and chopped fresh herbs.

Steak

Steak is, of course, expensive but potentially delectable. There are a few simple rules about buying and cooking it.

(i)   If you are buying for two and can't afford a lot of meat buy one largish piece rather than two small ones. The meat will be juicier and probably less fatty.

(ii)   Steak should be at room temperature before it is cooked. Chilled meat has less flavour.

(iii) Only very good steak can be grilled — most needs to be fried.

(iv)   Do not use salt in the cooking — it draws moisture out of the meat.

(v)   Gently beat cheaper cuts with the flat of a Chinese chopper or the bottom of a clean saucepan to 'tenderize'. Apply constant pressure rather than 'beating it up' and losing precious juices.

(vi) If there is a rim of thick fat running around the edge of the meat, as in rump steak, clip it every 2" (5 cm.) or so or it will contract during cooking and the meat will curl up.

Times: Approximate times for ½" (1 cm.) thick steaks.
Very rare — 2 to 3 minutes on each side.
Rare — 4 minutes on each side.
Medium — (pinkish inside) 6 minutes on each side.
Well cooked — 8 to 10 minutes on each side.
Approximate times for 1" - 1½" (2.5 - 3 cm.) thick steaks
Very rare — 4 minutes on each side.
Rare — 6 minutes on each side.
Medium — 8 minutes on each side.
Well cooked — 10 to 12 minutes on each side.

Cooking
Grilling: heat the grill for 5 minutes before starting cooking. Brush the meat with a little olive oil or melted butter first.
Frying: heat ½ oz. (15 g.) of butter or 2 tablespoons of olive oil in a frying pan. A mixture of the two will give a higher temperature without burning the butter. The fat needs to be hot to seal the outside of the meat.

Steak au poivre

Crush two or three tablespoons of black peppercorns in a pestle and mortar. You can improvise by putting the peppercorns in a paper bag and crushing them with a rolling pin. Press the crushed peppercorns into the steak and fry.

Steak with lemon & garlic (Gina's recipe)

Finely chop a clove of garlic. Spread into both sides of the steak with the flat blade of a knife. Just before the steak is cooked squeeze the juice of half a lemon into the pan and turn the heat up until the liquid in the pan thickens.

Steak with wine or brandy

Remove the meat from the frying pan and set aside in a warm place. Add about a small wine glass of brandy or dry red wine to the pan and boil fiercely for 3 minutes. You will need to add a knob of butter if there is only a little meat juice in the pan. Pour over the steak. If you use stock instead of alcohol simmer only. Use this method for making gravy for pan-fried liver or chops.

Chops

(These recipes are not suitable for lamb chump chops, which need longer cooking)

Lamb chops with rosemary

Rub lamb chops with crushed garlic and sprinkle with rosemary. Squeeze with a little lemon juice and grill or fry for 10 - 12 minutes on each side.

Lamb chops with mushrooms & spinach (for 2)

½ lb. (225 g.) cooked chopped spinach
¼ lb. (115 g.) sliced mushrooms
2 lamb chops
1 clove garlic (optional)
2 oz. (55 g.) of butter or 4 tbs. of cooking oil

Peel and crush the garlic and rub into the lamb chops. Heat the oil or butter in the frying pan. When a mushroom sizzles in the fat it is hot enough. Add mushrooms and chops and cook for 8 to 10 minutes on each side. Stir in the spinach. Cook on a gentle heat for another 8 minutes. Add a squeeze of lemon or a knob of butter if the spinach is sticking to the bottom of the pan. Season with salt and pepper. You could crumble Greek feta cheese over the chops and brown the whole dish under the grill.

Lamb chops with mustard

Peel and crush 1 clove of garlic into a tablespoon of grainy mustard and 1 teaspoon of olive oil. Spread the mixture over the chops and grill or fry.

Pork chops in mustard & yogurt (for 2)

½ carton of plain yogurt
2 tbs. of grainy mustard
2 pork chops
salt and pepper

Beat the mustard into the yogurt with a wooden spoon. Lightly grease a shallow ovenproof dish with butter or oil. Place the chops in the dish and coat the flesh but not the fat with the yogurt and mustard mixture. Cook under the grill for 15 minutes each side recoating the chop with yogurt and mustard when you turn it over. Alternatively cook at gas mark 5 (375°F) in the oven for 35 - 40 minutes.

Pork chops with apple & onion (for 2)

1 medium-sized eating apple
1 medium-sized onion, peeled
2 pork chops
1 oz. (25 g.) of butter
2 or 3 cloves (optional)
salt and pepper

Rub a shallow ovenproof dish with a little butter. Slice the onion and apple and place them in a thick layer at the bottom of the dish. Dab with butter and drop in the cloves. Season the chops with salt and pepper and lay on top of the apple and onion. Cook at gas mark 7 (475°F) for 10 minutes and then turn down to gas mark 5 (375°F) for 35 - 40 minutes. Turn the chops halfway through the cooking. Use this recipe for cooking pork or beef sausages at gas mark 5 (375°F) for 25-30 minutes.

Gammon with walnuts

Crush 2 walnuts and 5 or 6 black peppercorns and press into a thick piece of gammon with a rolling pin. Fry in hot butter or oil for 8 minutes each side.

Liver & sage

Dip 6 - 8 oz. (170 - 225 g.) of liver per person into wholemeal flour seasoned with salt and pepper. Sauté in 1 oz. (25 g.) of butter and 1½ tablespoons of oil for 4 - 5 minutes on each side with fresh sage leaves or a few sprigs of dried sage leaves. The liver should be pale pinky brown inside.

Chicken

Note on cooking chicken
If you are cooking frozen chicken it is absolutely essential that the piece is completely defrosted before it goes in the oven. You should carefully examine the inside which takes much longer to defrost. The temperature of the meat has to be raised to about 190°F during cooking to ensure that any dangerous bacteria — salmonella in particular — are killed off. That is why in these chicken recipes a period of cooking at a moderate temperature is preceded by a short blast at a higher temperature. Always remember to turn the oven on before starting to prepare a dish. Most ovens take a good 5 - 10 minutes to come up to the required temperature. Before serving chicken always pierce through to the bone with a knife point to make completely sure that the inside is not pink or bloody. If it is, continue cooking (more about poultry, page 9 Choosing Poultry).

Buttered chicken

1 chicken piece per person
1 peeled and sliced onion
1 lemon slice per person
½ oz. (15 g.) butter per person
thyme
salt and pepper

Lift the edge of the skin of the chicken with the point of a knife to make a little pocket. Push in a lemon slice and a knob of butter.

Fold back the skin and work the butter into the flesh with the fingers. Lay the chicken on a bed of onion slices in a buttered baking dish. Dot liberally with butter and sprinkle with a little thyme. Cook without a lid for 7 minutes at gas mark 7 (425°F) and then turn down to gas mark 5 (375°) for 30 - 40 minutes, turning the chicken over halfway through the cooking. Test to see if it is cooked by pushing the point of a knife through to the bone — if there is any suggestion of pinkness or blood continue cooking. This is a very rich buttery dish and needs a fairly plain vegetable like new potatoes or rice to absorb all the juices.

Chicken & apricot skewers

1 chicken breast per person
¼ lb. (115 g.) dried or fresh apricots (tinned ones are too sugary and will not do)
1 large courgette

Soak the apricots overnight in water. Cut the chicken into cubes. Cut the courgette into fairly thin slices. Thread the chicken, apricots and courgette onto skewers. Season with salt, pepper, mixed herbs and lemon juice and grill. 'Baste' with butter while they are cooking. ('Basteing' means keeping moist with the cooking fat, in this case butter.) They will only need 15 to 20 minutes.
(Juliette Compston's recipe)

Grilled chicken

Season chicken pieces with salt and pepper and rub a little garlic and/or grainy mustard into the skin. Dot with butter or brush with cooking oil and put under a hot grill for 5 minutes each side. Turn down the grill to a medium heat and continue cooking for 15-20 minutes each side.

EGGS

Use free-range eggs where possible. Battery hens are raised in disgusting conditions and their eggs have very little flavour.

Boiling eggs
Unless you want hard-boiled eggs, you must spoon eggs into boiling water. Eggs kept in the fridge tend to crack when placed in boiling water, resulting in the whites coming out in long streamers, and water taking their place inside the shell. Best to try and avoid this by either taking them out of the fridge long enough before cooking to allow them to regain room temperature or warming them between your hands while the water is boiling. The alternative, of course, is not to keep them there in the first place. Slip them gently into the water from a spoon, and bring the water back to the boil. It is a great culinary art to boil an egg so that yolk and

white are cooked as you want. One rule is: know your egg; fresh
ones take longer, and so do bigger ones.
Soft: 3½ minutes in boiling water.
Mollet: 4½ minutes in boiling water.
Hard: 8-10 minutes in boiling water.
For use in salad put in cold water after removal from the pan, this
prevents a dark ring forming around the yolk.

Coddled
Put the egg into cold water and bring to the boil. Turn off the heat
and allow to stand in the water for 7 minutes (soft) or 12 minutes
(hard). If you have an electric stove, take the pan off the ring or
the water will continue to heat as the ring only gradually loses
heat. The white of coddled eggs stays soft and is more easily diges-
ted than that of boiled eggs. Coddled eggs finely mashed with salt
and pepper and chopped spring onions or herbs can be used as a
dressing for salads.

You can buy porcelain egg coddlers: you put the egg in the
coddler with a knob of butter and season with salt and pepper and
herbs. Put the coddler in boiling water for 8 minutes.

Poached Eggs
In a poacher: fill the bottom of the pan half full with boiling water.
Rub a little butter around the metal cups and allow a small knob
to melt in each. Break the eggs in and cover. Cook until the white
is firm and the yolks are filmed with white but still runny.

Variation
Sams' recipe. Lightly fry a little chopped garlic and parsley and
drop into the cups before putting in the eggs.

Eggs with cheese
Butter a shallow baking dish. Put in one medium (mollet) boiled
egg per person. Cover with a thick layer of grated cheese and
brown under the grill.

Eggs with spinach, ham & cheese
Butter a shallow baking dish. Line with a layer of warm, cooked,
chopped spinach. Season with salt and pepper. Add 1-2 soft-boiled
or lightly poached eggs per person. Cover with slices of ham spread
with a little grainy mustard. Finish with a thick layer of grated
cheese and maybe a little grated raw onion. Brown under the grill.

Eggs in a pot
Butter an individual ovenproof pot per person. Crack an egg into
each one and top up with single cream. Scatter chopped chives on
the top and season with salt and black pepper. Put the pot or pots

in a shallow ovenproof dish half filled with boiling water and put in a medium oven (gas mark 5, 375°F) for 10 - 12 minutes. If you prefer you can do this on the top of the stove in a covered saucepan for about the same length of time. Be careful not to overcook or the egg becomes solid and very unappetising.

Variation
Dollop a little cheese sauce or grated cheese into the bottom of the pan under the egg.

Scrambled eggs

Beat at least 2 eggs per person in a mixing bowl with a wire balloon whisk or fork until the yolk and white are totally blended into one another. Add a little salt and pepper. Melt 1 tablespoon of butter per person in a frying pan. When the butter is frothy pour in the eggs and stir gently with a rubber spatula over a medium heat pushing towards the centre. Serve on brown buttered toast immediately the eggs are thick and creamy. A second too late and they will be unpleasantly rubbery. Garnish with watercress.

Variations
(i)   Blend fine strips of smoked salmon — the cheap scraps are ideal — into the eggs before cooking. You can use ham instead of smoked salmon.
(ii) Sauté a few chopped mushrooms or a chopped spring onion in the butter before adding the egg.
(iii) Some people add a tablespoon of single cream to the raw egg.
(iv) As the eggs begin to thicken in the pan add 1 tablespoon of milk per person.

Egg & onion salad

Chop together 3 hard-boiled eggs and a small peeled white onion while the eggs are still hot. Season with black pepper, salt and ¼ teaspoon of dry English mustard.
    You can add a knob of butter or a tablespoon of mayonnaise if you wish.

Eggs & bacon cooked in the pan

Lay 2 or 3 slices of streaky bacon in an individual, flameproof, cast iron enamelled dish. Cook over a gentle flame until the fat begins to run out of the bacon. Turn the heat up a little and just before the bacon is cooked to your satisfaction break in 1 or 2 eggs. When the egg white is cooked serve directly to the table. If the bacon is very lean and looks as if it may stick, butter the dish first.

BREAD

Bread (no, don't panic, you don't have to make it)
Use wholemeal breads for preference.

Garlic & herb bread

Beat crushed or finely chopped garlic into softened butter. (Take butter out of the fridge and leave in a warm place one hour before needed). How much garlic you use is a matter of personal taste. One large peeled and crushed clove beaten into 1 oz. (25 g.) of butter would be adequate for 4 - 5 slices of bread buttered on both sides. Slice a whole or half loaf in thick wedges but do not cut through the base. The loaf should still be joined together along the length of the base. Spread both sides of each slice of bread with garlic butter. Seal in aluminium foil. Bake for 20 minutes at gas mark 6 (400°F) or with whatever else is already cooking in the oven. Open the top of the foil for the last 4 - 5 minutes of cooking to crisp the crust. The more butter that you can spare for this the better.

Herbs
Substitute a mixture of chopped *fresh* herbs for garlic or use a mixture of both. Parsley, sage, thyme and chives would all be good.

Tomato bread

Use the pasta sauce alla piquante on page 39. Leave out the chillis if you prefer. Slice a French loaf lengthways but don't cut all the way through the back. Spread in the tomato sauce and fill with any combination of sliced ham, salami, mortadella or cold meats, cheeses and sausages. Sprinkle with chopped stoned black olives, capers and a little dried oregano, black pepper and a dribble of olive oil. Seal in foil for 1 - 2 hours before serving. Delicious for summer picnics.

Eileen Gorman's medieval oyster loaves

This is a medieval recipe that Eileen Gorman of the Old Bakery in Woolpit, Suffolk, dug up for a feast.

Cut dinner rolls halfway across. Hollow out the soft insides and crumble into breadcrumbs. Gently sauté half the breadcrumbs in a frying pan with ½ oz. (15 g.) of frothing butter and 1 small finely chopped onion and a crushed clove of garlic. Add the chopped flesh of half a dozen oysters or half a pint of mussels (see Shellfish page 9): and cook gently for 5 more minutes. Stir in 3 or 4 tablespoons of single cream and some finely chopped parsley. Pile the mixture back inside the rolls — this quantity will fill 8 to 10 — and put in a medium oven at gas mark 5 (375°F) to crisp for 5 minutes.

PUDDINGS

This bit of the book seemed destined to create problems since I have a marked dislike for puddings. But laying personal considerations aside and recognizing the distinct unreality of being able to produce a cookbook that quietly ignored a whole course I set to work with a bad grace. And, of course, was soon forced to admit to the number of occasions when the yearning for just a small mouthful of sweetness had forced me to plunder the currant packet or my companion's plate. So here are some of the puddings that have bypassed my puritan dislike for sugar and starch. They aren't very sweet or very starchy and I would recommend serving just enough to tease the senses rather than a great dollop.

Whipping cream
Use only double cream for whipping.

Let the cream chill for a couple of hours before whipping.

Pour cold water into the bowl that you are going to use. Tip it out and dry it.

Use a large bowl. The cream expands in volume as you beat air into it so you will need plenty of room. Also that way you don't get covered in splashes. Beat the cream with a balloon whisk or hand or electric beater. Remember that you are beating the cream *not* the bowl. Lift the whisk through the cream so that air is trapped in it. Stop beating when the cream will stand stiffly by itself in little peaks. If you go on it will go grainy and buttery.

Marion's banana & chestnut pudding

Mash 1 or 2 bananas into the contents of a small tin of sweet chestnut purée. The banana takes away the cloying sweetness of the chestnuts. Top with whipped cream. You could add chopped walnuts or hazelnuts to the purée or sprinkle them over the cream.

Yvonne Gold's raspberry & grape pudding

This was a dish invented for Sunday breakfast but it would be equally refreshing as a dessert. You must have glass dishes to serve it in or half the charm is lost.

tiny seedless green grapes
fresh raspberries
plain yogurt

Rinse the raspberries and push a whole grape into the centre of each one. This sounds fiddly but it's not. Stack the raspberries around the sides of a glass serving dish so that the green of the grapes can be seen from the outside. Fill the centre with plain yogurt.

Banana cream pudding

Beat or liquidize bananas into 4 oz. (115 g.) of cream cheese. Add one small carton of single cream, lemon juice, 2 tablespoons of caster or soft brown sugar and a little nutmeg to taste. Chill in the fridge for half an hour before serving. Decorate the top with flaked almonds.

Rice pudding

¾ tbs. of pudding rice (the round, short-grain kind) or round-grain brown rice
¾ tbs. of brown or white sugar
¾ pint (430 ml.) of milk
1-2 cardamom pods (optional: if you do use them, you must first remove the outer shell of the cardamom, inside which are the pods)

Cover rice with a little boiling water. Leave to stand for 5 minutes and then drain. Add sugar, cold milk and the ground seeds from inside the cardamoms and the empty pods. Cook at gas mark 1½ (275 - 300°F) for 4½ hours. This makes a light, creamy pudding delicious hot or cold. My mother's recipe.

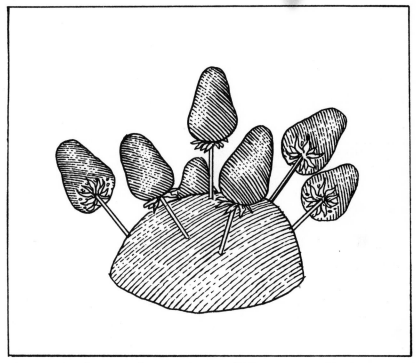

Chocolate covered strawberries

This most delicate and sensuous of delights was 'poached' on a visit to a confectioners in the CitiCorp building in New York where they have a glorious machine that spins an endless stream of melted black chocolate.

½ lb. (225 g.) of strawberries in peak condition
6 - 8 oz. (170 - 225 g.) of black chocolate
1 pkt. of cocktail sticks
1 large apple or potato

Rinse the strawberries and cut away any discoloured bits. Don't pull off the leaves. Break the chocolate into squares and place in a

heatproof basin in a saucepan of boiling water. Don't fill the saucepan too full or the water will bubble into the chocolate. As the
chocolate melts, stir it with a wooden spoon. Turn the heat down
when the chocolate is completely melted, since it will lose its
lovely glossy, runny quality and become dry and bitty if the heat
is too high. Cut the apple or potato in half and place each half cut
side down on a saucer. Spear each strawberry through the leaf on
a cocktail stick and, holding it over the bowl of melted chocolate,
dribble chocolate over the strawberry leaving the leaves sticking
out at the end. Push the other end of the cocktail stick into the
apple or potato. Don't let the strawberries touch each other. Leave
to chill in the fridge until the chocolate is hard. Pull out the sticks
and serve a couple to each person with their coffee.

Other fruits to try: tangerine segments, small whole apricots, fresh
pineapple chunks. Take care to pat off all the moisture or chill;
otherwise the chocolate will not stick.

Fruit salads

The conventional fresh fruit salad is made by cutting fruit into
small chunks and covering them with a syrup made with water,
sugar or honey and fruit juice. This is a very adequate but not a
very exciting way to serve fruit salad. An inventive alternative
follows, which also provides you with a much more attractive
answer and the only skills it demands are care in choosing the
absolutely freshest fruit and a little dexterity with the knife.

a selection of fresh fruits in perfect condition
lemon juice
optional sugar

Cut the apples, pears, melon, peaches, apricots, strawberries,
plums, nectarines, bananas, etc., into fairly delicate slices. Break
oranges and tangerines into segments. Leave grapes and the smaller
berries whole. Arrange the fruits on individual plates. Don't mix
them up, make small piles of the whole berries — redcurrants for
instance should be left on the stem — and fan out the sliced fruits
rather like a hand of cards. If you are not going to put the plates
straight onto the table, sprinkle with a fine spray of lemon juice
to stop the fruit turning brown. Serve with a little caster sugar
for those with a sweet tooth and thin continental biscuits like
Langues de Chat or tiny pastry shapes.

Dried fruit salad

Soak ½ lb. (225 g.) of mixed dried fruit — wild apricots, prunes,
apples, pears, peaches — overnight in ¾ pint (430 ml.) unsweetened
grapefruit or orange juice. The fruit will absorb the fruit juice and

58

leave a thick syrupy coating. Serve with fresh cream or plain yogurt.

Tinned *green figs* are scrumptious served with smetana (buttermilk).

Baked apples

Core 1 cooking apple per person and place in a generously buttered baking dish. Fill the hollow with honey or brown sugar, raisins and chopped nuts. Add a teaspoonful of brandy for special occasions. Bake at gas mark 6 (400°F) for 30 - 35 minutes. They taste equally good cold.

Strawberry & orange dessert

½ lb. (225 g.) strawberries/raspberries
5 oz. (140 g.) pack of cream cheese
juice and grated rind of 1 orange
2 tbs. caster sugar (or to taste)

Liquidize all ingredients together. Pour into individual glass bowls or tulip wine glasses, chill and serve.

Chapter 3

Simple Basic Methods

and Ways to Use Them

STARTERS

Soft roes on toast

1 lb. (450 g.) herring roes
plain or wholemeal flour seasoned with salt and pepper
2 rashers of bacon (optional)
wholemeal toast
2 oz. (55 g.) butter

Wash the roes and pat them dry. Dip into the seasoned flour.
Melt the butter in a frying pan and when it bubbles add the roes
and cook on a medium heat for 8 - 10 minutes. If you are using
bacon reduce the amount of butter to 1 oz. (25 g.) and chop the
bacon until it begins to crisp and then add the roes. Serve on
hot buttered wholemeal toast for breakfast, tea or as a starter.
You could also try using chopped mushrooms instead of bacon,
and maybe sprinkling the whole lot with chopped parsley.

Italian antipasto

To make a really satisfying plate of Italian hors d'oeuvres, you
need to have an Italian delicatessen within easy reach. The essence
is to include mouthwatering snippets of vegetable, meat and fish
delicacies. Enough to tease the palate, but not too much or you'll
be too full to move on to another course, although with lots of
fresh bread and butter and a salad you could expand it to make a
whole meal. Some things you could include: fresh or tinned
sardines, any of the Italian salamis, Mortadella, mozzarella cheese,
hard-boiled eggs with fresh mayonnaise, tomatoes dressed with
olive oil, parsley and garlic, a white or red bean salad, pickled red
peppers or long green pickled chillis, olives, anchovies, Italian
risotto rice with butter, ricotta cheese, pickled dried tomatoes,
bottled artichoke hearts, Parma ham, tuna and a selection of
crudités (raw, sliced vegetables).

Mussels in garlic butter

½ pint/½ lb. (225 g.) mussels per person
1 oz. (25 g.) butter per person
1 clove of garlic each
a handful of chopped parsley

Peel and chop the garlic and then crush with the flat of a knife (or put through a garlic-crusher). Melt the butter in a large heavy bottomed saucepan until it foams and then stir in the garlic. Allow them to bubble together for 2 - 3 minutes. Keep the heat low. Clean the mussels. Scrape any barnacles off the shells and scrub. Pull off the beard; this is a tuft of hairy suckers that the mussel attaches to the place where it grows. Throw away any cracked or damaged mussels and any which will not open when you tap them with another mussel. Drop the mussels into the pan with the chopped parsley. Don't fill the pan too full, do two batches if necessary. Cover and cook for 5 minutes giving the pan an occasional shake. When the mussels are open, remove from the pan and strain the juice in the pan through a fine sieve to make sure there is no sand floating in it. Discard any mussels that are still closed. Serve on individual plates with the hot butter and garlic and lots of fresh crusty bread.

Mushrooms in garlic butter

6 oz. (170 g.) mushrooms per person
½ oz. (15 g.) butter per person
1 small clove of garlic per person
2 -3 tbs. of chopped parsley
salt and pepper
4 - 5 coriander seeds

Wipe the mushrooms with a damp cloth. Trim off the tips of the stalks. Keep the mushrooms whole for this dish unless they are very large, in which case cut in two. Peel and chop the garlic finely and crush with the flat side of a heavy knife or put through a garlic-crusher. Melt the butter in a frying pan until it foams and then sauté the mushrooms, garlic and parsley until soft with the coriander. Serve on wholemeal toast.

Mushrooms à la grecque

1 lb. (450 g.) mushrooms
4 spring onions
2 cloves garlic
¼ pint (145 ml.) dry white wine
1 chopped stick of celery
salt and pepper
juice of half a lemon
4 tbs. olive oil/2 oz. (55 g.) butter
chopped parsley

Peel the spring onions and chop finely. Peel and chop the garlic and crush with knife or put through garlic-crusher. Heat the oil or butter. Sauté the onions and garlic until they soften. Chop the mushrooms and the celery. Squeeze the lemon. When the onions are soft add all the other ingredients to the frying pan and cook covered at a gentle simmer for 15 minutes. Chill and serve sprinkled with chopped parsley.

Avocado mousse (from Madame Rochon of Chez Solange)

4 ripe avocados
2 small pots plain yogurt
juice of 2 lemons
1 large or 2 small spring onions
salt and pepper
2 oz. (55 g.) of button mushrooms for garnish

Chop the spring onions. Liquidize together the yogurt and chopped spring onion. Peel and stone the advocados. Squeeze the juice from the lemons. Add the advocado flesh and lemon juice, and liquidize again. Season with salt and pepper. Chill in the fridge for at least 2 hours before serving. Cut the mushrooms into little umbrella slices and sauté in a little butter for a couple of minutes and then add a tiny squeeze of lemon juice. Arrange on top of the mousse.

Grapefruit, melon & avocado slices

2 large grapefruit
2 large avocados
1 melon (any sort will do, even watermelon)

Peel the grapefruit like an orange; if you can't be bothered you could, instead of breaking the grapefruit into segments, cut it into pieces *through* the flesh. It makes the grapefruit easier to eat. Peel the avocados and cut in two. Remove the stones and cut lengthways into thin half-moon slices. Cut the melon into thin lengthways slices. Remove the seeds. On individual plates make 'wheels' of alternating slices of grapefruit, melon and avocado slices. Squeeze a little lemon juice over the avocado slices or they will go brown. Serve sprinkled with chopped mint leaves.

Tandoori prawns

¼ lb. (115 g.) of prawns per person
½ oz. (15 g.) butter per person
jar of either tandoori paste or tikka paste
either 2 slices of wholemeal toast each or a bed of brown, long
grain or Basmati rice. Use 1 - 2 level tablespoons of uncooked
rice per person
lemon slices/plain yogurt (optional)
chopped green coriander (when available)

The simplest way of making curried food at home is to use one of the commercially produced curry pastes sold in jars in Indian shops and increasingly in ordinary grocers. They come in a variety of flavours including the very hot vindaloo, madras and just plain curry paste. You can also buy two pastes that are particularly suitable for grilling or barbecueing: tikka and tandoori paste. For a really subtle flavour you can marinade meat or fish in the seasoning for several hours before cooking ('marinade' merely means to soak in liquid before cooking), but spreading it on just before grilling is certainly perfectly adequate.

Put the rice on to cook (see p. 43). Brown rice will take 40 minutes, Basmati rice only 20. While the rice is cooking, remove the heads and shells from the prawns if necessary and arrange the meaty part in a shallow heatproof dish. Dot with knobs of butter and sprinkle with tikka or tandoori paste. Cook gently under a *medium* grill for 10 minutes. Take care, if the grill is too high the prawns will toughen. Chop the coriander leaves and mix into the cooked rice, pile on to individual dishes and top with prawns and a little of the sauce from the dish. Serve with lemon slices and plain yogurt.

If you are using toast instead of rice simply spread with butter and a little sauce from the dish, pile the prawns on top and sprinkle with chopped coriander.

Taramasalata

Is a pâté of smoked cod's roe and milk-soaked bread. It now seems to be quite widely available in delicatessens and is usually quite good, but I find the rather garish, shocking pinkness of commercially produced taramasalata a trifle off-putting. It's not at all difficult to make, but you might find it easier to use a blender.

½ lb. (225 g.) smoked cod's roe (cooked)
2 slices white bread
3 tbs. milk
1 - 2 cloves of garlic
5 tbs. of olive oil or salad oil
juice of half a lemon
salt and pepper
chopped parsley

Spoon out the cod's roe from the skin. Peel and chop the garlic very finely or put through a crusher. Cut the crusts off the bread and leave to soak in the milk. Liquidize the cod's roe and garlic to a fine, smooth paste. Squeeze the milk from the bread and add the bread to the garlic and roes. Add the oil and lemon juice gradually. Season and serve. The amount of garlic and lemon juice that you use is a matter of your taste; some people prefer just a hint of each, others prefer a really strong garlicky taste. Keep adjusting the quantities until you find the best flavour for you. This dish is usually served with Greek pitta bread warmed in the oven and slices of lemon. Fish always tastes better with brown bread — you may be lucky enough to have a shop near you that sells wholemeal pitta; if not, wholemeal toast will do.

Skordalia

4 large potatoes
4 cloves of garlic (or more if you like)
salt
¼ pint (145 ml.) olive oil
juice of 2 lemons

Boil the potatoes in their skins and then peel. While the potatoes are cooking, peel and chop the garlic very finely and then crush with about 1 level teaspoon of salt with the flat of a knife. Otherwise, put through a crusher and add the salt later. Beat together with the potatoes, garlic and salt and then add the olive oil and lemon juice drop by drop. You can do this in a blender on a slow speed if you like. Check the seasoning — it *is* supposed to be very, very garlicky — and serve with hot pitta bread or long cos lettuce leaves. Unless you have real garlic fiends eating with you it's probably a good idea to have another blander dish as well as *skordalia* — a large plate of crudités would be ideal.

Fried aubergines

One of the nicest ways to serve *skordalia* is surrounded by fried slices of aubergine. You could also serve them alone or with almost any dip, hot or cold.

1 large aubergine (more if you are serving it alone)
plain flour
sea salt
cooking oil (olive for real flavour, but a cheaper one will do. Be
    careful because the flavour of the oil is really an integral part
    of this dish)

Slice the aubergine across in ½" (1 cm.) slices. Salt heavily on both sides and leave to drain for at least 1 hour. Rinse and pat dry with paper kitchen towel. Dip into the flour on both sides. Heat the oil until it gives off a pale blue haze — you will need ½" - ¾" (a generous cm.) in the bottom of a frying pan. Aubergines are capable of soaking up a huge amount of oil so you must be sure that the oil is hot so that it seals the outside without seeping through to the centre. Try a little of the aubergine before you dump the whole lot in, and make sure that it is sizzling quite fiercely. Fry the aubergine slices until they are a crisp golden brown and then drain on crumpled paper towel.

Chopped liver

½ lb. (225 g.) chicken livers
2 oz. (55 g.) chicken fat or butter
salt and pepper
1 chopped hard-boiled egg
3 - 4 spring onions/1 small chopped onion

Chopped liver is the simplest of pâtés. Strictly it should be cooked with chicken fat or at least vegetable oil rather than butter. But chicken fat is difficult to get unless you have a kosher butcher nearby and often they don't have a great deal. I dislike the taste of vegetable oil for cooking chicken livers; also there is a danger of overcooking the livers to the point of toughness because it is capable of a higher cooking temperature than butter. However, if you use oil just try not to let it get too hot.

Pick through the livers to make quite sure that a green bile gland has been removed. If you leave it in the livers will taste bitter and disgusting. Chop them roughly. Melt the butter or chicken fat in a frying pan. The liver should bubble quite gently when you drop it in. Cook it, giving the occasional stir, until it is a pale pinky brown. While the liver is cooking, chop the onion and hard-boiled egg as finely as you can. Mash the liver into the cooking fat with the back of a fork and turn into a mixing bowl. Mix with the chopped onion and egg and season with salt and pepper. Allow to cool and serve with brown or rye bread, preferably — if you've managed to avoid it so far — without butter. You can make this in a blender if you like, but I find the texture too creamy, the egg and onion spread evenly throughout and rather dominate the taste of the liver. You can also cook the livers with just salt, pepper and fat and make a separate egg and onion salad.

Smoked salmon & cream cheese

Smoked salmon and cream cheese
A treat for special occasions.

½ lb. (225 g.) smoked salmon
½ lb. (225 g.) cream cheese
black pepper
lemon slices
brown bread or bagels

An alternative to making cream cheese and smoked salmon sandwiches is to cut the smoked salmon into strips about 2″ (5 cm.) wide by 5″ (13 cm.) long and roll them around a table-spoonful of cream cheese. Arrange on a flat serving dish with a dusting of coarse black pepper and lemon wedges.

Cheese, avocado & cucumber dip

½ lb. (225 g.) cream cheese
½ cucumber
1 avocado (it can be an old one)
salt and pepper

Peel the cucumber and spoon the flesh from the avocado. Either liquidize all the ingredients together and season with salt and pepper, or, for a rougher blend, grate the cucumber and beat together with the avocado and cream cheese. Try varying the seasoning with lemon juice, crushed garlic, chopped mint or chives or a very little chopped green chilli. Serve with bread, biscuits and crudités (raw, sliced vegetables).

Olives

The best olives to buy are the ones that you find loose in Italian and Greek delicatessens, where there are several different varieties that you can taste before buying. The big juicy green ones are good and you may be lucky enough to have a deli near you that sells rather hard wrinkled green olives in a strong herby lemon dressing. You can make lots of different dressings at home.

Garlic dressing

This sounds fearfully strong and garlicky, but is very good. Provide lots of crusty fresh bread to mop up the juices. For 4 oz. (115 g.) of olives, mix together 2 peeled and crushed cloves of garlic, the chopped flesh of 3 olives, 3 tablespoons of olive oil. Mix with the olives in a small deep dish and serve sprinkled with parsley after leaving to stand for 1 hour.

Lemon & coriander dressing

1 lemon/lime
about 20 coriander seeds
3 tbs. of olive oil
8 oz. (225 g.) green olives

Cut the lemon into two halves. With a potato peeler very finely strip off the top layer of peel from one of the lemon halves. The slivers should be almost transparent with no bitter yellow pith on one side. With a sharp knife cut the slivers of lemon peel into tiny bits. Squeeze the juice from the lemon half. Crush half the coriander seeds with the flat of a heavy knife. Beat together the olive oil, lemon juice and crushed coriander seeds. Season with a little salt and pepper and pour over the olives with the slices of lemon and whole coriander seeds. Cover and leave to stand overnight. Serve with brown bread — you can eat the whole lemon slices or not as you prefer. You can also add garlic to this dressing.

Egg & anchovy dressing

6 - 8oz. (170 - 225 g.) of black olives
5 - 6 anchovy fillets
1 hard-boiled egg

Crumble the yolk of the hard-boiled egg and chop the white as finely as you can. A Mouli parsley mill does this job really beautifully. Chop the anchovies into tiny slivers. Mix with the crumbled egg and olives, sprinkle with parsley and serve with hot French bread and lots of butter.

Pickled red pepper & tuna dressing

4 oz. (115 g.) black olives
4 oz. (115 g.) tinned tuna
4 oz. (115 g.) pickled/bottled/tinned red peppers
chopped parsley
a few capers
salt and pepper

Flake the tuna, and cut the peppers into long thin strips. Toss together with the olives, parsley and capers and season with salt and pepper. Serve with bread, salad and hard-boiled eggs.

Olives are also delicious served in a couple of spoonfuls of cold tomato sauce left over from making pasta or with a garlicky vinaigrette with fresh chopped herbs.

Fresh sardines

Fresh sardines are terrific when you can buy them. One or two per person makes a good starter to a meal. Cut the heads off and slit open the belly. Rinse it out with cold water and pat dry. Then score two or three diagonal cuts across each side of the fish, rub with a little butter and then grill under a hot grill for 4 to 5 minutes on each side. Serve with brown bread and butter and chunks of lemon.

Whitebait

Whitebait are very simple to cook, but you *must* have a proper chip pan with basket. You can buy them frozen if there are no fresh ones available. You will need 4 - 6 oz. (115 - 170 g.) per person, or more if you are feeling greedy. Thaw first if you are using the frozen kind, and then pat dry. While 4" - 6" of oil is heating in the chip pan, dip the fish first in milk and then toss in a paper bag with some plain flour. When the fat has a pale blue haze rising from the surface lower the fish in the basket into the oil. They are cooked when they turn a pale crispy golden brown. Serve with brown bread and butter and lemon wedges. Decant the oil when it has cooled through a strainer into a jar and keep it to re-use for whitebait and other fish dishes (not for anything else or it will end up tasting of fish). It will only taste OK while it retains its pale gold colour, once it starts to turn darker brown it will begin to taste slightly burnt.

Tinned sardines

The big fat Portuguese sardines in olive oil are wonderful served on hot buttered wholemeal toast. They make an irresistible hors d'oeuvre and if you feel mildly guilty about turning out a tin for your guests' delectation you can serve them with a few capers and slices of lemon and pickled cucumber.

Sashimi

Sashimi is the Japanese way of serving only the absolutely freshest of fish. It has to be very fresh because it is eaten raw. When this was first suggested to me, I, like a lot of people, recoiled in horror; but, staying with friends in New York who were *sashimi* addicts, I finally overcame my distaste and, in the interests of science, tried it. It is delicious. Not to be missed at any cost. Buy a small thick cutlet of any firm fish, the best is tuna, but abalone, monkfish, sea bass, bluefish, salmon and cod are all good. You will also need two other vital ingredients — soy sauce and a small tin of Japanese green horseradish powder, called *wasabi*. You can buy *wasabi* in Japanese and Chinese shops. When choosing soy sauce look carefully at the label for the ingredients. Avoid soy sauces that include sugar. The cheapest places are Chinese supermarkets where, for the price of a tiny bottle in most grocers, you can buy a whole litre (2 pints). A more expensive but better quality alternative is to buy soy sauce, often labelled 'Tamari' or 'Shoyu', in health-food stores.

Cut the fish across, not along, the flesh with a sharp knife into very thin slices. Mix a couple of teaspoons of the *wasabi* powder with a little water to the consistency of English mustard. The correct way to serve it is smeared in a little lump on the side of a tiny bowl full of soy sauce. You use chopsticks to pick up the sliver of fish and then dip it into the soy and *wasabi*. It all sounds very fiddly but it is worth it and if you become an enthusiast it is a rather calming ritual. Serve the fish with fine strips of spring onion cut lengthwise.

(An alternative – sardines & *wasabi*)

Cut the heads off the sardines (they must be fresh) – one each will probably be sufficient – scrape away any loose scales and then cut down the belly, clean out the innards and press down flat from the back. The backbone will come away quite easily; throw it away. You will see that the sardine falls into four long segments. Cut between them. In a frying pan heat 2" (4 - 5 cm.) of milk until it shivers gently. Season with black pepper and drop in the strips of sardine. Cook for 4 - 5 minutes at the same gentle simmer until the flesh is opaque. Remove and serve with *wasabi* and soy.

STOCK

Stock is most used in soups, sauces and stews, but there are very few people who actually go to great lengths to make their own for cooking; most people use stock cubes. They're not too bad as long as you remember to use the minimum amount – usually far less than the packet suggests – and remember not to add any salt to your cooking until you have tasted it. Unless you have a large family or a freezer, or entertain a great deal, stock cubes are obviously a great deal more convenient, but there are alternatives to going the whole hog and making a huge pan of stock. Miso, which is a paste of fermented soya beans and grains is a better substitute for beef stock than a stock cube. Add a couple of tablespoons towards the end of cooking, but don't bring it to the boil. Tamari or soy sauce is another alternative. White wine or cider make a delicious substitute for a pale stock and a dark beer or red wine for a darker one; add a tablespoon of tomato purée for extra bite. Recipes that include alcohol need to be simmered or boiled until their bulk is reduced by half or they will be very indigestible and raw tasting. Alternatively, for a pale stock, the juice of a lemon added 5 minutes before the end of cooking will add extra piquancy.

A more expensive, but subtler flavour for stocks would be to use tinned consommé instead of beef stock or one of the brands of kosher clear chicken soup as a chicken stock. Both of these are delicious in their own right as soups. Hot consommé is even more of a treat with a tablespoon of sherry added for each person and a sprinkling of chopped parsley. To the chicken soup you could add a squeeze of lemon and some fine vermicelli. Cook for 5 minutes until the noodles are soft. A tablespoon of plain boiled rice is good too if you have some left over from another dish.

Vegetable or herb stock cubes are now quite widely available but fresh vegetable stock is really very simple to make. You can use the water out of cooking any root vegetables as the base.

Vegetable stock

1 chopped onion
1 chopped potato
1 chopped carrot
1 chopped parsnip or turnip
1 chopped leak
juice of a lemon
1 bay leaf
4 tbs. of chopped parsley
2 chopped cloves of garlic
1 tsp. of yellow mustard seed
1 oz. (25 g.) of butter

Melt the butter in a large saucepan. Throw in the mustard seeds and let them pop in the butter. Don't forget to cover the pan or they will shoot all over the kitchen. When they have popped put in the onions and garlic and cook gently in the butter until they are transparent. Toss in all the other ingredients except the lemon juice. Sauté the vegetables in the butter. If you want a pale stock don't let the vegetables brown or catch on the bottom of the pan. If you want a dark stock, let them catch but keep turning them all the time with a wooden spoon. You want them brown, but if they blacken at all you will get a nasty bitter taste. When the vegetables are golden or brown, depending on what you want, add two pints of cold water, and bring to the boil. Turn down and simmer for 30 minutes. Add chopped parsley and lemon juice. Add seasoning. For a thick stock purée or liquidize. For a thin stock strain and serve vegetables separately.

SOUPS

Tomato & orange soup

1½ oz. (40 g.) butter
1½ pints (860 ml.) of chicken stock
2 lb. (1 kilo) tomatoes/a large tin of tomatoes
grated rind of 1 orange
fresh chopped basil or a small pinch of dried basil
salt and pepper
1 onion
2 cloves of garlic

Chop the tomatoes very finely. Heat 1 oz. (25 g.) butter in a heavy bottomed saucepan. When it bubbles, add the tomatoes and cover on a low heat. Simmer until the tomatoes are mushy (about 20 minutes) and then liquidize. Give the tomatoes the occasional stir while they are cooking to be sure that they are not sticking on the bottom of the pan. While the tomatoes are cooking finely chop the onion and the garlic. Grate the peel from the orange, taking care not to grate the bitter white pith. Chop the fresh basil. In another saucepan melt the remaining butter and sauté the onions and garlic until they are transparent and then add the tomatoes, basil, orange rind, stock and salt and pepper. Bring to the boil and simmer covered for 20 minutes. If you want a very smooth soup you could liquidize the whole lot again. Serve with croutons (see below).

Omit the grated orange peel for a plain tomato soup.

Croutons

3 slices of bread (preferably stale)
½ oz. (15 g.) butter and 2 tbs. oil

Cut the bread into little cubes. Heat the butter and oil in the oven until, when you drop a piece of bread into it, the bread sizzles. Then add all the bread, toss it around to coat it with fat and put it back in a hot oven, gas mark 7 (425° F). At this temperature the croutons will be done in about 5 minutes but you should shake them during that time. If your oven is at gas mark 5 (375° F) they'll take about 15 minutes. Croutons can also be made garlicky, by adding crushed garlic to the fat.

Good with all soups, or in salads.

Fish soup

8 oz. (225 g.) filleted white fish
4 oz. (115 g.) streaky bacon (optional)
2 large onions
1 large potato
2 sticks of celery and their leaves/2 stalks of fennel with leaves
*   or a little of both*
2 cloves of garlic
a sprig of fresh or dried thyme
a handful of chopped parsley
salt and pepper
a bay leaf
juice of 1 lemon/½ pint (290 ml.) dry white wine
2 pints of water (a generous litre)
4 oz. (115 g.) shrimps or prawns (not frozen; optional)
2 oz. (55 g.) of butter
a handful of fresh or frozen peas (optional)
a fine round slice of lemon per person
a little chopped chives if available

Peel the onion and garlic and chop the vegetables into little chunks. Melt the butter in a large saucepan and sauté the vegetables

71

and chopped bacon bits. Add the garlic and herbs. When the vegetables are a pale golden brown, add 1 pint (575 ml.) of water and bring to the boil. Turn down to simmer covered for ¾ hour. While the vegetables are cooking cut the fish into 3 or 4 large chunks and soak it in the wine/lemon juice and enough water to cover. When the vegetables are tender, liquidize them with the stock in which they have cooked and return to the saucepan. Drain the liquid from the fish. If you have used wine, add it to the vegetable stock and cook at a bubbling boil for 10 minutes or there will be a raw taste of alcohol. Turn down to a gently trembling simmer and add the fish, peas and prawns; you can leave their heads and shells on but be sure to rinse them first in cold water. If you have used lemon juice for the marinade you can add it with the fish to the simmering vegetable stock. Cook for 10 to 12 minutes or until the fish is tender and opaque but not breaking up. Serve with a lemon slice and a sprinkling of chopped chives.

Cream of
mushroom soup

*1 lb. (450 g.) mushrooms. Flat mushrooms have a better flavour
  for soup than button mushrooms*
3 oz. (85 g.) butter
1½ oz. (40 g.) plain or wholemeal flour
1 small peeled and finely chopped onion
1 pint (575 ml.) milk
¼ pint (145 ml.) of water/chicken stock
salt and pepper

Wipe the mushrooms with a damp cloth and cut off the ends of the stalks. Chop half finely and half into quarters or fat slices. When the butter is bubbling in the saucepan throw in the finely chopped onion and sauté gently until the onion is floppy and transparent. Add the mushrooms and keep sautéing over a fairly low heat until their juices start to run into the butter. Cover and turn the heat as low as it will go. The mushrooms will begin to stew gently in a mixture of their own juice and the butter. Leave for about 10 minutes, giving the pan an occasional stir to prevent them sticking. If they are sticking the chances are that the heat is too high. After 10 minutes gently shake the flour over the mixture and then with the heat turned up a little gradually work the flour into the juice and mushrooms. You can beat the flour in quite vigorously for 3 to 4 minutes. If you heat the milk and water together in another saucepan to just below boiling it makes the blending easier. But you can use cold milk. Tip a little milk into the mushroom mix and blend it in thoroughly with the back of a wooden spoon. It won't blend in completely smoothly because of the onions and mushrooms but there should be no lumps of flour. Gradually add all the milk and when the soup has thickened to a creamy consistency turn down the heat, cover and cook for 20 minutes. Correct the seasoning and serve. If you feel extravagant, a spoonful of sour cream is good in the soup at the end; or a drop of sherry.

Brown lentil soup

2½ pints (1½ litres) beef stock/water
4 oz. (115 g.) of brown lentils
3 - 4 rashers of streaky bacon (optional)
1 large onion
2 cloves of garlic
2 carrots
2 leeks
1 small potato
1 tsp. of yellow or brown mustard seeds
¼ tsp. of cumin seeds
salt and pepper/bay leaf
2 oz. (55 g.) of butter/4 tbs. of cooking oil

Peel the onion and garlic and chop the vegetables. Sort through the lentils to make sure that there are no small stones or twigs mixed in with them. Rinse in cold water. Heat the butter or oil in a large saucepan. Throw in the mustard seeds and cumin seeds. Cover the pan and let the seeds pop in the oil. If you don't cover the pan they will shoot all over the kitchen. Be careful not to burn the oil while it is covered; it should go brown and develop a lovely nutty smell but should not burn. Cut the bacon into little strips and sauté gently with the onions in the pan. When the onions and bacon are a pale brown, add the other vegetables and continue sautéing for 5 minutes and then add the lentils and stir over the heat for a couple of minutes. Add the stock and bring to the boil. Turn the heat down until the soup is simmering and then cover and allow to cook for 1 hour. The lentils will gradually break down as they cook. You may wish to serve the soup with the lentils soft but still whole, or you can wait until they break down completely into a thick, rich purée. A short cut is not to wait until the lentils break up, but liquidize when they're soft. Serve sprinkled with chopped parsley.

You can make this soup with the smaller orange lentils as well, but you may find chicken stock more suitable than beef stock.

To make Indian lentil soup — *dhall* — add a few coriander seeds with the mustard and cumin seeds, a chopped fresh green or dried red chilli and ½ tsp. of Garam Masala (a curry powder you can buy ready mixed). Serve sprinkled with fresh green coriander leaves or mint.

Vegetable soup

2 oz. (55 g.) butter/4 tbs. of cooking oil
2 onions
2 carrots
2 leeks
¼ small head of cabbage
2 potatoes
1 clove of garlic
1 - 2 tbs. of pearl barley
2 pints (a generous litre) of chicken/beef/herb stock
salt and pepper
chopped parsley or other fresh herbs

You can use any other vegetables that you like but summer ones like aubergine and capsicums are not really suitable.

Peel the onion and garlic, scrub the carrots and chop the vegetables into small chunks. Sauté in a large saucepan in the hot oil or butter. Add the stock and pearl barley and bring to the boil. Turn the heat down, cover and simmer for 1 to 1½ hours. Add the cabbage 20 minutes before the end of cooking. If you wish, you can entirely liquidize or sieve this soup, or just half of it, or you can leave it as it is.

Minestrone soup

4 - 5 tbs. of olive oil/cooking oil/3 oz. (85 g.) butter
2 carrots
2 large onions
1 potato
3 sticks of celery
a handful of peas (they can be frozen) or beans. Use broad beans whole with maybe a little of the shell finely chopped if it is tender Break other beans into little chunks.
a handful of dried red kidney beans, white beans or chick peas (or tinned)
1 x 14 oz. (400 g.) tin of tomatoes/1½ lb. (675 g.) fresh tomatoes
2 - 3 cloves of garlic or more if you like a lot
a handful of chopped parsley
a handful of one of the tiny pastas (annellini, nochette, conchigliette) or some broken spaghetti
Parmesan cheese

These are suggestions for some of the vegetables to include, but you could also use any of the winter root vegetables, except beetroot, and cabbage cut in fine strands. If you use cabbage, add it to the soup at the end with the pasta.

If you are going to use dried beans soak them in water the night before and cook in their soaking water for three quarters of an hour until you are ready to add the tomatoes to the soup.

Peel the onions, scrub the carrots, and then chop all the vegetables into small chunks. Heat the butter or oil in a large saucepan and sauté the vegetables, leaving aside peas, beans and cabbage if you are using it. When the vegetables are golden brown, add the parsley, salt and pepper, and leave to cook for a couple of minutes while you chop the tomatoes into little chunks (if they're fresh). Add the tomatoes if they are fresh, and, 1½ pints of water. If you are using a tin, you can use the juice plus water to make up the 1½ pints. If you have used a great many more vegetables you will need more water or you will end up with a stew not a soup. Add any dried, cooked beans and their cooking water. If using tinned beans, drain them and add. Bring to the boil and then turn down to simmer, covered, for 1 hour. Stir occasionally, since as this is a thick soup there is a danger of it sticking on the bottom of the pan. After 1 hour add the peas or beans, cook for another 10 minutes and then add the pasta and any cabbage. Sprinkle the pasta in and give the soup a good stir to be sure that it doesn't stick together or drop to the bottom. Normally soup pastas only need 10 minutes to cook but because this is a fairly thick soup you may allow up to 20 minutes. When the pasta is cooked serve with grated Parmesan.

Nettle soup

2 lb. (900 g.) of nettle tops
1 large peel and chopped onion
2 pints (a generous litre) of chicken, beef or vegetable stock
1 chopped clove of garlic
juice of half a lemon
1 large potato
salt and pepper
4 tbs. of cooking oil

If you find yourself in the country in the spring, or you're weeding the garden, this is a delicious way to use nettles. Unless you have a very large scales you'll find it difficult to weigh this quantity of nettle heads. A large plastic carrier bag of the sort that you get with your groceries will hold about the right quantity. Pick just the top two inches of small juicy leaves, wearing gloves of course, in the spring. You can use nettles at any time but the flavour is best in the spring. Wash in lots of cold water and salt. Wear rubber gloves to do it. Peel and chop the onion and scrub and chop the potato. Peel and crush garlic. Heat the oil in a very large saucepan and throw in the potato, onion and garlic. Cook until they are soft and golden brown. Add the nettles and turn down the heat. Cover and allow to stew in their juices until the nettles are limp. Add the stock, season and bring to the boil. Turn down to simmer. Cook for at least 1 hour and then liquidize or pass through a food mill. Return to the pan, add the lemon juice and simmer for another 20 minutes. Serve with croutons (see p. 71) or grated cheese.

Nettle soup may sound a nasty idea but it has a wonderful strong, almost meaty, taste and isn't the slightest bit prickly. Don't pick the nettles near the road where they may be polluted by cars and dogs.

Egg & lemon soup

2 pints (a generous litre) herb or vegetable stock
6 oz. (170 g.) small pasta
3 eggs
1 clove garlic
grated Parmesan cheese
1 oz. (25 g.) butter
salt and pepper
a little chopped parsley or chives
the juice of one lemon

Heat the stock to boiling point and sprinkle in the pasta. While the pasta is cooking — it should take about 10 minutes — beat together the eggs, peeled and crushed or chopped garlic, herbs and softened butter. When the pasta is cooked whisk the egg mixture into the hot stock. It will break up into fine ribbons. Stir in the lemon juice and serve.

Watercress soup

2 oz. (55 g.) butter
3 large bunches watercress
1 large onion
1 large potato
2 cloves of garlic
1½ pints (860 ml.) water/chicken stock
1 small pot of sour cream/2 oz. (55 g.) cream cheese
juice of half a lemon
salt and pepper

Peel and finely chop the onion. Peel and crush the garlic. Scrub and dice the potato. Wash the watercress, cut off any yellow leaves and the very coarsest stalk ends. Chop half the watercress finely and half in quite large sprigs. Melt the butter in a saucepan and sauté the onion, potato and garlic until they begin to soften and then add the finely chopped watercress. Cover, turn down the heat and allow to stew for 10 minutes. Add the stock to the vegetables. Bring to the boil and then turn down to simmer, covered, for 25 minutes. Liquidize or sieve and then return to the saucepan and reheat. Add the extra watercress and cook for a final 10 minutes. You may need a little lemon juice to sharpen the flavour. Serve with thin slices of fried bread or thin brown toast and either a spoon or two of sour cream or some knobs of cream cheese.

Cream of celery soup

1 large head of celery
1 large onion
1 large potato
2 cloves of garlic
2 pints (a generous litre) of chicken stock/water
salt and pepper
2 oz. (55 g.) of butter

Scrub the celery and cut into bite-size chunks. Peel and chop the onion. Scrub the potato and cut into small chunks. Crush the garlic. Melt the butter in a large saucepan and when it bubbles gently sauté the vegetables in it until they are pale golden brown. You can include some of the chopped celery leaves if you like quite a strong flavour. Add the stock and bring to the boil. Turn the heat down to a gentle simmer and cover. Cook for at least 1 hour. The tougher outer ribs of celery may take longer to cook — test them after an hour. Liquidize and reheat. Add a little cream or milk at this stage if you wish, or even sherry. Serve sprinkled with chopped parsley.

You can use a large head of celeriac for this recipe instead of celery.

Jerusalem artichoke soup

2 lb. (900 g.) Jerusalem artichokes
1 large onion
2 pints (a generous litre) chicken stock/water
2 oz. (55 g.) of butter
salt and pepper
2 cloves of garlic
4 - 6 tbs. of single cream or top of the milk

Scrub the Jerusalem artichokes and peel off any rotten bits of skin. Peel and chop the onion. Crush the garlic. Melt the butter in a large saucepan and gently sauté the vegetables in it until they begin to soften. Don't let them brown. Add the stock and bring to the boil. Turn down to simmer. Cover and allow to cook for 1 hour. Liquidize or pass through a food mill. Return to the saucepan and reheat with the cream. Bring it to just below boiling and leave to simmer for a couple of minutes. Serve sprinkled with chopped chives or mint. For richer tastes, you can add cream, sour cream or perhaps some sherry.

Carrot soup

1 lb. (450 g.) carrots
1 large onion/3 leeks or both
1 large potato
2 pints (a generous litre) stock/water
2 oz. (55 g.) butter
salt and pepper
4 -6 tbs. single cream or top of the milk
1 clove garlic (optional)

Wash the carrots, cut off the ends and chop into rounds. Scrub the potato and chop. Peel and slice the onion or leeks and garlic. Melt the butter in a large saucepan and when it bubbles throw in the vegetables and garlic. Let the vegetables slowly melt into the butter until the onions are limp and translucent and the potato and carrots are beginning to soften. Do not let the vegetables brown, this is a pale orange, creamy soup. Take as long as you like for this bit of the preparation; the hot butter will bring out the sweet, rich taste of the vegetables. If you have time, you can turn the heat down after the vegetables soften and cover the pan with a lid and allow the vegetables to stew in their juices for 10 minutes. Add the stock or water and bring to the boil. Season. If you are using packet stock cube do not add any salt until the end of the cooking. Gently simmer for 1 to 1½ hours until the vegetables are tender. Rub through a sieve or food mill or liquidize in an electric blender. If you want a coarser texture, leave a couple of tablespoons of the vegetables whole. Return to the saucepan and stir in the cream, reheat to just below boiling. Draw it off the heat when little bubbles start gathering around the rim of the pan. Sprinkle with chopped parsley or mint and serve. This soup is delicious served with crispy fried bread or thin brown toast.

Creamy onion soup

2 lb. (900 g.) onions
1 lb. (450 g.) potatoes
2 cloves garlic
2 pints (a generous litre) chicken or vegetable stock/water
salt and pepper
½ pint (290 ml.) milk
2 oz. (55 g.) butter

Peel the onions and potatoes and slice. Melt the butter in a large saucepan. When it bubbles throw in the chopped vegetables and crushed garlic and continue stirring until they soften. Do not allow the vegetables to brown, this is a pale soup. Season and slowly add the stock or water, gradually bringing to the boil. Cover and turn the heat down until the soup is gently simmering. Cook for 1 to 1½ hours and then liquidize or pass through a food mill. Pour back into the saucepan and reheat to simmering with the milk for 15 minutes. Do not allow to boil. Sprinkle with chopped chives, parsley or mint and serve. Grated cheese is also good.

French onion soup

2 lb. (900 g.) onions
3 cloves garlic
2 pints (a generous litre) of beef or vegetable stock/water with
*   2 tbs. miso added at the end*
salt and pepper
3 oz. (85 g.) of butter
1 slice of buttered brown bread per person (use French bread if
*   you prefer)*
1 - 2 oz. (55 g.) grated Cheddar or Swiss cheese per person

Peel and slice the onions. Peel and chop the garlic. Melt the butter in a large saucepan. When it bubbles, stir in the onions and garlic. Turn up the heat. French onion soup should be a lovely rich dark brown colour so you can fry the onions over quite a high heat and even let them burn a little as they are cooking. The sugar in the onions will caramelize in the hot butter and give a strong, sweet taste to the soup. When the onions are brown, soft and smell very delicious, slowly pour in the hot stock and bring to the boil. Cover and turn down the heat. Allow to simmer for 1 to 1½ hours. While the soup is cooking, toast the slices of bread on one side and spread the other side with butter and grated cheese. When the soup is a thick rich dark brown, pour it into either a large ovenproof casserole or individual ovenproof serving dishes, float the bread and cheese on the surface and put in the oven at gas mark 5 (375°F) for 10 to 15 minutes for the cheese to brown or put the dish under a hot grill. This makes quite a hearty meal by itself and if you want to make it even more substantial you could crack an egg into each dish before putting the bread and cheese on top. It will poach in the soup.

Spinach soup

2 lb. (900 g.) spinach or ½ lb. (450 g.) frozen
2 large potatoes
1 large carrot
2 pints (a generous litre) chicken, herb or vegetable stock
a small carton of single cream
2 chopped cloves of garlic
2 oz. (55 g.) of butter
grated cheese

Wash the spinach (if using fresh) very carefully. Peel and chop the onion and garlic and scrub and chop the potato. Melt the butter in a large saucepan and gently sauté the vegetables until they are soft and pale golden. Add the spinach, turn the heat down very low and allow to stew until the spinach is limp. Add the stock, bring to the boil, season and then turn down to simmer for half an hour. If you want a fine, creamy soup, liquidize at this stage; if not, roughly chop the spinach against the side of the saucepan with a knife. Add the cream and heat to just below boiling point. Serve with grated cheese or croutons (see p. 71.)

Cold cucumber soup

2 cucumbers
5 - 6 large sprigs of mint
juice of half a lemon
2 small cartons of plain yogurt/1 carton of yogurt and 1 of sour
  cream
2 tbs. of olive oil
10 spring onions
1 medium-sized potato
1 pint water
salt and pepper

Peel the potato and onions, and chop both. Boil the potato in the water with salt, the chopped spring onions and a sprig of mint. When the potato is cooked (about 15 minutes), liquidize with the cooking water, onion and mint. Leave to cool. Grate or liquidize the cucumbers and add with all the other ingredients to the potato liquid. Beat together. Season and sprinkle with chopped mint leaves. Chill for at least 1 hour in the fridge before serving.

Split-pea soup

Split-pea soup is one of the simplest and most nutritious soups that you can make. You can either make up your own combination of split peas, lentils and grains, or you can buy ready-mixed packets in health-food stores and groceries.

   The proportions that I use are roughly 1 level tablespoon of peas, lentils or grains to ½ pint (290 ml.) of water or stock. But you can of course just use one kind of split pea.

1 level tbs. of *red lentils*
              yellow split peas
              green split peas
              pearl barley
              barley flakes
optional: *aduki beans*
              brown lentils
              short-grain brown rice
              millet

Bring to the boil with the water and simmer for 1½ to 2 hours. Add salt and/or tamari soy sauce before serving. Do not add salt at the beginning of cooking, it will prevent the beans and lentils from softening. This will make a delicious, almost meaty tasting, soup as it is; if you like, you can also add chopped carrot, onion, parsley, thyme, garlic, other root vegetables and celery.

Miso soup

Serious macrobiotic eaters have miso soup for breakfast. The idea of a rich, dark vegetable soup first thing in the morning may seem a little hard to take, but it is very comforting on a cold winter morning and one can fast become an addict. It is also incredibly easy to make.

1 carrot
1 onion
¼ head of cabbage
2 tbs. of miso
2 tbs. of cooking oil
generous pinch of salt
1 pint (575 ml.) water

Peel the onion and scrub the carrot, then chop them finely with the cabbage. Sauté in the oil until soft. Add the water, bring to the boil and then turn down the heat to a fairly vigorous simmer for 20 to 25 minutes. Mix in the miso. It does tend to be very sticky; the easiest way to mix it is probably to blend it in a small bowl with some of the vegetable water, beating it with the back of a wooden spoon and then gradually stirring it into the saucepan. Cook for 5 minutes but do *not* bring to the boil. Check seasoning and serve.

These are really the minimum ingredients for miso soup. You could also add peeled and chopped parsnip, turnip, spring onion, swede, celeriac, celery, watercress, whole beanshoots, chopped parsley, kale, cauliflower or broccoli. It is the ideal way of using up leftover vegetables. Potatoes, tomatoes and aubergine are members of the nightshade family and are not used in macrobiotic cooking. If you wish you can also add one of the dried seaweeds — a small strip of *wakame* or a few strands of *arame*.

SAUCES

An unwarranted air of mystery tends to surround the making of sauces. This may proceed from the contemplation of puzzled and occasionally enraptured faces struggling to discern the ingredients of a particularly fine, subtle mixture or from simple exploration of what's on your plate. How does the transformation of butter, flour and milk into a creamy, smooth liquid happen? How do you make a fresh tomato sauce that bears no relation to its tinned equivalent? Once you've mastered a couple of the basic sauce recipes a whole range of simple, fast dishes are yours to do with as you wish.

The most useful and adaptable sauce recipe is based on a 'roux'. This is a mixture of equal proportions of fat, usually butter or margarine, and flour heated together whilst stirred. White and golden sauces are kept on a low flame, a higher flame will brown the butter and flour and make a darker base for meat sauces and thickening some soups and stews. Beating milk, stock or wine into the flour and fat will give you a simple sauce capable of endless variations — from a thin white pouring sauce used to lightly coat vegetables to the first step on the way to making a soufflé. Egg yolks can also be used for thickening sauces. They are beaten and added to the warm liquid, not hot or they will 'curdle' (break up into a fine grainy texture with the liquids and solids separating; not recommended).

White sauce (Béchamel)

This is a splendid basis for lots of other sauces — flavourings can be added to it.

2 oz. (55 g.) butter/margarine
2 oz. (55 g.) flour
1 pint (575 ml.) milk/white stock/stock and milk

Method 1
Melt the fat slowly over a low heat in a small deep saucepan. Stir in the flour with a wooden spoon. Keep stirring until the flour and fat are completely mixed together with no lumps or little pockets of flour. This should take about 2 minutes. The mixture should be golden *not* brown. Remove from the heat and add about 1/3 of the liquid. Either whisk or beat with a wooden spoon — whichever suits you best. When the mixture is smooth return to the heat and keep stirring until it comes to the boil. Slowly stir in the rest of the liquid, keeping in mind how thick you want the finished sauce to be. Season with salt and freshly ground black pepper. Let the sauce bubble for another 5 minutes (longer if you want it to thicken more). Give it an occasional stir. If you don't cook it, you'll find the flour tastes 'raw'. If it ends up lumpy, the only remedy is to strain it.

Method 2
The truly reluctant method. Put all the ingredients in a liquidizer and blend at high speed. Pour into a saucepan and heat slowly, stirring all the time until thick and creamy. Gently bubble from 5 - 10 minutes, giving the occasional stir.

Thicker and thinner sauces
For a thicker sauce, use ½ - 1 oz. (15 - 25 g.) more of both flour and far. For a thinner sauce use ½ - 1 oz. (15 - 25 g.) less. Use the same amount of liquid.

82

Cheese sauce

Beat in 3 - 4 oz. (85 - 115 g.) of strong, grated Cheddar before serving. Make sure the cheese is all melted. This is the *minimum* amount of cheese. Good cheese sauce can take up to ½ lb. (225 g.) of grated cheese.

Pour over cauliflower, leeks, macaroni, potatoes, broccoli, spinach.

Mushroom sauce

Sauté 6 oz. (170 g.) sliced mushrooms (the flat ones are best) in 2 oz. (55 g.) of butter until the mushroom juices run into the butter. Stir into the sauce.

Parsley sauce

Add 3 oz. (85 g.) of washed, finely chopped parsley to the sauce a few minutes before serving. Serve with fish, white meat, or vegetables.

Caper sauce

Add 1½ tablespoons of chopped capers and 1½ teaspoons of the vinegar they were pickled in to 6 oz. (170 g.) of thick white sauce. Serve with hot or cold fish.

Herb sauces

Chop fresh, mixed or individual herbs into simmering sauce. Stir for 1 - 2 minutes and serve with vegetables, fish or meat.

Celery sauce

Slice 5 or 6 celery sticks, including the leaves, into ¾ pint (430 ml.) of water. Season and simmer until the celery is mushy. Rub through a fine sieve or liquidize and use as the liquid to add to a roux in making a white sauce. Cream can be added after the sauce is removed from the heat.

Onion sauce

Boil 2 peeled and chopped onions in water or stock. Remove them when they are tender. Boil the liquid furiously until it is reduced to ½ pint (290 ml.) Mix with ½ pint (290 ml.) of milk and gently beat into the roux. Add the chopped onions and ½ - 1 teaspoon of dry English mustard. You could also experiment with adding grated cheese or chopped chives.

Fennel sauce

Either substitute fennel for celery in the celery sauce recipe or chop a small handful of feathery green fennel leaves into ½ pint (290 ml.) of thick white sauce. Add a few drops of lemon juice. Serve with fish, especially mackerel.

Shrimp sauce

Make the white sauce with equal proportions of milk and fish stock. Gently sauté 1 pint (575 ml.) of peeled shrimps or prawns, roughly chopped in 2 oz. (55 g.) of butter for 4 - 5 mins. Stir shrimps and butter into the sauce. Try seasoning with cayenne, lemon juice and/or anchovy essence.

Wine, cream

All these sauces can be made richer by substituting cream for milk; they can be made tastier by substituting white wine for some of the milk.

Bordelaise sauce

Is a rich tomato and wine sauce that is usually served poured over steak.

2 shallots or a small onion, peeled and finely chopped
1 oz. (25 g.) tomato purée
3 tbs. chopped tinned tomatoes, drained
1 bay leaf
3 oz. (85 g.) butter
2 oz. (55 g.) plain flour
¼ bottle red wine
¼ pint (145 ml.) chicken stock or water

Put the chopped onion in a thick bottomed saucepan with the butter. Melt over a high flame. Turn down the heat when the onions are golden and add the bay leaf. Remove from the heat, add the flour and keep stirring until the flour is completely blended in. Add the tomatoes and the tomato purée, stirring all the time until the ingredients are well mixed. Take care not to burn the bottom. Stir in the wine and slowly add the stock. The sauce should be thick, so don't add too much stock. Simmer over a low heat until the sauce thickens and turns slightly brown. Stir from time to time: 20 minutes.

Hollandaise sauce

8 oz. (225 g.) of butter
3 egg yolks
salt, pepper, vinegar, lemon juice
Melt 4 oz. (115 g.) of the butter in a double saucepan, with water boiling in the lower part. If you don't have a double saucepan, put a pudding basin in the top of a saucepan of boiling water. Skim off any froth from the butter and cool to tepid. Gradually whisk in the egg yolks and put back over the heat. As it thickens, cut the rest of the butter into little knobs and add one by one, gently whisking all the time. Season with salt, pepper and vinegar or lemon juice when the sauce has thickened. This sauce is very rich and particularly delicious with vegetables or with cold fish.

84

Curdling

This sauce will curdle if it is too hot. If it does, there are several remedies but they will not work if the egg has hardened into grainy lumps. Watch carefully for any sign of curdling and remove from the heat the moment the butter and egg begin to separate. The sauce will have to be thrown away if the curdling goes too far or it can be used in sandwiches.

Emergency measures
(i)   Drop an ice cube into the sauce and whisk until it melts.
(ii) In a clean pan whisk together 1 tablespoon of water and one egg yolk until the two thicken together and then slowly whisk into the curdled sauce drop by drop.

Mousseline sauce

large carton of whipping cream
Hollandaise sauce (as above)

Beat the cream until it is stiff. Fold into the Hollandaise sauce while it is still hot. Correct seasoning, as the cream will make it a little bland.

MEAT

STEWS & CASSEROLES

Stewing is a slow way of cooking the cheaper cuts of meat; you cut the meat into chunks, brown them in oil, top them up with stock or other liquid and then cook for several hours at a low temperature. It is no good trying to hurry along a stew; raising the temperature so that the liquid cooks at above simmering point will toughen the meat. So you do have to allow plenty of time for cooking, although the preparation period is quite brief. The paler stews and casseroles made with chicken, veal and pork tend not to need such a long time in the oven, nor do liver or kidney. Stews improve in flavour out of the oven; they are nearly always richer and tastier the next day, although the vegetables tend to go rather mushy and unpalatable and you may have to spoon them out and throw them away. Keep covered in the fridge for up to three days if you can keep temptation at bay that long. Always bring to the boil before re-serving. The flavour can be improved even more by marinading (i.e. soaking) the meat in some sort of alcohol, tamari soy sauce and herbs and spices the night before you are going to cook. The liquid from the marinade will provide a strong base for the stock.

Heavy cast-iron casseroles are ideal for cooking stews because both stages of the cooking can be carried out in the same dish. The meat is browned on the top of your stove and then the liquid is added and the dish is transferred to the oven and none of the juices are lost. If you are using a frying pan and then transferring everything to a pottery casserole, which cannot be put on top of the stove, when you've put the meat and vegetables into the casserole, add a little stock or water to the frying pan and over a medium heat stir with a wooden spoon to free all the scraps of meat that are sticking to the pan into the stock. Add this liquid to the casserole; the meat should be covered, but not drowned. It is better to use the minimum of liquid and check for evaporation during the cooking, since too much liquid will dilute the flavour and give you a thin, watery gravy reminiscent of school dinners. All is not lost, though, if this does happen. Spoon out the stock into a saucepan and boil it furiously until the quantity reduces and then pour it back over the meat.

Allow between 4 - 6 oz. (115 g. - 170 g.) of meat per person. If you are using meat which includes bones increase this quantity by a couple of oz. to make up for the weight of the bones.

You can ask the butcher to cut the meat into chunks suitable for stewing or do it yourself. The ideal size is about 2" (5 cm.) square. Trim the fat away first, although you may wish to leave a little in to thicken the gravy. Cut across the bunches of muscle; the short strands will cook more tenderly than long strips.

Pat the meat dry before browning or the juices will leak into the oil and the outside of the meat will not seal. Browning the meat improves the flavour of the stew and helps to keep the meat in neat chunks. You can dip the meat into seasoned flour before frying. This will help to seal the outside and the flour will thicken the stock. Only add herbs, spices and pepper to the flour, salt will draw out the moisture from the meat and there will probably be enough salt in the stock anyway. Don't add salt to the stew until the end of the cooking. Packet stocks are quite highly salted and the strength increases as the liquid evaporates and becomes more concentrated.

Heat the butter or oil until meat dropped into it cooks quite fiercely; some people prefer to brown the onions first and then cook the meat in the onion-flavoured oil. You can either remove the onions or leave them in the pan but don't brown too many things at once because the temperature of the oil will drop and the meat will steam instead of sealing. Carrots cook much quicker in a stew if they are sautéd first, so the sequence for browning meat and vegetables would be: onions first, then meat and then any root vegetables. When the onions are transparent and the meat is sealed on all sides and beginning to brown add the stock and bring to just below boiling point. The first couple of bubbles to rise to the surface will indicate that it is time to move the casserole into the oven. The oven should have been turned on to heat at the beginning of preparations. Cover the pot during cooking and check once or twice to be sure that not too much liquid is evaporating. Top it up with warm stock or water. Stir to the bottom of the casserole to be sure that nothing is sticking to the bottom. You can if you wish continue cooking the stew on a very low heat on top of the stove, instead of in the oven, but be sure to check every half hour or so that the bottom is not sticking. Some stews, like Lancashire hot-pot, have a layer of vegetables on top and should be uncovered to brown for the last half hour of cooking.

The white meats — pork, veal and chicken — are not browned before stewing but gently sautéd to a pale gold.

Serve stews with something absorbent like rice (see p. 43) or mashed potatoes.

Lancashire hot-pot

Lancashire hot-pot is one of the few stews where it is not absolutely necessary to brown the meat before putting it in the oven. You may if you wish though.

1½ lb. (675 g.) lamb chops (small ones from the middle neck are fine)
2 lb. (900 g. - 1 kilo) potatoes
2 large onions, peeled and sliced in fine rings
1 leek, peeled and sliced in rings (optional)
salt and pepper
½ pint (290 ml.) water or beef stock
½ tsp. of thyme
½ tsp. dried English mustard
½ oz. (15 g.) butter

You can use stewing steak for this dish if you prefer. Warm the oven to gas mark 4 (350°F). Trim most of the fat from the meat and cut into even-sized portions. Scrub the potatoes and slice them into rings. Peel and slice the onions and the leeks. Rub a little butter or oil around the sides of the casserole.

Cover the base of the casserole with a layer of potatoes, season with a little salt, pepper and thyme and then cover with a layer of onions and leeks and then a layer of meat and so on to the brim of the dish. The top layer should be potatoes. You should try and save the neatest circles for this topping. Whisk the dried mustard into the stock or water. Pour it down the side of the potatoes. It should just touch the bottom of the top layer of potatoes. Dot a little butter on the potatoes and cover. Bake for 1½ to 2 hours, checking occasionally that the stock is not drying up. When the meat gives easily to the point of a knife and the potatoes are tender, remove the lid and cook at gas mark 6 (400°F) for another 20 minutes to half an hour until the potatoes are crisp and golden. Serve sprinkled with a little chopped parsley, with peas and baby carrots.

Beef stew

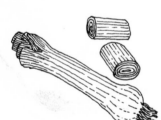

1½ lb. (675 g.) stewing steak
2 large onions
4 large carrots
2 leeks
2 cloves garlic (optional)
1 tsp. of yellow mustard seed
salt and pepper
2 oz. (55 g.) wholemeal flour
a bay leaf
4 tbs. of cooking oil
¾ pint (430 ml.) of beef stock (include some red wine if you wish)
1 tbs. of tomato purée
2 large potatoes
¾ tsp. of dry English mustard

Preheat the oven to gas mark 2 (300°F). Trim the fat from the meat and cut into cubes. Scrub the potatoes and cut into quarters. Peel and slice the onions and leeks, scrub the carrots and chop into chunks. Peel and crush the garlic. Dip the meat into the flour seasoned with ground black pepper and dry mustard. Heat the oil with the fat trimmed from the meat over a low heat. When the fat has gone transparent and fizzled up, fish it out with a perforated spoon and discard. All this business with the fat is a bit fiddly and you can leave it out if you wish, but it does give the stew extra flavour. Heat the oil until a piece of onion sizzles in it and then fry the onions until they begin to brown a little. Add the meat and sauté it until it is brown on all sides. At this stage it smells really delicious. If you are going to continue cooking the stew in the

88

same pan, add the chopped vegetables, mustard seed and garlic and keep sautéing until they begin to soften. Cover and turn down the heat and leave to stew gently in their own juices for 5 minutes. Pour the stock over the meat and vegetables, add the bay leaf and tomato purée, cover and put in the centre of the oven. Cook for at least 2 hours. Check halfway through cooking that the stock is not evaporating too quickly.

Try making this stew with other root vegetables — turnips, swedes, parsnips, Jerusalem artichokes. You could also add tinned or fresh tomatoes if you like.

Summer stew

This is a tomatoey beef stew made with courgettes, green peppers and celery.

1 oz. (25 g.) butter/3 tbs. olive oil
1 lb. (450 g.) braising beef
20 spring onions
4 sticks of celery
2 green peppers
4 courgettes
1 x 14oz. (400 g.) tin of peeled tomatoes/1 lb. (450 g.) sharp red
*   tomatoes or big Mediterranean tomatoes*
2 cloves garlic
pinch of oregano
½ pint (290 ml.) water
salt and pepper

Preheat the oven to gas mark 3 (325°F). Cut the meat into cubes. Cut the hairy ends off the spring onions and just the last couple of inches of really coarse green leaves. Wash to remove any grit. Scrub the celery and chop into 2″ (5 cm.) chunks. Cut the ends off the courgettes and slice. Remove the stalk from the green peppers and slice, cutting away any white pith and throwing out the seeds. Peel and crush the garlic. Heat the oil or butter in the casserole or frying pan and sauté the meat until it browns on all sides. Add the onions, celery, courgettes, garlic and herbs and continue sautéing until they soften. Chop the tomatoes and add to the meat and vegetables. If you're using tinned tomatoes, you don't need to chop them, just add the whole lot with the liquid and break them up roughly in the pan. You'll probably need to add another ½ pint (290 ml.) of water to cover the meat and vegetables properly. More, if you used fresh tomatoes. Cook in the oven with a lid on for 1 hour, and then add the green peppers and a little extra water if it seems dry. Serve when the peppers are soft but not mushy. Another 25 to 30 minutes should be long enough. Serve with rice or pasta.

Use red or white wine instead of water if you have it.

Chicken casserole

1 piece of chicken per person
2 large onions
2 large carrots
2 large potatoes/or even better 1 lb. (450 g.) tiny new potatoes
2 - 3 cloves of garlic
sprig of fresh thyme — dried will do
1½ - 2 pints (860 - 1150 ml.) water/chicken stock/dry white wine or still dry cider
juice of half a lemon
salt and pepper
½ tsp. of dried English mustard
2 leeks (optional
2 sticks celery (optional)
2 oz. butter
¼ lb. (115 g.) button mushrooms (optional)

Preheat the oven to gas mark 5 (375°F), unless you wish to cook this casserole on the top of the stove.

Dry the chicken, patting gently with paper kitchen towel. Clean, peel if necessary, and chop the vegetables. Don't peel the potatoes, the flavour is much better with them left intact. Melt the butter in the casserole or saucepan and sauté the chicken pieces, turning all the time until they are pale gold and beginning to take on a slightly opaque look. Add the onions, herbs and garlic, and keep sautéing until they are soft and transparent. Add the remaining vegetables except the mushrooms, which should not be added until the last 10 minutes before serving. Cover and turn down the heat, allow to stew gently for 5 minutes. Pour the stock over the vegetables and chicken until they are just covered. Check seasoning. Bring to the boil for 2 -3 minutes and then put in the middle of the oven and cook for 1 hour. Test the chicken with the point of a knife, cutting right through to the bone to be sure that the inside is cooked. If the flesh looks pinky or blood runs from the meat, continue cooking. Add the lemon juice and mushrooms. Cook for another 10 minutes and serve. If you are cooking this dish on top of the stove cover with a tight fitting lid and simmer for 1 hour.

This makes a complete meal in itself. You can serve the juice first as a soup, or together with the chicken.

Sausage stew

I invented this recipe for a friend who didn't eat pork sausages, because beef sausages seemed pallid just grilled or fried. They are very tasty in this rich tomato sauce. You can use pork sausages if you wish, the big fat Italian ones would be ideal and so would tiny lamb sausages or venison ones, if you could get them. Boil Italian and venison sausages for 10 minutes before using them.

1 lb. (450 g.) sausages
2 large onions
3 cloves garlic
pinch of oregano
3 carrots
salt and pepper
1 x 14oz. (400 g.) tin of tomatoes
pinch of chilli powder/half chopped fresh chilli/dash of Tabasco
  (optional)
wholemeal flour
2 tbs. of cooking oil
½ pint (290 ml.) water

Preheat the oven to gas mark 4 (350°F). Cut the sausages into chunks about 1½" long (4 cm.), roll in your hands, having dipped your hands first in flour. Peel and slice the onions into rings. Chop or crush the garlic. Cut the carrots in chunks. Heat the oil in a casserole or saucepan and sauté the onions, garlic and sausages until the onions are translucent and the sausages are beginning to brown. Add the carrots and continue sautéing until they begin to soften. Add the tin of tomatoes and roughly break up tomatoes in the pan. Season with salt, pepper, oregano and chilli. Add water to cover and bring to the boil. Cook in the oven for 35 - 40 minutes or at a gentle simmer on top of the stove for about the same time. Serve when the carrots are tender, with pasta or rice.

Lamb & spinach stew

1½ lb. (675 g.) of chump chops of lamb. If your butcher does slices of leg of lamb you could use this instead. It will be more expensive, but takes less time to cook.
1 lb. (450 g.) fresh spinach
juice of 1 lemon
½ pint (290 ml.) dry white wine/1 pint (575 ml.) dry cider
½ pint (290 ml.) water/chicken stock
3 cloves garlic
2 sticks finely chopped celery
2 large onions
pinch of dried rosemary
2 tablespoons of olive oil
wholemeal flour

Preheat the oven to gas mark 5 (375°F). Cut the meat into cubes, trimming off the fat. Keep the bones. Shake bones and meat with wholemeal flour. Peel the onions and chop with celery into fine pieces. Heat the oil until a piece of onion sizzles pleasantly when dropped in. Sauté the onions, meat and celery until the vegetables are soft and the meat is beginning to brown. Add the whole, peeled, cloves of garlic and the rosemary. Add the wine or cider and only enough stock or water to cover the meat. If you are using cider you will only need a very little extra water. Cook in the oven for 45 minutes to 1 hour until the meat is tender. Wash the spinach while the meat is cooking and break into large pieces. Keep all but the very toughest stems. When the meat is cooked and breaks easily apart with a fork stir in the spinach, cover and cook for 5 to 10 minutes with the lemon juice. Serve with rice or new potatoes sprinkled with mint.

Beef Stroganoff

1 lb. (450 g.) braising steak
2 large onions
½ lb. (225 g.) mushrooms
2 cloves of garlic
2 small cartons sour cream
wholemeal flour
salt and black pepper
pinch of tarragon
½ pint (290 ml.) dry white wine/beef stock
1 oz. (25 g.) butter
2 tbs. olive oil

I think that it is simplest to make this dish in a deep frying pan or flame-proof casserole on the top of the stove.

Cut the meat into fine slivers 2″ (5 cm.) long by 1″ (2 cm.) wide, across the grain. It is easier to cut meat when it has been chilled in the fridge for a couple of hours. Douse the strips in flour. Peel and slice the onions in fine rings; peel and chop or crush the garlic. Wipe the mushrooms with a damp cloth, cut off the tips of the stalks and slice into umbrellas; or you can leave them whole if they are very small. Heat the oil and butter together and sauté the strips of meat with the garlic. When the meat is evenly browned on all sides, add the onions and cook until they are beginning to brown around the edges. Season with a generous grind of black pepper and a pinch of dried tarragon. Tarragon seems unpredictable in its strength, depending on freshness, so start with a small pinch and add more if you can't taste it. This dish should have a distinct, sweet taste of tarragon, but it can be unpleasant if it is overpowering. Stir in 1 pot of sour cream. Cover with a minimum of wine or stock and cook covered at a gentle simmer for 45 minutes. When the meat is tender, add the mushrooms and continue cooking for 5 - 10 minutes until they are tender. Stir in the remaining sour cream, taste and correct the seasoning. The sour cream can make everything a little bland so it is important to check that there is enough salt and pepper before serving. Add ¼ teaspoon of dried mustard if it seems to lack bite. Reheat after adding the sour cream and serve with rice or buckwheat (see p. 152).

Couscous

Is one of my favourite warming winter dishes. I don't think eating it at home is quite up to sitting in an Algerian café in Saint Germain, but it comes quite close. It doesn't seem to matter how large a dish of this you make, it always gets finished down to the last scrap. It has four components — couscous, which is a highly processed wheat cereal, bought dried in little granules which fluff up into light, buttery tasting golden grains when soaked and steamed; a vegetable, tomato and chick-pea stew; a fierce chilli and garlic paste called *harissa*; and a portion of grilled lamb, a kebab or a piece of chicken. You can leave out the meat if you prefer; the grain and chick peas together are an excellent source of protein. You can cook the meat in the stew but I prefer it separate unless it is something like *kalamaras* (squid). It may sound like a lot of work, but the three or four components make a whole meal.

Unless you have a pressure cooker, preparation should ideally start the night before or at least in the morning before work. But it is only one simple step, the chick peas need to be soaked in lukewarm water. A pint (575 ml.) to a teacup of chick peas is fine. If you want a short cut, use a tin of chick peas.

Vegetable stew

1 cup of chick peas (either tinned or dried)
1 x 14oz. (400 g.) tin of tomatoes
2 onions
4 - 5 potatoes
4 - 5 carrots
parsnips or turnips if you wish
2 - 3 leeks
¼ head of cabbage
2 tbs. of olive oil
salt and pepper
a handful of chopped parsley
¼ tsp. of cumin seeds
pinch of chilli powder

If you are cooking dried chick peas, throw away the water that they have soaked in and cook them in 2 pints of boiling water for half an hour without salt. Slice the onions into rings. Peel and chop the garlic. Scrub the potatoes and carrots and any other root vegetables. Chop, wash and cut the leeks into long strips. Chop the cabbage into rough chunks. Heat the oil in a large saucepan and sauté the onions, carrots, garlic, potatoes, parsnips, turnips and leeks until they are soft and beginning to brown. Add the tin of tomatoes and the chick peas with the water that they have been cooking in. (If using tinned chick peas, drain them and add some water.) Sprinkle with cumin seeds and season with salt and pepper.

93

Add a little chilli powder. Bring to the boil and then cook covered at a gentle simmer for about an hour. By the time that everything else has been prepared the stew will be cooked. It will only improve with time.

Couscous

Buy couscous in 1 lb. (450 g.) packets. It swells enormously when soaked, and 1 lb. is a generous amount for four; it would certainly serve six. The only time that I have ever followed the elaborate and hilarious instructions on the packet I ended up with a soggy cake instead of a light fluffy glistening pile, so I now use a method which seems to work perfectly each time. For every cupful of couscous take 1½ cups of water. Soak the couscous in the water for about 30 minutes until the grains are soft. Drain through a fine wire sieve and steam, covered, in the sieve for 10 to 15 minutes over a pan of boiling water. Gently turn the grains from time to time to be sure that the ones nearest the water don't go soggy. Serve with plenty of butter. Buy couscous in Italian, Middle Eastern and health-food shops.

Harissa
Some shops do sell tiny, brightly coloured tubes and tins of *harissa,* but it is easy to make. The proportions sound ridiculous, but you'll be surprised how it disappears from people's plates. Mix together:

2 finely chopped or crushed cloves of garlic
4 tbs. of chilli powder
2 tbs. of olive oil
2 tsp. of lemon juice
a pinch of ground cumin seed
a pinch of ground coriander seed

It should be the consistency of a thick, oily paste. You can add chopped mint or parsley too if you wish.

Meat

Chicken
Use one piece of chicken for each person. Wash the chicken and then pat dry. Rub a little butter into the skin or brush with cooking oil and put under a hot grill for 10 - 15 minutes on each side. Turn down the grill and cook at a medium heat for another 15 - 20 minutes on each side.

Lamb
Buy one or two lamb chops per person, depending on the size of the chops. Squeeze a little lemon juice over them and a grind of pepper and grill for 10 - 12 minutes on each side.

Lamb kebabs
8 oz. (225 g.) of lamb cut from the leg, per person
lemon juice
pepper

Cut the lamb into 2″ (5 cm.) cubes, leaving a small piece of fat on each if possible. Thread onto skewers and grill brushing each time you turn with lemon juice. They will take between 10 and 12 minutes to cook.

Lamb or chicken stew
If you prefer to cook the meat in with the vegetable stew, buy lamb chump chops or chicken pieces and sauté them in the oil for the stew before adding the vegetables and then continue cooking as for the vegetable stew.

Fish stew
6 - 8 oz. (170 - 225 g.) of white fish — cod, whiting, halibut — per person. Fifteen minutes before you are ready to start serving the vegetable stew, turn the temperature down to a gentle simmer and add the fish either whole or in chunks. It is cooked when the flesh comes easily away from the bone. Sprinkle with parsley.

Grilled fish
One cutlet or fillet of fish per person — cod, whiting, halibut or coley. Paint with melted butter and grill gently until the flesh turns white and opaque and the bone starts to come away from the centre. Turn once during 8 or 9 minutes' cooking.

Liver casserole

1½ lb. (675 g.) lambs' or calves' liver
2 onions
3 red peppers
5 tomatoes/small 8 oz. tin (225 g.) of tomatoes
½ pint (290 ml.) beef stock/stock and red wine mixed
2 oz. (55 g.) butter/3 tbs. of olive oil
1 clove of garlic
salt and pepper
wholemeal flour

Preheat the oven to gas mark 4 (350°F). Rinse the liver in cold water and pat dry with kitchen towel. Cut in thin slices. Dip in flour. Melt the butter or oil in a frying pan and gently fry the liver for 2 minutes on both sides. Transfer to a casserole. Peel and slice the onions, slice the red peppers, peel and crush garlic and chop tomatoes (if fresh). Sauté in the oil, adding the tomatoes for only the last couple of minutes. If you are using tinned tomatoes, add the juice as well. Pile in the casserole with the liver. Pour the stock and wine into the casserole. Cook at gas mark 4 (350°F) for 1 hour. Correct the seasoning and serve with rice or pasta.

Liver & onion casserole

1 lb. (450 g.) sheeps' or calves' liver
1 lb. (450 g.) onions
2 large potatoes
salt and pepper
½ pint (290 ml.) beef stock/water
wholemeal flour

Wash the liver under cold water. If there are any tubes running through it, cut them out. Pat dry and cut in thin slices. Dip in the flour. Peel and slice the onions. Scrub the potatoes and slice in rings. In a lightly greased casserole build up layers of liver, onions and potatoes in rotation, starting and ending with potatoes. Season with pepper and a little salt as you go. Pour the stock into the casserole. Dot the top layer of potatoes with a few knobs of butter and cover. Cook at gas mark 4 (350°F) for 1 hour.

Lamb & white bean casserole

2 oz. (55 g.) butter or 3 tbs. of olive oil
1 lb. (450 g.) of stewing lamb fillet
2 cups of white haricot beans (soaked)/large tin haricot beans
2 large onions
2 carrots/parsnips
2 cloves garlic
salt and pepper
2 pints (a generous litre) of stock, mixed with white wine
½ tsp. cumin seeds
½ tsp. coriander seeds
juice of 1 lemon
wholemeal flour

Preheat the oven to gas mark 4 (350°F). Soak the haricot beans overnight, if you're cooking dried ones. Cook for 1 hour in un-salted boiling water. While the beans are cooking, cut the meat into cubes and dip in the flour. Peel and slice the onions, cut carrots or parsnips in rings. Peel and crush the garlic. Heat the oil or butter and sauté the cubes of meat until they begin to brown at the edges. Add the chopped onions and carrots, parsnips and garlic. Sprinkle with coriander and cumin seeds. Season with salt and pepper. Cover, turn down the heat and leave to stew gently for 10 minutes. Drain the beans and, if you cooked them, use the water as stock. If using tinned beans, drain them. Put the beans, lemon juice, vegetables and meat in a casserole, cover with stock and move to the oven. Cook for 1 hour and then check that the beans and meat are tender. Continue cooking for another half hour if they are still firm.

Serve with plain yogurt and a sprinkling of chopped mint leaves.

Pork & red cabbage stew (for 6 to 8)

This dish is made on top of the stove in a large saucepan. Substitute venison or pork sausages for pork fillet if you like.

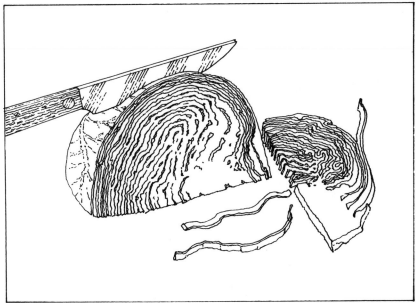

1 lb. (450 g.) pork fillet
1 large red cabbage – about 1½ lb. (675 g.)
2 large onions
2 large cooking apples
2 oz. (55 g.) butter or 3 tbs. of cooking oil
salt and pepper
1 tsp. of grainy mustard
2 tbs. red wine/red wine vinegar
3 cloves
½ tsp. of caraway seeds

Cut the meat into 2″ (5 cm.) squares. Peel the onions. Slice the red cabbage, onions and apples finely. You may have to wash the cooking apples under warm water – the skins are often sticky with chemical sprays. Heat the butter or oil in a large saucepan and sauté the meat until it turns pale gold. Scatter with caraway seeds. Add the onions and continue to sauté until they are limp and transparent. Add all other ingredients, turn the heat down as low as it will go and cover. Stir from time to time. This dish does have a tendency to stick to the bottom of the pan. As the apples and cabbage soften it becomes more and more moist and cooks in its own juice. Cook for 1½ to 2 hours. You may wish to omit the meat altogether and serve as a vegetable. It's delicious with a little sour cream. This dish improves if kept overnight.

MINCED MEAT DISHES

Meat sauce

This is a basic meat and tomato sauce for use with pasta in lasagne or with spaghetti.

¾ lb. (340 g.) minced beef
2 onions
2 cloves garlic
salt and black pepper
1 x 14 oz. (400 g.) tin of tomatoes
pinch of basil or oregano
½ pint (290 ml.) water or stock
3 tbs. of olive oil

Peel and slice the onions; peel and chop or crush the garlic. Fry the onions and garlic until they begin to turn transparent and then add the meat. Heat the oil in a large, deep frying pan over a medium heat. The meat should not fry very fiercely or it will brown and harden but it may lower the temperature of the oil when you first put it in the pan, so turn the heat up a little. Spread it over the surface of the pan rather than keeping it in a lump. Use a wooden spoon or a spatula and keep stirring the meat and turning it until it is an even, pale brownish grey, with no lumps of pink raw meat. A lot of fat tends to run out of minced meat; the cheaper the meat the more fat there will be. Push the meat to one side of the pan and tilt it towards you. The fat will gradually run down and form a pool; spoon it out, trying only to get rid of the top clear layer and leaving the meaty juices in the pan. Season with salt, pepper and herbs and add the tomatoes and a little stock or water. Roughly break up the tomatoes. This should be a thick, meaty sauce when it is cooked so only add extra stock when it is needed to stop the meat sticking to the bottom of the pan. Bring to the boil and then turn down to simmer, covered. It will cook satisfactorily in about 35 minutes, but the flavour improves the longer you cook it.

Variations
— Add sliced red or green peppers or courgettes at the same time as the tomatoes.
— Add button mushrooms 10 minutes before serving.
— Add olives or capers with the tomatoes.
— Add sliced carrots with the onions.
— Add peas (frozen will do) for the last 10 minutes of cooking.
— Use red wine instead of stock.

Chilli con carne

Chilli con carne is the same basic meat sauce as the above, but with the addition of red kidney beans and chilli, which makes the dish fiery.

Soak 2 cups of red kidney beans overnight. Cook in boiling, unsalted water for 1½ hours until the skins peel back when removed from the water. You can use tinned kidney beans to save time. Drain and add to the meat sauce at the same time as the tomatoes. How much chilli powder you use depends on your taste buds. It is very hot, so start with a pinch and work your way up to the right strength for you. Use the water that the beans have cooked in instead of stock. Add sliced red or green peppers with the tomatoes, if you like.

Serve with rice sprinkled with parsley and a bowl of plain yogurt which will sooth enraged palates.

Shepherd's pie

This is traditionally made with the leftovers of a leg of lamb, minced the following day; but I know very few people who can afford to buy a big enough leg of lamb to have enough left over to make this dish, so most people use minced beef instead.

1½ lb. (675 g.) minced beef
2 large onions
2 large carrots
1 pint (575 ml.) beef stock/water/Guinness or dark beer
1 lb. (450 g.) potatoes
salt and pepper
½ tsp. of dry mustard
dash of Worcestershire sauce (optional)
2 tbs. cooking oil
1 oz. butter
2 tbs. of milk

Peel and chop the onions and slice the carrots. Heat the oil in a large saucepan and fry the onions until they begin to brown. Add the meat and keep sautéing until it is an even brownish grey with no raw pink lumps. Add the carrots, cover the pan, turn the heat down and allow to stew for 10 minutes until the carrots begin to soften. Season with salt, pepper and mustard. Pour in the stock, water or beer and bring to the boil. Add a bay leaf if you wish. Splash in a little Worcestershire sauce. Turn down to simmer for half an hour.

Meanwhile, peel the potatoes (sorry, yes, this time you must peel them) and slice in two. Cover with cold water with a pinch of salt and bring to the boil. Turn down to a bubbling simmer and cook until tender. Mash with the back of a fork or an electric beater with salt, pepper, butter and milk. There should be no lumps in the mashed potato but this is sometimes easier said than done.

Lightly grease a deep pie dish. Preheat the oven to gas mark 4 (350°F). Tip the meat into the casserole. If there is a considerable amount of stock, strain some of it off into a small saucepan, don't throw it away, you can use it later as gravy.

Cover the layer of meat with a thick layer of mashed potato, score with a fork and dot with butter. Bake until the potato topping is tipped with rich golden brown peaks.

You can add 4 oz. (115 g.) of garden or frozen peas to the meat before topping it with the potato. I have a friend who won't eat shepherd's pie without a small tin of baked beans stirred into the meat. I think this is pretty yucky but he likes it.

Moussaka

1 lb. (450 g.) minced beef
2 onions
2 cloves chopped garlic
1 x 14 oz. (400 g.) tin of tomatoes
small handful of chopped parsley
2 large aubergines
6 oz. (170 g.) grated mature cheese
Parmesan cheese
3 tbs. of olive oil
½ oz. (15 g.) butter
salt and pepper
3 tbs. of milk
½ tsp. dry mustard

Slice the aubergines into thin long slices and sprinkle with salt. Leave to stand for 1 hour. The salt will draw moisture and the slightly bitter taste from the aubergines and also speed up the cooking time. Rinse and pat dry.

Peel and slice the onions and peel and chop or crush the garlic. Finely chop the parsley. Heat the olive oil in a frying pan and sauté the onions and garlic until they are transparent. Add the minced meat and continue stirring until the meat has browned. Add the tomatoes with their juice and a little water rinsed around the tomato tin to gather up the last drops of juice. Break up the tomatoes and gently bubble the whole lot together, covered, for 35 - 40 minutes checking from time to time that the tomatoes have not stuck to the bottom of the pan. While the meat is cooking, grate the mature cheese and beat together with the egg and milk. Season with salt, pepper and dry mustard. Preheat the oven to gas mark 4 (350°F).

Lightly grease a deep pie dish and line with a layer of aubergines. Pour in a layer of the meat sauce. Top with another layer of aubergine, another layer of meat, and a final layer of aubergine. Spread the egg, milk and cheese mix on top and scatter with Parmesan cheese. Cook, covered, for 1 hour and then remove the cover and allow the top to brown for 15 minutes. Serve sprinkled with parsley.

Basic minced meat curry

1 lb. (450 g.) minced beef
2 onions
2 carrots
1 small (8 oz.; 225 g.) tin of tomatoes
2 cloves of garlic
1 tsp. of black or yellow mustard seeds
pinch of coriander seeds
pinch of cumin seeds
pinch of ajvain seeds, which can be bought from Indian grocers
  (optional)
1 green fresh chilli/1 dried red chilli/¼ tsp. chilli powder
1 tbs. of curry paste
2 tbs. of cooking oil/butter and oil/if you really love curries invest
  in a tin of ghee *(special Indian cooking fat)*
small knob of fresh ginger (about ½''; 1 cm.) ¼ tsp. ground ginger
a few fresh coriander leaves if you can get them

If feeling very reluctant, or without the ingredients, you can omit the spices and just use curry paste and chilli. Peel and slice the onions and cut carrots into rings. Peel and chop the garlic finely or crush. Peel the pale brown papery skin off the knob of ginger, if using fresh, and chop finely. Heat the oil in a large saucepan. Throw the cumin, coriander, ajvain and mustard seeds into the oil and cover the pan with a lid. The seeds will pop in the oil, infusing it with their flavours. When they stop popping throw in the ginger, garlic and a small piece of chilli. Go carefully with the chilli; use a minute amount and add more later to your taste. Add the onions and stir in the oil until they begin to brown and soften. If you are not using all the extra spices start here. Add the meat and the carrots and continue stirring and turning the meat until it is thoroughly browned. Add the tomatoes to the meat with their juice and the same amount again of water. Roughly break up the tomatoes in the pan. Sitr in the curry paste (double the quantity if you have not used seeds). Simmer in a covered pan for 1 hour. Correct the seasoning, scatter with the chopped coriander leaves if you have them and serve with rice, pickles, chutneys and *raita* (see page 21).

Curry variations
— Use chopped potato as well as carrot. Add at the same stage.
— Omit carrot and stir in ½ lb. (225 g.) spinach (it can be frozen) 10 minutes before serving.
— Use chopped ladies' fingers instead of carrots. ½ lb. (225 g.) should be enough.

— Stir a small carton of yogurt into the curry before serving.
— Saute a chopped aubergine in a little oil and add instead of carrots.
— Omit the carrots and stir in ½ lb. button mushrooms (225 g.) 10 minutes before serving.
— Add ¼ lb. (115 g.) peas 10 minutes before serving.
— Use 1 sliced green pepper and 1 sliced red pepper instead of the carrots.
— Stir in half a head of cauliflower broken into flowerets halfway through cooking.

Easy onion chutney

1 medium-sized onion
1 small tomato
pinch of chilli powder
a few fresh coriander leaves finely chopped or parsley

Peel and slice the onion very finely; a grater or mandolin will do this job perfectly. Slice the flesh of the tomato very finely. The seeds and juice can go in the curry. Mix together onion and tomato and sprinkle with fine chilli powder and coriander leaves. Parsley will do, but it's not such a treat. To vary this, mix the whole lot into a small pot of plain yogurt.

Pappadums

Pappadums always seem such a miracle when you have them in Indian restaurants, it seems incredible that they are easy to make at home. But they are. You buy them in tins or packets; be sure to buy the kind that can be roasted as well as fried. Frying is very tricky, but if you merely toast them under a medium grill, they will erupt in tiny bubbles and go a pale golden brown. They have a slightly different taste to fried pappadums but it is very delicious. Beware — they are very easy to burn. Turn halfway through grilling.

ROASTING MEAT

Roasting meat is one of the easiest processes in meat cooking. There is barely any preparation to do and the result — if the meat is tender — is invariably irresistible. A meat thermometer is an invaluable aid for the reluctant cook.

Lamb

There are several cuts of lamb that can be roasted — some more expensive than others. There will be more fat on the cheaper cuts e.g. breast and shoulder, but this will contribute to the flavour. Lamb should be crisp and pale brown with streaks of dark red on the outside when roasted and slightly pink towards the bone. Allow 6 oz. lamb per person; 8 oz. per person if the meat is on the bone.

Roast shoulder of lamb or leg of lamb

Shoulder of lamb tends to be a cheaper, fattier cut of meat than leg of lamb, but lots of people prefer it for flavour. Both are simple to cook and suitably impressive. Try to let the meat regain room temperature, if it's been in the fridge, before cooking.

1 x 3 - 4 lb. (1½ - 2 kilo) leg or shoulder of lamb
2 — 3 cloves garlic
a little flour
salt and black pepper

Preheat the oven to gas mark 9 (500°F). Either rub the lamb all over with a cut clove of garlic or make tiny shallow cuts in the meat and fat and slide in thin slivers of garlic. Sprinkle with salt and black pepper and dust with flour. The flour will trap any escaping juices from the meat and form a thin crust. Put the lamb in a roasting tin. If you have a meat thermometer push it into the thickest part of the meat. Do not have it resting on the bone or fat because you will not get a true reading.

Roast for 10 minutes and then reduce the temperature to gas mark 3 (325°F).

Timings
For a rare joint, cook for 1 - 1¼ hours: 145° on the thermometer.
Medium rare — 1½ hours: 155/165°.
Well cooked — 1¾/2 hours: over 175°.

Opinions differ about 'basting' roasting meat: that means scooping the juices from the bottom of the roasting pan and spooning them over the meat to prevent it drying. The danger is that every time you baste you wash more of the juices from the joint into the bottom of the pan, whereas what you want to do is keep the juices inside the joint. Try both ways and see which you prefer. If you do baste, a spoon is adequate but you can buy a baster which is a rather obscene looking long plastic tube with a bulb on the end. They look a little weird but they work wonderfully efficiently. You suck the juice up using the bulb, and then let go and the juice runs out over the meat.

Variations
— Use slivers of lemon rind instead of garlic.
— Sprinkle the joint generously with rosemary (lamb and rosemary go together rather like beef and Yorkshire pudding).

Stuffed breast of lamb

Some butchers do have this inexpensive cut of meat ready stuffed to go in the oven but if yours does not, try this simple stuffing.

103

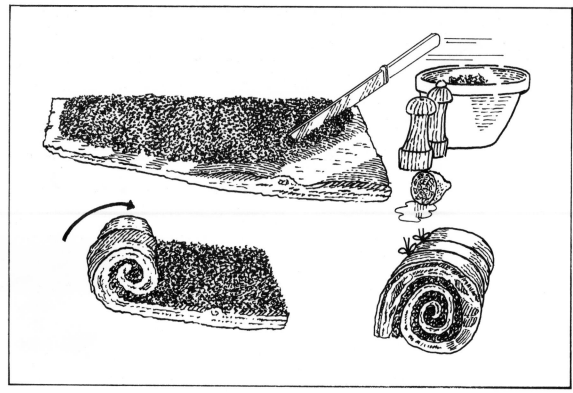

1 small onion
1 small eating or cooking apple
1 cup of wholemeal breadcrumbs
1 tbs. porridge oats
2 finely chopped cloves garlic
handful chopped parsley
pinch of dried rosemary
salt, pepper and dry mustard
1 oz. (25 g.) butter
1 egg

Grate the breadcrumbs either with the roughest side of a grater or in a liquidizer. Finely chop the onion, garlic and apple. Heat the butter in a frying pan and sauté the vegetables until they are soft. Add the breadcrumbs, chopped parsley, oats, salt, pepper and a little dry mustard. Stir until the breadcrumbs have absorbed the butter. Remove from the heat and allow to cool. Beat the egg and stir into the breadcrumb mix.

Ask the butcher for a 1½ - 2 lb. (675 - 1 kilo) breast of lamb (a generous amount for 4) and ask him to bone it for you. Preheat the oven to gas mark 3 (325°F). Sprinkle the inside of the meat with salt, pepper and maybe a squeeze of lemon juice. Spread the stuffing in a thick layer over the meat and then roll it up. Tie it once or twice around the centre with string, but not too tightly. Lightly dust with a little flour and place in a greased roasting pan. Cook for 1½ hours and then for the last 20 minutes turn the gas up to mark 5 (375°F). Remove from the roasting pan. Now comes the gravy process, which floors many of the inexperienced. You can just serve the juices from the pan if you prefer. But if you want gravy, this is what to do. Drain the meat juices into a saucepan; add ¼ pint (145 ml.) of vegetable cooking water or dry cider and bring to the boil. Boil for 5 minutes if you are using cider. Thicken if you wish by beating in a rounded teaspoon of cornflour.

Roast beef

Use sirloin or wing rib on the bone, top rump or topside. With a bone allow ½ to ¾ lb. (225 g. - 340 g.) per person, off the bone 6 to 8 oz. (170 g. - 225 g.). Most people choose joints of roasting beef just by looking at them in the butcher's window, and you have to be pretty expert to do more. Do at least check that the size is suitable for the number of people that you are inviting. Cold roast beef, if any is left over, is of course wonderful in sandwiches and salads. Keep it covered but outside the fridge or the flavour will take a while to recover from chilling.

This is quite a slow method of cooking roast beef but is very easy. Let the meat come up to room temperature. Preheat the oven to gas mark 3 (325°F). Rub the joint with salt and pepper and dust with flour. Place the meat with the fat side up in the pan. If you wish, you can surround it with par-boiled potatoes, (boiled for about 10 minutes), small whole onions, halved parsnips or carrots to roast with the meat. There is really nothing else to do except put it in the oven and wait until it is done, although if you have used vegetables they will need the occasional turn to stop them browning too much on one side. Push a meat thermometer into the thickest part of the meat but not touching the bone.

Timings
For meat with a bone allow 30 minutes per lb. for a rare joint, 35 for medium, and 40 minutes for well done. Unboned, reduce these times by 5 minutes.

Meat thermometer readings
Rare: 120°.
Medium: 130°-140°.
Well done: 150° and over.

Gravy
I like the French way of serving roast meat with just the

juices from the pan as gravy, but it's hard to deflect the English from their brown gravy. If you want gravy, then move the beef from the pan and set aside on a carving board for a few minutes before serving. Set the roasting tray on the top of the stove and on a medium flame stir in either 1 teaspoon of corn-flour (which is easiest to mix in) or gently shake in 1 teaspoonful of plain flour. Stir with a wooden spoon until the juices thicken and then gradually stir in hot beef stock or vegetable cooking water to the consistency desired. Continue cooking for 5 to 10 minutes so that there is no taste of raw flour. Adjust the season-ing with salt, pepper and mustard.

Roast pork loin

1 x 4 lb (2 kilo) loin of pork (this will do for 6 - 8 people)
salt, pepper
1 tsp. of dried thyme/sage/rosemary
2 cloves garlic (optional)
½ tsp. of dry mustard
half a lemon sliced finely
juice of half a lemon
½ pint (290 ml.) stock
2 oz. (55 g.) lard

Preheat the oven to gas mark 8 (450°F). Choose which herb you are going to use. Peel the garlic and cut into fine slivers. Mix together the herbs, salt, pepper and mustard, and rub into the fat of the meat. Insert the slivers of garlic into little cuts in the meat and fat. Lay slivers of lemon on the fat. Put the lard and the meat in a roasting tray and bake for 20 minutes. The fat should have begun to turn golden brown. If it hasn't, bake for a few more minutes. Turn the oven down to gas mark 4 (350°F), and continue cooking, allowing 35 minutes per pound (450 g.) of meat and an extra 35 minutes. When the meat is done, drain the meat juices and fat from the pan into a saucepan, skim off most of the fat with a spoon and thicken the juices that are left with a teaspoon of cornflour. Beat in ½ pint (290 ml.) of beef stock or vegetable cooking water and the juice of half a lemon. Season to taste and serve.

For the last hour of the cooking time, you could surround the meat with cored apples filled with raisins and topped with a knob of butter. Pour 2 tablespoons of water into the pan. Run the point of a knife around the centre of the apples to split the skin so they do not burst during cooking.

Roast gammon

1 x 4 lb. (2 kilo) unsmoked gammon corner

Rinse the gammon with cold water and dry. With a sharp knife mark with criss-cross diagonal cuts all over. Preheat the oven to gas mark 4 (350°F). Wrap aluminium foil around the gammon and set in the centre of a roasting dish. Cook for 20 minutes and then open the foil and fold back. Cook for 20 minutes for each pound (450 g.) with an extra 20 minutes overall. Turn the heat up to gas mark 6 (400°F) for the last 15 minutes of cooking to crisp the crackling.

Roast chicken

There is not a deal of fat on most chickens and what there is is not where you want it. The chicken will dry out around the breast and legs while cooking if you do not add extra fat. Butter has a wonderful affinity with chicken and can be used liberally. The best method is to lift the skin around the neck opening and push little knobs of butter under the skin, massaging it into the flesh from the outside. This is a bit revolting so you may prefer either to dot the outside with butter or to run melted butter over the chicken. In any case lightly grease the roasting tray and put some inside the bird.

1 x 3 lb. (1½ kilo) chicken (for 4 hungry people)
salt and pepper
a sprig of fresh thyme or a tsp. of dried thyme
clove of garlic
2 oz. (55 g.) butter

Preheat the oven to gas mark 8 (450°F). Rinse the chicken with cold water and pat dry. It may sound obvious, but even the most experienced cooks from time to time forget to look inside the chicken to be sure that there isn't a plastic bag full of giblets. Either melt the butter in a saucepan and pour over the chicken or try the under-the-skin method. Put the rest of the butter inside the bird with some thyme and a peeled and chopped clove of garlic. You could also put in a peeled onion, which will help to keep the chicken moist from the inside. Sprinkle with salt, pepper and thyme. You can also slip slivers of garlic or lemon under the skin.

Put the chicken in the middle of the oven and cook for 20 minutes. Baste with the juices in the pan and turn the heat down after 20 minutes to gas mark 6 (400°F). Turn the chicken on to its side. Continue basting and turning every 20 minutes until the bird is glistening golden brown. Allow 20 minutes per pound (450 g.) cooking time plus 20 minutes overall. With a sharp knife point cut through to the joint underneath the leg or wing to be quite sure that the inside of the bird is not pink or bloody; if it is cook for another 10 to 15 minutes.

Cook roast potatoes around the chicken or in a separate baking tin on the shelf above.

Boiled chicken

1 boiling fowl (about 3 - 4 lb. or the equivalent in chicken pieces). A battery fowl will give a very inferior result. Giblets and feet should also be used; the feet will make the stock more gelatinous. Kosher chickens are best for this.
2 large onions
3 or 4 carrots
salt, pepper
4 - 5 pints (2 - 2½ litres) cold water
(optional kosher chicken stock cube)

Peel and chop the onions. Scrub and chop the carrots. Put everything in a large pan on the stove and bring to the boil. Skim off any froth that rises to the surface. Turn the heat down until the stock is gently simmering. Cover and cook for 2 hours, a little longer for a larger bird. Take out the chicken. Let the stock stand until cold, when a layer of fat will form on the surface. Skim this off and discard. If you want a concentrated stock continue the simmering for another 2 hours.

Serve the chicken as it is. You can serve the liquid as chicken soup with the vegetables, or vary it by adding a little of the chopped chicken, or cooking a little pasta or rice in it. Use the liquid as stock where a pale stock is required.

FISH

Rose's smoked fish pâté

1 smoked mackerel
1 small pot of cottage cheese
1 small pot of sour cream
2 tsp. lemon juice
ground black pepper

Flake the flesh off the skin of the mackerel and either whizz up until smooth in a blender with all the other ingredients or mash together with a fork. Chill before serving with brown bread or toast.

Fried fish

Wash one whole fish per person and pat dry. Melt 1½ - 2 oz. (40 - 55 g.) butter in a thick frying pan. The fat needs to be very hot so it is a good idea to add a couple of tablespoons of olive oil to the butter. This will give you a higher temperature. Watch the butter carefully as it is heating and when the first tiny specks of brown appear put the fish in the pan. The fish is less likely to stick to a heavy bottomed frying pan. Cook for around 5 minutes each side. Once the fish is in the pan you can turn the heat up a little as the cold fish will reduce the temperature of the oil and butter. It is cooked when the sharp point of a knife slides easily into the fleshiest part of the fish. Serve straight from the pan with a knob of butter and lemon wedges. A large fish will take up the whole frying pan so you would need to be very adept at managing a couple of pans at once if you chose to fry fish for more than a couple of people. Pour the butter from the pan over the fish when serving. Whole fish have a tendency to part with their skins during the process. Apart from appearances, this doesn't matter too much.

Suitable fish: trout, mackerel, herring, sole, whiting, place, small cod or cod steaks, skate, sprats and sardines (4 - 6 oz.:115 - 170 g.) per person.

A la Meunière

Dip the fish first into milk and then flour before frying. Set aside in a warm place after cooking. Add 2 - 3 oz. (55 - 85 g.) of butter to the cooking liquid with the juice of half a lemon. Stir with a wooden spoon until the butter turns a light golden brown. Pour over the fish and serve with finely chopped parsley.

With almonds or mushrooms

Throw a small handful of slivered almonds or sliced mushrooms into the pan after turning the fish.

With oatmeal

Oily fish like herring or mackerel can be dipped in milk and then in fine oatmeal flakes before frying. The oatmeal has a tendency to fall off the fish, but don't panic — it doesn't matter. Just continue to cook the fish and the oatmeal till it's brown, and serve it on top of the fish.

Fish baked in foil

One of the simplest methods of cooking fish is to seal it in a parcel of aluminium cooking foil with a little butter and fresh herbs and bake in the oven. The foil seals in all the precious juices from the fish, which cooks in its own steam.

Salmon steaks

Wrap individually in foil with a knob of butter on each side and finely chopped mint or fennel leaves. Cook at gas mark 5 (375°F) for 20 minutes.

Cod steaks

Wrap in foil with butter, chopped capers and chopped green gherkins. Cook at gas mark 5 (375°F) for 20 minutes.

Baked trout

use 1 small whole trout for each person
1 oz. (25 g.) butter for each fish
1 tbs. of split almonds each
salt and pepper

Toss the almonds under a hot grill until they begin to toast around the edges. Preheat the oven to gas mark 4 (350°F). Very lightly rinse the trout and sprinkle the insides with salt and pepper. Dot with butter inside and out and use a little of the butter to grease a piece of aluminium foil. Sprinkle inside and out with toasted almonds, wrap in the foil and seal the edges. Cook for 20 minutes at the top of the oven. Serve with watercress and new potatoes.

You can bake herring or any of the oily fleshed fish — mackerel, sprats, sardines — in exactly the same way as trout. Use rather less butter, as the flesh is already oily, and use instead of almonds a

110

herb stuffing made with wholemeal breadcrumbs, chopped fresh herbs, garlic and lemon peel. Bind the stuffing together with a little beaten egg or milk and pack into the split fish. Bake for 20 to 30 minutes at gas mark 5 (375°F) depending on the size of the fish. Mash the herring roe into the stuffing.

White fish & cider

1 small fish per person/fillets or cutlets of cod, whiting, sole,
*   flounder or plaice*
½ oz. (15 g.) butter
1 bunch of spring onions
½ pint (290 ml.) dry cider
2 oz. (55 g.) grated cheese

Cut the heads off the fish or get the fishmonger to do it for you. Rinse. Preheat the oven to gas mark 5 (375°F). Wash the spring onions and cut off the hairy root ends. Slice in fine lengthways strips. Butter a shallow ovenproof dish and make a bed of spring onion strips. Lay the fish on top of the spring onions and fill the dish half full of cider. Sprinkle with grated cheese and dot with any remaining butter. Cook covered for 20 minutes or until the bone is coming away from the fish.

Monkfish in tomato sauce

Monkfish is a firm, very white-fleshed fish with a flavour very much like lobster. It does tend to be rather expensive. This recipe can be varied to use as little or as much fish as you like; use whatever vegetables you like.

1 lb. (450 g.) monkfish
1 x 14 oz. (400 g.) tin of tomatoes
1 large onion
8 oz. (225 g.) carrots — preferably baby ones
3 sticks of celery
¼ lb. (115 g.) packet of frozen peas
2 cloves garlic
salt and pepper
pinch of oregano
3 tbs. olive oil

Preheat the oven to gas mark 4 (375°F). Wash the fish and cut into large pieces. Peel and slice the onion. Scrub the celery and carrots and cut into chunks. Peel and crush the garlic. Heat the olive oil in an ovenproof, flameproof casserole and saute the onions, garlic, carrots and celery until golden. Stir the tomatoes into the vegetables, and roughly break up. Season and leave to simmer for 10 minutes. Put the fish into the tomato sauce, add enough water to cover the fish and vegetables and place in the middle of the oven. After 20 minutes, take it out and add the frozen peas. Cook for 30 minutes or until the fish is tender and coming away from the bone.

Any cutlets of white fish can be used for this recipe. Served cold with olives it's delicious.

Whiting with vegetables (for 2)

This is a very easy method of cooking any whole white-fleshed fish.

1 x 8 oz. (225 g.) whiting
1 rib of celery
3 carrots
2 onions
1 stick of fennel (optional)
¼ lb. (115 g.) packet of frozen peas
½ pint (290 ml.) dry white wine/wine and water mixed
pinch of tarragon/clove of garlic
2 chopped long white radishes/salsify (optional)
2 oz. (55 g.) butter

Get the fishmonger to cut off the head of the fish and clean the insides. Preheat the oven to gas mark 4 (350°F). Wash the celery, carrots and fennel and dice. Peel and chop the onions and the clove of garlic. Melt half the butter in a frying pan and sauté the vegetables (not the peas) until they are a pale golden brown. Grease a deep ovenproof casserole and turn the vegetables into it. Or use a flameproof casserole for both frying and baking in the oven. Season with salt, pepper and tarragon. Add the peas. Pour in the wine and water and bury the fish in the vegetables. Cook covered for 20 minutes, dotted with the rest of the butter, until the bone at the centre of the fish is falling away from the flesh. Serve with rice or pasta and scattered with parsley.

Vary the vegetables and herbs according to what you have in the kitchen.

Goujons

This is a recipe best suited to the owners of a chip pan. It can be made in an ordinary frying pan, but isn't so simple to do.

4 - 6 oz. (115 - 170 g.) of sole or cod per person
¼ pint (145 ml.) milk
2 oz. (55 g.) wholemeal flour
lemon wedges

Cut the fish into strips about half the thickness of fish fingers. Dip into the milk and then into the flour. Heat the oil in the chip pan until it has a blue haze rising from the surface. Place the fish in the chip basket and dip into the hot oil; cook until the strips are golden brown. Serve immediately with lemon quarters.

You can cook this with potatoes at the same time, but start cooking the potatoes before the fish and only add the fish as the potatoes are beginning to turn pale gold.

If you are using a frying pan instead of a chip pan, fry in unsalted butter, not oil.

Scallops in their shells

You will need 1 scallop shell for each person and the flesh of 1 to 2 scallops each.
1 lb. (450 g.) potatoes
2 oz. (55 g.) grated cheese
1 oz. (25 g.) butter
chopped mint, parsley or chives
½ pint (290 ml.) milk
salt and pepper

Wash the scallop shells. Peel and cut the potatoes into halves. Place in a pan of cold water with a pinch of salt. Bring to the boil. Turn down to simmer until tender. While the potatoes are cooking, heat the milk until it is just shivering – no hotter. 'Poach' the scallops in the milk for 10 minutes until they are tender (i.e. cook them in the milk, just below boiling point); if you have the milk too hot they will go hard. Use the milk later for mashing the potatoes. When cooked, cut the scallops into little chunks. Lightly butter the scallop shells and fill with scallop flesh. Mash the potatoes with butter and the hot milk. Beat the chopped herbs into the potatoes and spread on top of the fish. Sprinkle with grated cheese, dot with butter and brown under the grill.

EGGS

The most important thing to remember when cooking eggs is that, as with all animal protein, they go hard when overheated. I fear that I have often stood in grave danger of making myself an un-welcome guest when generous and busy friends have said, 'Oh, let's just have scrambled eggs/omelette.' They have been met with a blank refusal on my part. The prospect of a potentially rubbery yellow pile on my plate has led me to contravene the basic rules of good guesthood. My explanations are usually dis-missed with, 'Well, you've never had them made properly,' followed by instructions on how to achieve light, frothy, creamy, mouth-watering confections. The explanations, the magic-absolutely-not-to-be-omitted-infallible-tricks, are all different. I have my own set and they don't work each time either. Maybe the variables are just too numerous to formulate a totally fool-

113

proof, or eggproof, way. The freshness of the eggs, the source of the heat, the temperature and quality of the oil, the suitability of the pan all play their part in sabotaging the most experienced cook's best endeavours. Ah well, it's not as gloomy as it sounds and the rewards are great, not just in flavour but in the versatility, the hordes of sweet and savoury recipes in which eggs play a part. They can be an individual ingredient, as say a boiled egg in a Salade Niçoise, a binder in mixtures that need to hold together, the yolks can be used to thicken sauces, custards and quiche fillings, the whites will hold expanded air bubbles to fluff up a soufflé or meringue.

A few facts
(i) Eggs start to cook at 70°C (158°F), which is a fairly low temperature.
(ii) Once they start cooking they cook quickly, so pay careful attention, in a matter of moments the texture and taste can change (perhaps for the worst).
(iii) Most egg dishes should be served straight away or they will toughen. Keep prepared dishes away from direct heat if they have to stand for any time. Undercooking a little will help. Don't serve omelettes or scrambled eggs on a hot plate, the heat will continue to cook the eggs.
(iv) The number of eggs that you serve for each person depends on how you are cooking them. One egg, poached or boiled, is enough for a starter if it is served with toast, fried bread, a helping of a vegetable like spinach or a slice of cold meat. The taste of a plain egg unrelieved by another texture or taste is a bit unsatisfying. With egg mixtures served as a main course you need to allow at least 2 eggs per person and possibly another one for the pot.
(v) If your household gets through eggs quickly don't store them in the fridge; they dehydrate there more quickly than outside. But do try to store them in the coolest place in the kitchen.
(vi) Egg whites can be kept for up to three weeks in the fridge and they whip up much more easily if they are cold. Egg yolks form a stiff and unappetizing crust if left; either add another whole egg to them or cover the yolk with a little cold water which can be drained off later.

Separating whites and yolks
This is a slightly tricky operation. The first pitfall is cracking the egg; it is very easy to break the yolk as you break the shell. Hold the egg in the palm of your hand and give a sharp bouncing tap to the centre of the shell with a knife or any sharp edge. You want to crack it, not penetrate it. Insert your two thumbnails into the

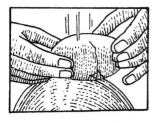

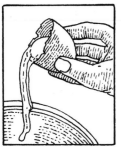

crack and gently lift apart the two halves. There are several small plastic gadgets on the market for separating egg yolks and whites and they are fairly foolproof. They are constructed a little like a tea strainer with a central unperforated cup into which you drop the yolk; the white should then fall away through slits around the edge. A perforated spoon will do if you don't have one of these gadgets or you can do it the lazy and hazardous way. Crack the egg and hold it end up in one hand over a basin. The yolk will fall into the bottom half of the shell and the white will tumble over the edges. In theory that is. In practice, the white will often spin the yolk in the shell as it falls and can bring the whole yolk with it or a large pool of white will be left in the shell with the yolk and you will very carefully have to tip the yolk from one half shell to the other, allowing the white to fall through the gap. This is quite fun when you get good at it but a good way of wasting eggs if you're not.

Egg whites will not beat up if there is even a trace of yolk mixed with them, so it is important to separate each egg individually. Break them one by one into a small bowl and after setting aside each yolk tip the white into a large bowl. You will need a large bowl in order to whisk them properly. Once you have cracked four whites into a bowl for a soufflé and then botched the fifth and had to throw the lot away you will always use this two-stage method. Even if you are skilled at keeping the yolk out imagine how you would feel if the last egg was bad!

Beating eggs

The most common way to beat eggs is to whisk with a fork. The best and most tiring way to beat eggs is to use a wire balloon whisk. Hold the bowl in the crook of one arm — a bit like a baby — and, holding it at an angle, beat the eggs with the whisk. And I don't mean beat the bowl. The whisk should move through the eggs lifting them through the air to incorporate it in the mix. A common mistake is to stop beating before the yolks and whites are indistinguishably mixed together. There should be no long strings of white. If you don't mix them enough you will get scrambled eggs marbled with streaks of white and the white cooked by itself is much more liable to be rubbery. A small pinch of salt will help the whites break up.

Beat egg whites in a chilled bowl with a pinch of salt.

Using an electric beater is faster and easier but the result will be slightly denser. Take care not to beat whites for too long or they will start to break up and will eventually flatten. They are ready when you can remove the whisk leaving stiff peaks of white that do not bend or dissolve. As you beat, check that there is not a pool of unbeaten white underneath the frothy top. Use beaten whites immediately; if you leave them, they revert to their liquid state.

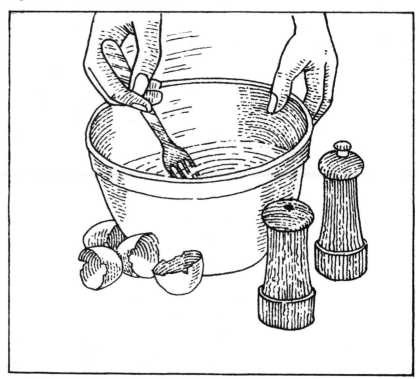

How to treat beaten egg whites

Beaten egg whites need to be treated with great care. If they are to be used to hold up a heavy mixture as in a soufflé you have to try and fold them into the mixture without letting it squash all the air out. Use a light plastic or rubber spatula and gently lift the flour, butter and milk mixture through the whites until they are blended together. Don't attempt to beat them together or you will flatten the whole thing. The purpose of beating egg whites is to incorporate as much air in them as possible in the form of tiny bubbles which will expand when heated. The whites will stiffen as they cook and form a sort of scaffolding to hold up a heavier mix.

Omelettes

Allow 2 - 3 eggs per person (you can make individual omelettes or one large one)
salt
black pepper
2 tbs. of butter

Place the serving plates where they will be warm but *not* hot.

116

Beat the eggs and salt and pepper with a fork until they are completely blended together. Melt the butter in the pan over a medium flame. As it foams and bubbles, gently pour in the eggs. Stir quickly with the fork until they cover the base of the pan and start to thicken. With a spatula gently push the cooked egg at the edges of the pan towards the centre, tipping and angling the pan so that the uncooked liquid centre then runs to fill the spaces around the edges of the pan. If you prefer the centre of your omelette runny, stop when there is a firm layer covering the bottom of the pan, because the omelette will continue to cook in the hot pan. Let the base brown for 15 seconds or so. Add filling

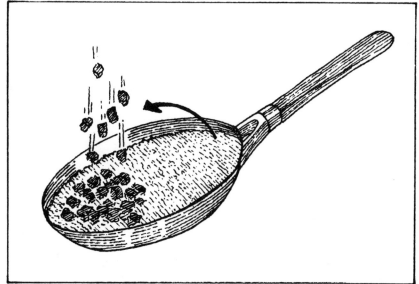

if you have one and fold. Folding is where most omelettes come to grief. If you are using a well prepared pan you are less likely to fail – don't worry if it falls apart, it will taste good anyway. Tip the pan away from you and slide a palette knife underneath the top edge of the omelette. Flip it over the bottom half. Slide the turned omelette to the edge of the pan and on to a waiting plate. This is a technique that does tend to take everyone ages to perfect, so don't be perturbed if you find it difficult. Serve as quickly as possible.

Omelette pans
The best aid to perfect omelettes and pancakes is a well prepared pan. Keep one pan specially for these purposes. A thick iron pan with a heavy, perfectly flat base is what you need. Curved sides will help you slide the cooked mixture out of the pan on to the serving plate. Wash the pan in warm soapy water as soon as you buy it and then dry and fill with a thick coating of vegetable oil and salt. Leave to stand overnight. Heat until the oil is very hot

and just beginning to smoke. Clean out the oil and salt and wipe
dry. Do not wash at this stage. If you carefully clean the pan with
paper towelling after each use you will not need to wash it.

Fillings

Herbs
Mix chopped fresh herbs into the egg mixture and cook as above.
Try chives, parsley, mint, fennel leaves. If you are using dried
herbs you will get a more distinctive flavour if you stick to one
kind. Oregano, basil, thyme, sage and marjoram are all good.

Eggs go wonderfully well with garlic and parsley. Finely chop or
crush a clove of garlic and fry until golden in a little butter and
then add the eggs. Scatter the parsley over the eggs as they are
cooking and fold as usual.

Tomatoes
Chop a small tomato for each omelette and sauté until soft in
½ oz (15 g.) butter. Remove from the pan but leave as much of
the tomato-flavoured butter as you can. Cook the eggs in this
butter as above, and just before you are ready to fold the omelette,
spoon the tomatoes on to one side of the omelette, season with
salt, pepper and a pinch of basil and fold. Alternatively, fill the
omelette with chopped raw tomato.

For an onion-flavoured tomato filling scatter chopped chives
or finely chopped spring onion over the tomato or chop a small
onion and sauté in butter until golden before cooking the tomato.

Mushrooms
Sauté 2 oz. (55 g.) of sliced mushrooms for each omelette in ½ oz.
(15 g.) butter until soft. Remove from the pan, leaving as much
of the mushroom flavoured butter as you can. Set aside in a warm
place and cook the eggs. Add the mushrooms to half the omelette
just before folding.

Cheese
Grate 2 oz. (55 g.) of cheese over the middle of the omelette.
Allow to melt and then fold. Include a little dry mustard in the
egg mix. Eggs and cheese are both fairly hard to digest and the
mustard will help.

Ham
Cut 2 oz. (55 g.) of ham into ribbons and add to the omelette
before folding.

Tuna and capers
Flake 2 oz. (55 g.) of tuna and mix with 3 or 4 chopped capers.
Spread over half the omelette before folding.

Almost any cold cooked meat, chicken, sausage or even fish can be chopped and included in an omelette.

Fake Spanish omelette

This is a short-cut method for making Spanish omelettes, for 2.

8 oz. (255 g.) cooked boiled potato
3 tbs. olive oil
1 large onion
salt, pepper
1 egg

Boil the potatoes and allow to cool. Chop. Peel the onion and slice. Heat 1 tbs. of the oil in an omelette pan and sauté the onions until they are transparent. Add the chopped potatoes and keep turning until they are beginning to turn golden brown. Remove from the heat and allow to cool. Beat the egg in a large bowl with the salt and pepper. When the potato and onion mix has cooled, fold it into the egg. If you do this before the potato and onions have cooled, the egg will solidify. Heat another table-spoon or two of oil over a medium flame in the pan and when it is hot pour in the egg, potato and onion mixture in a thick layer. With the flat side of a palette knife, press down on the mixture until it is a flat cake. Gently neaten up the edges of the omelette by pushing in with the palette knife from the edges. Shake from time to time to make sure it has not stuck on the bottom. This omelette needs to cook fairly slowly as it is thick. When the edges turn a rich golden brown and there is a toasted smell coming from the bottom of the pan, slide the frying pan under a hot grill and brown the top of the omelette. Serve either straight from the pan or remove by putting a plate over the omelette and tipping

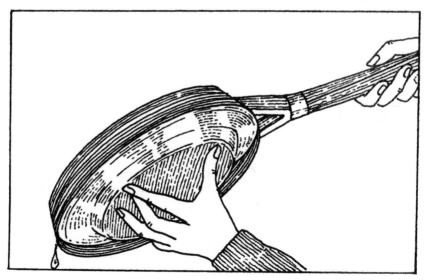

the pan upside down. The omelette should fall on to the plate. Hold the frying pan at an angle tipped away from you and preferably over a sink and then any hot oil that has not been absorbed will not drip on you. Leave to stand for at least 15 minutes before eating. The flavour is much better lukewarm or even cold. You can serve this with a tomato sauce or crispy fried bacon.

Spanish omelette is one of the dishes that will make a meal out of a few undistinguished scraps. Try adding peas, chopped ham and chopped peppers.

Soufflé omelettes

Separate the yolks and the whites. Beat the yolks with a fork and the whites stiffly with a whisk. Gently fold the two together. Cook as an ordinary omelette until the base of the pan is browned and then sprinkle with finely grated cheese and brown under a medium grill. Make a sweet version by whisking 1 teaspoon of sugar per egg into the whites.

Lemon soufflé omelette

1 lemon
3 eggs
3 teaspoons of caster sugar
1 oz. (25 g.) butter

Grate the rind from the lemon and then cut in half and squeeze out the juice. Separate the egg yolks and whites. Beat the egg yolks and gradually drop by drop beat in the lemon juice. Beat the egg whites and when they are stiff whisk in the sugar and grated lemon peel. Melt the butter in a frying pan until foamy. Gently fold together the egg yolks and whites, and pour into the pan. When you can smell the base of the omelette browning, remove from the heat and brown the top under the grill. This is a difficult dish to serve, but even if it falls apart, the light, feathery spoonfuls look and taste very good.

Use oranges, limes or half a grapefruit for a different flavour.

SOUFFLES

Soufflés are much easier to make than you imagine, but observing a couple of simple rules will help you to succeed.

(i)   Too much heat will curdle the egg yolks. The base (i.e. the mixture of butter, flour, milk and flavouring) should be at a temperature such that you can easily dip your finger in it without discomfort before you add the whites.

(ii) It is the beaten egg white that makes the soufflé rise, so you need to *fold*, not beat it into the base without squashing the pockets of air. It is best to do this in two operations. First fold half of the egg white into the base and mix well, and

120

then gently add the rest of the egg white with a spatula, lifting it through the base. It is better to have pockets of egg white than a too thoroughly blended flat soufflé; but don't have a solid well of unblended base at the bottom of the dish.

(iii) Butter the soufflé dish before pouring in the mix, or rub oil round with kitchen roll.

(iv) Very important. Preheat the oven. A soufflé in a cold oven is a potential flop. Literally.

It is best to serve a soufflé straight from the oven to the table but the timing in the oven is not crucial. There is at least 10 minutes difference between a soufflé that is runny inside and one that is firm all through and in their different ways they both taste lovely.

All of these soufflé recipes use 1 less yolk than white, to achieve real aerodynamics. Use the extra yolk in scrambled eggs or poached in butter and crumbled over salad.

Cheese soufflé

1½ oz. (40 g.) butter
1 oz. (25 g.) plain flour
¼ pint (145 ml.) milk
4 eggs
4 oz. (115 g.) grated cheese
salt, pepper, dry mustard
extra knob of butter for greasing the soufflé dish, or a bit of oil

Preheat the oven to gas mark 6 (400°F). Separate the egg yolks and whites. Melt the butter in a heavy medium-sized saucepan. Stir in the flour and when the two start to froth and bubble, remove from the heat. It is a good idea to heat the milk to just below boiling point, but you can add it to the roux cold. When most of the bubbles in the butter and flour have flattened out beat in the milk. Return to a very low flame and whisk until they are perfectly blended together. Drop in 3 of the egg yolks one by one, beating with a wooden spoon furiously as you go. When the sauce is thick, bring to the boil for a second stirring all the time and then take off the heat and stir in the cheese. Season with salt, pepper and mustard. While the sauce is cooling, beat the egg whites until the whisk leaves stiff points. Grease the soufflé dish, pour in the sauce mix and fold in half the egg whites and then fold in the remaining whites. Turn the heat down to gas mark 5 (375°F) and put the soufflé on a middle shelf. Bake for 25 to 35 minutes.

It does not hurt a soufflé to peek in the oven towards the end of the cooking time but don't leave the oven door open for too long.

Mushroom soufflé

½ lb. (225 g.) mushrooms
1½ oz. (40 g.) butter
1½ oz. (40 g.) plain flour
¼ pint (145 ml.) milk
4 eggs
salt, pepper
knob of butter to rub around the soufflé dish/drop of oil

Separate the egg whites from the yolks. Preheat the oven to gas mark 6 (400°F). Wipe the mushrooms with a damp cloth. Dice into tiny bits. Melt the butter in a saucepan and stir in the mushrooms. Allow them to stew in their own juices. When they are soft, beat in the flour. The mushrooms will make little lumps in the mixture but there should not be any lumps of flour. Cook, slowly stirring all the time, until the mushroom and butter mix thickens. If you can be bothered, heat the milk until it begins to bubble around the edges of a saucepan, otherwise, risk it and use cold. Stir into the mushroom mix and stir over a low heat until the milk thickens. Beat in three of the egg yolks, one at a time. Take off the heat and allow to cool. Beat the egg whites until the beater leaves stiff peaks. Butter a soufflé dish and turn in the mushroom mix and half of the egg whites. Fold together well and then add the remaining whites. Lift the whites through the base mix very gently. Level off at the top of the soufflé dish. Bake for 35 to 40 minutes with the heat turned down to gas mark 5 (375°F).

Cauliflower soufflé

1 small head of cauliflower
2 oz. (55 g.) grated cheese
1½ oz. (40 g.) butter
1 oz. (25 g.) plain flour
½ pint (290 ml.) milk
salt and pepper
¼ tsp. dry mustard
5 eggs

Boil the cauliflower in salted water or steam until very soft. Mash head and stalk, pass through a vegetable mill or liquidize. Separate the egg whites from the yolks. Preheat the oven to gas mark 6 (400°F). Grease a soufflé dish. Heat the butter in a saucepan and stir in the flour. When they start to froth remove from the heat. Warm the milk until bubbles start to appear around the edges of the saucepan, if you can be bothered, otherwise use cold milk and hope for the best. Whisk the milk into the butter and flour and stir over a low heat. Add 4 of the egg yolks one by one, beating as you go. Keep stirring until the mixture thickens. Stir in the mashed cauliflower and half the grated cheese, and pour into the dish.

122

Season with salt, pepper and mustard. Beat the egg whites until the whisk leaves stiff peaks. Fold half the egg whites into the cauliflower sauce. Blend well, but carefully, so as not to deflate the whites. Fold in the remaining whites. Sprinkle with the rest of the cheese. Bake for 45 minutes.

Spinach soufflé

1 lb. (450 g.) spinach (or ½ lb. frozen)
2 tsp. Parmesan cheese
2 oz. (55 g.) butter
1 oz. (25 g.) plain flour
¼ pint (145 ml.) milk
4 eggs
salt, pepper, nutmeg
knob of butter to grease the dish — drop of oil

Separate the egg whites and yolks. Wash the spinach thoroughly. Cook the spinach in a large covered saucepan over the lowest possible heat with ½ oz. (15 g.) butter cut in tiny pieces. The water from the washing will prevent the spinach from burning. Chop the cooked and drained spinach or purée in a vegetable mill. Be sure to drain off all the spinach water or else the soufflé will be watery, but don't throw the liquid away. If using frozen, defrost it.

Preheat the oven to gas mark 5 (375°F). Heat the remaining butter in a saucepan and stir in the flour when it bubbles. Blend well together and when they froth, take off the heat and wait for the bubbles to subside. Preferably, heat the milk with 3 or 4 tablespoons of the spinach juice until just below boiling. You can add it cold. Stir it into the butter and flour over a low heat and when it thickens drop in three egg yolks one by one, beating as you go. Stir in the spinach. Season with salt, pepper and grated nutmeg and leave to cool. Beat the egg whites until the whisk leaves stiff peaks. Grease a soufflé dish. Turn the spinach mixture into the soufflé dish and fold in half the egg white. Cut the rest of the egg white in using a spatula or knife blade. Sprinkle the top with Parmesan and bake for 35 minutes.

Prawn & lemon soufflé

8 oz. (225 g.) whole prawns
a few strands of saffron (optional)
1½ oz. (40 g.) butter
1 oz. (25 g.) plain flour
1/3 pint (190 ml.) milk
salt, pepper
grated rind of half a lemon
4 eggs
knob of butter to grease the soufflé dish/drop of oil

123

Preheat the oven to gas mark 5 (375°F). Separate the egg yolks and whites. Rinse the prawns and pull off the heads and tails. Put the heads and tails in a saucepan with the milk and gently simmer for 20 minutes. Do not bring to the boil. Strain the milk through a fine sieve. Finely chop the prawns. Grate the peel from half a lemon, taking care not to grate any of the white pith. Heat the butter and stir in the flour. When they bubble together take them off the heat and let the bubbles die down. Stir in the milk and keep stirring over a low flame until the mixture thickens. Drop in the strands of saffron, if you've got it. Beat in 3 of the 4 egg yolks one by one beating all the time. Remove from the heat to cool. Beat the egg whites until the whisk leaves peaks. Pour the chopped prawns into the butter and milk base and fold in half of the egg whites. Fold in the rest of the egg whites and transfer to the soufflé dish. Sprinkle the top with grated lemon peel but gently push it just beneath the surface. Bake for 35 minutes.

BATTER

Batter is an egg, milk and flour mixture as is a soufflé. The result however, is completely different. By using different proportions, batter itself can end up as pancakes or crêpes, Yorkshire pud, or a deep fried coating for chunks of fruit, vegetables, meat or fish. The rule that everyone agrees on when making batter is that it improves if allowed to stand for up to an hour before cooking. The old-fashioned way was to put the flour in a basin and mix in the egg, then slowly add milk. It's much quicker to liquidize the whole lot in your blender and let it stand so that the lumps dissolve.

Coating batter (for fritters)

4 oz. (115 g.) flour (plain, wholemeal, buckwheat)
3 tablespoons of oil (olive or good quality vegetable)
small cup of tepid milk/milk and water mix
pinch of salt
beaten white of 1 egg

Stir together the salt, flour and oil. Beat in the liquid to make a smooth cream or liquidize.
  Allow to stand. Beat the egg white and stir in just before using. Heat ½ - 1 pint (290 - 575 ml.) of oil in a deep frying pan. A blue haze will rise off the oil when it is hot enough. Watch carefully at this state — it only lasts for a couple of minutes. If the oil gets too hot it will burn, turn black and have to be thrown away. Test the heat of the oil by dropping in a tiny dribble of batter. If it hisses and bubbles and puffs up immediately then the oil is hot enough. Dunk the vegetable, fruit or meat chunk in the batter and drop into the oil. It will sink to the bottom at first and

then float up to the top. If it doesn't, the oil is not hot enough to seal the batter and the oil will leak through the batter and make the filling greasy. So throw that one away. Unless you have a very large pan only cook 2 - 3 pieces at once. Be careful to watch that the oil continues to bubble quite fiercely, the cold food may bring the temperature down and you will have to adjust the heat. Gently flip the chunks over to be sure that both sides are cooked. When golden brown and puffy (about 8 minutes) fish out with cooking chopsticks or a perforated spoon and set to drain in a warm place on crumpled paper towel. Between each lot of frying, clear any burnt bits of batter from the oil or they will stick to the food and give it an unpleasant burnt taste.

Fruit fritters

(i) *Apples*: peel and core and cut into rings ¾" (1 cm.) thick with a hole in the centre. Sprinkle with lemon juice if you are going to let them stand for any length of time before cooking. This will prevent them turning brown. Pat dry before dipping in the batter.

(ii) *Bananas*: peel and slice in half lengthways. Dip in batter and fry.

(iii) *Pears*: peel and cut into 4 long quarters. Cut out the pips and core. Pat dry before dipping in the batter.

(iv) *Pineapple*: cut into slices and peel off the rough outside. Cut into fan shapes. Pat dry and dip in batter. Or cut in circles as apples. Peel away the outer layer and core. Dip in batter and fry.

All fruit can be served with a fine dusting of caster sugar and lemon wedges. It's more fun to mix fruits.

Vegetable fritters

This is a delicious way of serving vegetables. They are crunchy without being raw. You can do one vegetable only; a mixture, especially if you also include some small pieces of fish, will make a whole meal. If you are serving vegetable fritters as a starter, cut them into smaller pieces. Serve with tamari soy sauce.

(i) *Onion rings*: peel the onion and cut it across in thick circles. Separate individual rings. Pat dry and dip in batter.

(ii) *Carrots and parsnips*: scrub and pat dry. Cut off the ends and cut in very thin sticks. Dip in batter and fry.

(iii) *Leeks and spring onions*: cut in 2" (5 cm.) chunks. Run water down the leaves to remove any grit and pat dry. Dip in batter.

(iv) *Courgettes*: cut lengthwise into quarters and pat dry.

(v) *Broccoli and cauliflower heads*: break into flowerets, dip in batter and fry.

Fish

Cut into chunks 3″ (8 cm.) long, dip in batter and fry. The best fish to use are the fleshy kind, not oily white fish: cod, coley, strips of plaice and sole, whiting and shrimps, prawns and squid are suitable.

Elderflowers

Wash elderflower heads thoroughly in cold water and salt. Remove stems and leaves. Shake dry. Dip in batter and fry. Shake with icing sugar and serve. They have a delicious, delicate flavour.

Pancake batter

Beat together or liquidize:

½ pint (290 ml.) of milk
1 egg
8 oz. (225 g.) of flour
3 tbs. of melted butter

If you use half buckwheat flour the pancakes will be crisper and darker. Heat a small amount of butter or a mixture of butter and oil in a heavy, flat bottomed frying pan, turning the pan to ensure the whole surface is coated. When it is hot, pour in a thin layer of batter and allow to cook for 2 minutes on a medium heat. Run a springy palette knife underneath and flip over onto the other side (or throw it up in the air and catch with the saucepan on Shrove Tuesday). Cook for 2 more minutes and either pile the pancakes up on a warm plate or serve straight away.

You can serve them with a sprinkle of caster sugar and a squeeze of lemon; with fruit and cream; or with a liqueur poured over the top, if you want a sweet dish; if you want a savoury dish, wrapped around a hot savoury filling or layered with chicken and mushrooms and baked in the oven.

Fillings

Use any of the omelette fillings in pancakes.

Asparagus & ham

2 - 3 sticks of asparagus per pancake
1 slice of ham per pancake
grainy mustard

Cook the asparagus before starting to make the pancakes. Cut the hard bits off the stalk ends. Cook by standing the tips upwards in boiling salted water until the thickest part of the stem is tender. Keep in a warm place. Spread each slice of ham with mustard, cream cheese or pickle as you prefer. As you make each pancake fold in the asparagus and the slice of ham. It doesn't matter if they stick out at the ends.

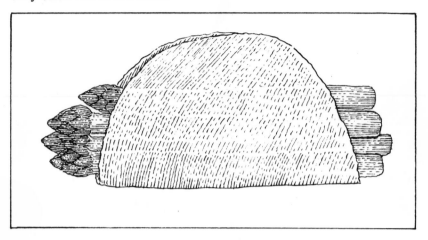

Cream cheese & onion

1 oz. (25 g.) cream cheese for each pancake
chopped spring onion/chopped chives/parsley/mint

Finely chop the spring onion or herbs and mix them into the cheese. After turning the pancake lay a line of filling down the middle and fold.

Smoked salmon & sour cream

1 - 2 oz. (25 - 55 g.) smoked salmon scraps per pancake
small carton of sour cream
lemon wedges
black pepper/cayenne pepper

Fold the smoked salmon scraps into the sour cream. Sprinkle with black or cayenne pepper. Fill the turned pancake and fold. Serve with lemon wedges.

Bacon, spinach & onion filling

6 oz. (170 g.) streaky bacon
½ lb. (225 g.) cooked chopped spinach (frozen if you like)
small very finely sliced onion
½ oz. (15 g.) butter
black pepper and salt

Wash the spinach and cook covered in a large saucepan with ½ oz. (15 g.) of butter and the drops of rinsing water trapped on the leaves. If using frozen, heat till thawed. Chop, drain thoroughly and keep in a warm place. Grill the bacon until it is crispy and then cut into small pieces. Slice the onion very finely and mix with the cooked bacon and spinach. Season with salt and black pepper.

Keep warm and pile 2 tablespoons of the mixture on the turned pancake and fold.

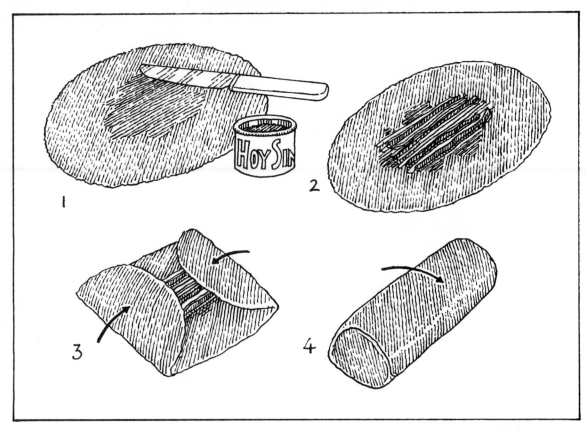

Put a pile of pancakes on the table and let the guests fill them themselves.

Fake Chinese pancakes

6 oz. (170 g.) cooked silverside of beef cut into strips
6 oz. (170 g.) of spring onions cut in fine lengthwise strips
a jar of Chinese Hoy Sin sauce (from Chinese supermarkets)

Spread a little Hoy Sin sauce on each pancake, fill with beef and spring onion and roll. In theory this should be done entirely with chopsticks.

Chicken & mushroom filling

8 oz. (225 g.) cooked chicken (approximately two raw pieces)
1 oz. (25 g.) butter
6 oz. (170 g.) mushrooms
small pot of single cream
salt, pepper, pinch of tarragon
flour to dust chicken pieces

This is a very quick filling to make with already cooked chicken; it will take quite a bit longer if you start from scratch.

With uncooked chicken, either grill and cut in small chunks off the bone or bring to the boil in enough water to cover, with a chopped onion, carrot and a bay leaf. Skim off any foam that rises to the surface and simmer for 40 minutes. Drain, keeping the stock and vegetables for soup and cut the chicken away from the bone and chop into chunks. An alternative would be to buy ready boned chicken breasts.

If you are using ready-cooked chicken, start here. Melt the butter in a frying pan and sauté the lightly floured chicken pieces until they begin to turn golden brown. Cover and leave to stew in the butter over a very low heat for 10 minutes. Chop the mushrooms into slices and add to the chicken; sprinkle with tarragon, salt and pepper and cover until the mushrooms give up their juices and the butter begins to turn black. Stir in the cream and correct the seasoning.

In a deep, round, buttered dish alternate layers of chicken and mushroom sauce with cooked pancakes, kept flat, not folded over. There should be a pancake covering the whole of the top. Sprinkle with Parmesan or grated cheese, dot with butter and bake at gas mark 4 (350°F) for 20 minutes or until the top turns golden brown.

Try different sauces and fillings between the layers.

Serve with a green vegetable or salad.

Yorkshire pudding batter

½ lb. (225 g.) plain flour
2 eggs
1 pint (575 ml.) of milk
2 tbs. of cooking oil/beef dripping
generous pinch of salt

Sift the flour and the salt into a deep basin. Make a well in the centre of the flour and add the eggs and 3 - 4 tablespoons of milk. Gradually stir the flour into the eggs and milk, slowly adding the rest of the milk. Beat with a whisk or electric beater for at least 5 minutes. The reluctant way is to liquidize everything. Leave to stand.

While the batter is standing, heat the fat in a deep baking dish until it just begins to smoke. For this amount of batter, your dish should be about 13" x 10" (30 cm. x 25 cm.). Pour in the batter and put the dish quickly back in the oven at gas mark 7 (425°F). Cook on a high shelf for about 45 minutes until the batter rises and is brown on the top. Move down one shelf and reduce the heat to gas mark 5 (375°F) for another 15 minutes.

This is quite a large quantity of batter suitable for a Sunday lunch party with roast beef or as a complete dish for Toad in the

Hole. Halve the quantities for less than 4 people, and reduce the cooking time by 15 minutes.

Toad in the hole

1 lb. (450 g.) of sausages
batter as above

Prick the sausages with a fork so that they do not burst.
As the fat in the pan is beginning to smoke add the sausages evenly distributed over the pan and then pour in the batter mix.
Bake for 40 - 45 minutes at gas mark 7 (425°F).

Apple batter

1 lb. (450 g.) cooking apples
2/3 tbs. brown sugar

Peel, core and quarter the apples and dip in the sugar. Use as above instead of sausages for a sweet pudding or an apple batter to serve with roast pork. Use cooking oil for puddings and dripping for meat dishes.

Mayonnaise

1 egg yolk
¼ pint (145 ml.) oil
2 tsp. wine vinegar/lemon juice
salt, pepper, mustard

If you have time, place all the ingredients and utensils in the fridge for half an hour before starting. Run cold water over them if you don't have time. Separate the yolk of an egg from the white. Drop the yolk into a cold clean basin and, drop by drop and stirring all the time with a balloon whisk or wooden spoon, beat olive oil into the yolk. Go very slowly with the oil at the beginning and keep beating until you have at least doubled the quantity in the bowl, then allow a fine stream of oil to build up. Use ¼ pint (145 ml.) of oil for each egg yolk. Finally beat in salt, pepper, 2 teaspoons of wine vinegar or lemon juice per ¼ pint (145 ml.) of oil, and mustard if you wish. If the mayonnaise curdles, start afresh with a new egg yolk and this time beat in the curdled mixture instead of oil. Do not store in the refrigerator as it may separate.

This whole business is much quicker and easier with an electric beater or liquidizer but the texture of the mayonnaise will be slightly different, lighter and fluffier.

N.B. Some people think that warming the utensils and the oil works better than chilling them! See which works best for you.

Variations
(i)   Add finely chopped fresh herbs, spinach, watercress or Brussels sprouts.
(ii) Add chopped anchovy, capers, gherkins, onion and tarragon.

Aioli – garlic mayonnaise

Cut the crust off a slice of white bread. Soak in milk until soggy. Crush 6 - 8 cloves of garlic. Blend thoroughly with the bread and add the mixture to the egg yolk before adding any oil.

Meringue

2 egg whites
pinch of salt
4 oz. (115 g.) caster sugar

You need a large mixing bowl to make meringue because the mixture expands a great deal. Whisk the egg whites and salt together until the whites stand in stiff peaks when you lift out the whisk. Whisk in 3 or 4 teaspoons of the sugar and then fold in the rest with a fork.

Meringue can be used as a topping for a fruit purée or tart, folded into a fruit purée or sweet soufflé mix, or cooked individually. If you want them to put together with a filling, spoon them onto Bakewell paper and cook at gas mark ½ (250°F) for 3 to 4 hours until crisp all through. If you can turn your oven down any further, leave them in to cook overnight. The Bakewell paper is essential; without it meringues fall apart and tempers fray.

Fillings for meringues
(i)   Whipped double cream.
(ii)   Chocolate filling: cream together 2 oz. (55 g.) butter, 2 oz. (55 g.) of grated chocolate or 4 heaped tbs. of cocoa and 2 oz. (55 g.) of soft brown sugar.
(iii) Orange filling: cream together 2 oz. (55 g.) butter, 2 oz. (55 g.) soft brown sugar and the grated rind and juice of half an orange.
(iv) Coffee and nuts: cream together 2 oz. (55 g.) butter, 2 oz. (55 g.) soft brown sugar, 1 tablespoon of strong black coffee and 1 teaspoon chopped roasted hazel nuts. To roast the nuts, shake under a hot grill until they turn golden brown on all sides.

Peach meringue pie

4 oz. (115 g.) cream cheese
4 peaches
2 egg whites
4 oz. (115 g.) caster sugar
8" (20 cm.) sweet or plain shortcrust pastry flan case (see p.163)

Bake the pastry blind (see p. 163) for 15 minutes at gas mark 8 (450°F). While it's cooking, peel and stone the peaches and chop the flesh finely and beat into the cheese. Or you can liquidize the peaches and cheese. Pour the fruit and cheese mixture into the flan case. Top with meringue (see above) and bake in a cool oven, gas mark ½ (250°F) for about ½ an hour to an hour — it's done when the meringue is pale brown and crisp. (You could experiment with other fresh fruit.)

Nut meringues

2 egg whites
4 oz. (115 g.) caster sugar/soft brown sugar
2 oz. (55 g.) finely chopped almonds/hazelnuts

Chop the nuts and toss under the grill until golden brown. This brings out their flavour. Whisk the egg whites until they stand in stiff peaks. Whisk in 2 or 3 teaspoons of the sugar, and then fold in the rest with a fork. Preheat the oven to gas mark 2 (300°F). Fold in the nuts and scoop into little peaks on Bakewell paper. Cook for 45 minutes to 1 hour until the meringues are hard and sound hollow when tapped on the bottom. Fill with whipped double cream and raspberries.

Fruit snow

½ lb. (225 g.) apples/pears/plums/apricots
3 tbs. of water
½ oz. (15 g.) butter
meringue made with 1 egg white and 2 oz. (55 g.) sugar

Peel, stone or core the fruit and chop into chunks. Place in a small saucepan with ¼ oz. (8 g.) butter and the water. Cover and allow to stew on a low light until soft. Purée or pass through a sieve. Allow to cool. Grease a shallow baking dish with the remaining butter. Preheat the oven to gas mark 4 (350°F). Make the meringue and fold into the apple, or whatever fruit you choose. Turn into the baking dish and cook for 20 minutes.

Baked egg custard

1 pint (575 ml.) milk
2 eggs
1 oz. (25 g.) raw brown sugar
knob of butter — drop of oil, to grease the pie dish

Beat the eggs with the sugar. Warm the milk until you can dip your fingertip in without discomfort but it still feels warm. Butter a deep dish. Preheat the oven to gas mark 4 (350°F). Whisk the milk into the eggs and then strain through a fine sieve into the dish. Stand the dish in another shallow dish containing warm water. Bake slowly for about 50 minutes until the custard is set.

Variations
— Flavour the custard before cooking with grated nutmeg, cinnamon or chopped cardamom seeds.
— If you want a richer custard, use single cream instead of milk.

132

VEGETABLES

Stuffed vegetable dishes

Stuffed vegetables — like stews and soups — are receptacles for leftovers and bits and pieces that most kitchens seem always to have in stock. They usually make use of a small amount of meat padded out with a grain like rice and a few vegetables and herbs. Most vegetables cook quicker if they have been steamed or cooked in a little boiling water before being stuffed.

Make up your own stuffings from rice, fish, vegetables and herbs. These are very basic recipes to start off with. You can substitute buckwheat, millet or couscous for rice. Leftover chilli con carne, shepherd's pie or any bean dish would make a good basis of a stuffing.

VERY EASY STUFFINGS

Tomato, onion & cheese

Mix together:

2 cups of cooked rice
1 finely chopped tomato
3 finely chopped spring onions
4 oz. (115 g.) of grated cheese
salt and pepper

Tuna, egg & caper

Mix together:

2 cups of cooked rice
4 oz. (115 g.) tuna
1 tablespoon chopped capers
1 raw egg
salt and pepper

Peas, cheese & ham

Mix together:

2 cups of cooked rice
4 oz. (115 g.) chopped ham
3 oz. (85 g.) frozen peas
3 oz. (85 g.) cottage/cream cheese
chopped fresh mint
salt, pepper, grainy mustard

Sausage, sage & onions

Mix together:

2 cups cooked rice
5 oz. (140 g.) uncooked sausage meat
1 teaspoon dried or fresh sage
4 chopped spring onions
salt, pepper, grainy mustard

Basic meat & rice stuffing

½ lb. (225 g.) minced beef
1 onion
1 small finely chopped carrot
1 finely chopped stick of celery
2 cloves of garlic
chopped fresh parsley and/or mint
1 cup cooked brown or white rice
¼ tsp. cumin seeds (optional)
salt and pepper
2 tbs. of tomato purée
2 tbs. of olive oil

Cook the rice while preparing the vegetables and meat. The stuffing will hold together much better if you take care to chop the vegetables very finely. Peel the onion and scrub the carrot. Dice onion, carrot and celery and then, holding the point of the knife with the fingertips on the chopping board, work the knife up and down across the vegetables until they are in tiny pieces. Peel and chop the garlic in the same way. Heat the oil in a frying pan and sauté the vegetables until they turn transparent. Stir in the meat and continue stirring and turning until the meat is browned all over. Season with salt, pepper and cumin seeds. Add the tomato purée and enough water to cover the meat and vege- tables. Cover and turn the heat down until the meat is simmering. Cook for 20 minutes. Check from time to time that the pan does not catch on the bottom. Try not to add too much water because you want to end up with a stiff, dry stuffing.

At this stage you could add chopped capers/olives/soy sauce/

Worcestershire sauce/chilli sauce or chopped green chilli/chopped anchovy/chopped herbs. If you can't get mint or parsley, oregano or basil would be good.

Add enough cooked rice to the meat and vegetable mix to absorb the extra liquid. You may have to raise the temperature and dry out any liquid by boiling. Stuff the mixture into the vegetables and bake.

This mixture could be used to stuff aubergines, marrows, courgettes, green or red peppers, vine leaves, cabbage leaves and onions.

Nut stuffing

6 oz. (170 g.) rice
1 x 14 oz. (400 g.) tin of tomatoes
1 green pepper
1 red pepper
1 large onion
2 oz. (55 g.) chopped mixed nuts
2 cloves garlic
2 oz. (55 g.) butter/3 tbs. of olive oil
salt, pepper
basil or oregano
half a chopped green chilli

Cook the rice. While it is cooking, peel and chop the onion and garlic and remove the stalks, seeds and white pith from the peppers and chop finely. Heat the butter or oil in a frying pan and sauté the onions and garlic until golden brown. Add the nuts and finely chopped peppers. Season with salt, pepper, basil or oregano and a very little chopped chilli. When the peppers are soft, add the cooked rice and the tomatoes, roughly breaking them up. Simmer hard until the mixture is very dry. Use to stuff vine leaves or any other vegetable.

Stuffed aubergines (starter or main course)

1 medium-sized aubergine per person (if they are large half will do)
half the meat and rice stuffing (see p. 134)/half nut stuffing
  (above)
4 - 6 oz. (115 - 170 g.) grated cheese
sprinkling of Parmesan cheese
1 oz. (25 g.) butter

Cut the aubergine in half lengthways and scoop out the insides with a spoon. Lightly salt the insides of the cases and the scooped-out aubergine. Leave to stand for half an hour and then rinse. Squeeze the water from the flesh and chop finely. When making the stuffing, add the chopped aubergine at the same time as the other vegetables and sauté with them. If you want to make a

135

vegetarian version of the meat stuffing, simply omit the meat.

While the stuffing is cooking, steam the aubergine cases for 10 - 20 minutes until they begin to go loose and floppy. Preheat the oven to gas mark 5 (140°F). Grease a shallow pie dish that will hold the aubergine cases lying side by side.

Fill the aubergine cases with stuffing mix and smooth down level with the top of the cases. Sprinkle with a thick layer of cheese and dot with butter. Cover and bake in the oven for 40 minutes. Uncover and allow the cheese to brown. Serve with rice; a thick tomato sauce (see p. 39) would be delicious too.

Stuffed marrow

a large marrow, about 1½ - 2 lb. (675 g. - 1 kilo)
half the meat and rice stuffing (see p134)/half nut stuffing (see
*   p. 135)*
8 oz. (225 g.) grated cheese (optional)
a little water
a little oil

You can either stuff the marrow whole, by cutting a hole at the stalk end, and scooping everything out through that, or slice lengthways and stuff hollowed halves, topping with grated cheese.

Cut off the stalk end of the marrow about 2" (4 cm.) down. With a long sharp knife or spoon hollow out the inside of the marrow leaving a layer of flesh ½" (1 cm) thick. Remove seeds and pith from the centre. Chop the flesh finely and add to the stuffing with the other vegetables, but watch out — marrow flesh is mostly water. Four or 5 tablespoons will probably be enough, unless you are not using meat. While the stuffing is cooking either steam the marrow case for 10 minutes if you have a big enough steamer or drop it into boiling salted water for 5 minutes and then rinse under cold water.

Preheat the oven to gas mark 5 (375°F). Lightly grease an oven-proof dish large enough to hold the marrow lying on its side. Fill the marrow with stuffing and replace the stalk 'lid'. Secure with toothpicks. Pour some oil over the outside of the marrow and place in the dish with about ½" (1 cm.) of water. Bake for 40 - 45 minutes and then open the lid and look inside. The flesh of the marrow should be watery and transparent. If it is still firm and white, cook for another 10 minutes. Slice and eat hot or cold.

Stuffed courgettes

As courgettes are usually quite small, this is probably better as a starter.

2 - 3 courgettes per person
half the meat and rice stuffing (see p. 134)/half nut stuffing (see p. 13.
6 oz. (170 g.) grated cheese
1 oz. butter

Slice the courgettes lengthways and scoop out the flesh, leaving an even layer of flesh about ¼" (½ cm.) thick next to the skin. Chop the flesh and add it to the stuffing mix with the other vegetables. Preheat the oven to gas mark 5 (375°F). Grease a shallow overproof dish with a little butter or oil. Lay the courgette shells in side by side and fill with the stuffing. Sprinkle with grated cheese. Cover and bake for 30 minutes and then take off the top and allow the cheese to brown slightly.

Stuffed Red & green peppers

1 pepper per person
meat and rice stuffing (see p. 134)/nut stuffing (see p. 135)
1 tbs. olive oil

Cut the stalk tops off the peppers, making a large lid. With sharp knife cut the white pith and seeds from the inside of the peppers. Drop into boiling water for 5 minutes while the stuffing is cooking. Lightly grease a deep ovenproof dish which will hold the peppers standing upright wedged against each other. Preheat the oven to gas mark 5 (375°F). Fill the peppers with stuffing, replace the lids, brush with a little olive oil and bake, covered, for 40 minutes.

Stuffed cabbage leaves

1 large green cabbage
1 oz. (25 g.) butter
½ pint (290 ml.) beef stock/cider
Meat and rice stuffing (see p. 134)/nut stuffing (see p. 135)

Prepare the stuffing and while it is cooking break the cabbage into individual leaves. Only the larger leaves can be used. Make a long V shaped cut to remove the hardest part of the stalk. Drop the leaves into boiling salted water for 5 minutes. Drain and rinse in cold water. Spread individual leaves flat on a chopping board and cross over the split ends. Place a small tablespoon of the stuffing mix in the middle of the leaf and roll up tucking the ends as you go. It doesn't have to be very neat.

Grease a shallow ovenproof dish with a little oil and lay the packages of meat and cabbage in rows. Pour in about 1" (2 cm.) of stock or cider. Dot with butter and bake for 40 minutes at gas mark 5 (375°F).

Variations
— Cover with thick tomato sauce and bake.
— Cover with cheese and bake.
— Cover with cooked sliced potato, dot with butter and bake.
— Lay strips of bacon over the top and bake.

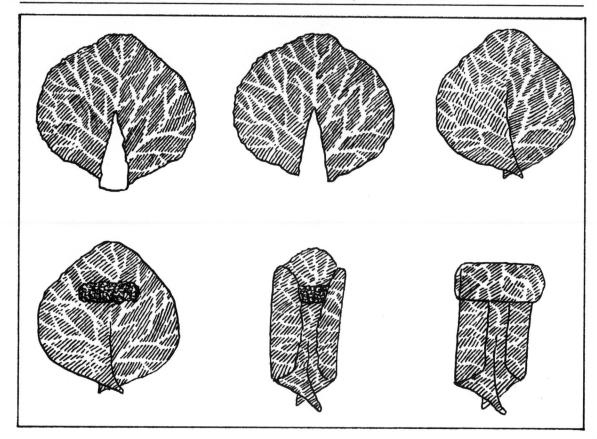

Vine leaves

The brine in which vine leaves are pickled makes them very easy to roll up. Vine leaves can be bought in 8 oz. (225 g.) vacuum packs; or some Greek delicatessens sell them loose in brine.

8 oz. (225 g.) vine leaves
meat and rice stuffing (see p. 134)/nut stuffing (see p. 135)
½ pint (290 ml.) beef stock/dry white wine
½ oz. (15 g.) butter/1 tbs. cooking oil

Soak the vine leaves in cold water for 10 minutes to wash away the brine. Grease a shallow dish with a little butter or oil and preheat the oven to gas mark 5 (375°F).

Spread individual leaves flat on a chopping board; you may need to spread out two together to make a large enough leaf but the brine will help them stick together easily. At the base of the leaf above where the stalk starts place a tablespoon of filling. Fold the sides of the leaf over and roll up, as with cabbage leaves (see p. 137). Place side by side in the baking dish. Fill halfway up with stock or wine and bake for 50 minutes.

Variations
— Cook in a thick tomato sauce.
— Sprinkle with crumbled feta cheese and bake.
—Serve with the following yogurt sauce.

Yogurt sauce

1 large carton of plain yogurt
½ oz. (15 g.) plain flour
½ oz. (15 g.) butter
3 tbs. of milk
salt, pepper, dry mustard

Melt the butter in a saucepan and beat in the flour with a wooden spoon. When it has thickened and is beginning to colour golden brown slowly beat in the milk and then the yogurt. Continue stirring for 5 minutes. Season with salt, pepper and mustard. Pour over the stuffed vine leaves and bake for 50 minutes. Sprinkle with chopped fennel leaves when serving.

Stuffed tomatoes

1 tomato per person (you must use Mediterranean-type large tomatoes)
meat and rice stuffing (see p. 134)/nut stuffing (see p. 135)
½ oz. (15 g.) butter/1 tbs. of olive oil

Preheat the oven to gas mark 5 (375°F). Slice the tops off the tomatoes and hollow out the flesh and seeds. Chop the flesh and seeds and add to the stuffing mix. Put the lids back on the tomatoes and place in a greased ovenproof dish. Cook for 35 minutes. Beware: do make sure you don't leave too much flesh inside the tomatoes or your oven will end up underwater.

Stuffed onions

1 largish onion per person
8 oz. (225 g.) stuffing (for 6 people)
4 oz. (115 g.) grated cheese
1 oz. (25 g.) butter
4 tbs. water/cider/stock/red or white wine

Preheat the oven to gas mark 5 (375°F). Peel the skin off the onions but leave them whole. Boil for 35 minutes in salted water until they are tender. Scoop out the insides, leaving a fairly substantial outer layer. Chop the insides and mix into the stuffing. Fill the onion shells with stuffing, place in a fairly deep, buttered ovenproof dish, sprinkle with grated cheese and dot with butter. Pour in the liquid, cover and bake for 30 minutes and then lift the cover and brown for 10 minutes.

Baking with cheese

Suitable for root vegetables, onions and potatoes.
(i)   Cut vegetables in thin slices, or they will take all night to cook.
(ii)   Layer in a greased baking dish with grated cheese and onions if you wish. Season with salt, pepper and mustard as you go.
(iii) Top with a layer of grated cheese and/or cheese sauce (see page 83).
(iv)   Pour 3 - 4 tablespoons of single cream/top of the milk over the top. Cooked vegetables will take 20 - 25 minutes to cook at gas mark 5 (375°F). Uncooked vegetables will take anything up to 1 hour. Test with a fork.

Carrots, onions & cheese

4 large carrots
4 large onions
8 oz. (225 g.) grated cheese
¼ pint (145 ml.) chicken/vegetable stock
1 oz. (25 g.) butter/oil
salt, pepper, dry mustard
pinch of tarragon

Scrub the carrots and cut off the ends. Slice into circles. Peel the onion and slice into circles. Preheat the oven to gas mark 5 (375°F). Bring the carrots to the boil in lightly salted stock or water and simmer for 10 minutes. Grease a 2" - 3" (5 - 8 cm.) deep baking dish with butter or oil. Drain the carrots and keep the cooking water. Line the dish with carrots and build up alternate layers of carrots, onions and cheese. The top layer should be onions and cheese. Season as you go with salt, pepper, dry English mustard and a little tarragon. Pour the carrot water or stock down the edges of the dish to just below the top layer of vegetables. Dot the top with the remaining butter and bake for 45 minutes to 1 hour.

Variations
— Use a mixture of carrots and parsnips.
— For a creamier dish use milk or cream instead of stock.

New potatoes, mangetout peas & lettuce

1 lb. (450 g.) new potatoes
6 oz. (170 g.) mangetout peas/very tender young broad beans
1 head of lettuce
1 clove garlic
1 oz. (25 g.) butter
salt and pepper
a few fresh mint leaves (optional)
2 oz. (55 g.) grated cheese
¼ pint (145 ml.) chicken stock/vegetable water

Preheat the oven to gas mark 5 (375°F). Butter a fairly deep oven-proof dish. Scrub the potatoes and bring to the boil in the stock or water. Simmer for 10 minutes. Allow to cool and slice. Wash the lettuce and top and tail the peas or beans. Use only very young beans, and use them whole in the pod. Peel and crush the garlic. Line the dish with lettuce leaves and cover with a layer of peas, then a layer of potatoes, another layer of lettuce and so on to the top of the dish, seasoning as you go. Finish up with a layer of potatoes. Sprinkle with cheese and fill about 1/3 full of stock. Dot the top with butter and cover. Bake for 5 minutes at gas mark 5 (375°F) and then turn down to gas mark 4 (350°F). Cook until the potatoes and peas are tender — about 35 minutes — and then uncover for 10 minutes to allow the cheese to melt.

Tiny whole pickling onions with just their skins removed can be included.

Sweet potatoes, potatoes & celery

2 large potatoes
1 large sweet potato
4/5 large ribs of celery
2 oz. (55 g.) butter
6 oz. (170 g.) grated cheese
¼ pint (145 ml.) of stock/vegetable water/milk
1 clove garlic
salt and pepper

Preheat the oven to gas mark 5 (375°F). Grease a deep ovenproof dish. Scrub the potatoes, sweet potato and celery. Bring to the boil in the stock and cook for 5 minutes. Drain and keep the stock. Slice the sweet potato and potatoes into circles. Chop the celery into chunks. Build up layers of potatoes, sweet potato and celery in the baking dish, ending with a layer of potatoes. Season with salt, pepper and chopped garlic as you go. Sprinkle a layer of grated cheese on the top and pour in vegetable water, stock and milk until it reaches halfway up the vegetables. Bake for 45 minutes uncovered until the potatoes are cooked.

You could place thin layers of ham between the vegetables or a layer of streaky bacon rashers on top.

Bacon & potato bake

1 lb. (450 g.) potatoes
6 oz. (170 g.) streaky bacon
1 large sliced onion
1 oz. (25 g.) butter
salt and pepper
3 tbs. milk

Preheat the oven to gas mark 5 (375°F). Scrub the potatoes and bring to the boil in salted water. Simmer for 10 minutes. Peel and slice the onion into rings. Cut the potatoes into slices. Grease a deep ovenproof dish and layer with potatoes, chopped bacon and onion slices. Lay potatoes and bacon rashers on the top and dot with butter. Season with salt and pepper and pour 3 tablespoons of milk in between the potatoes. Bake for 45 minutes or until the potatoes are completely tender.

Aubergine pizza

1 large aubergine
small tin of tomatoes
small onion cut in fine slices
6 or 8 olives
a few anchovies/or sliced salami (optional)
1 small mozzarella or 4 oz. (115 g.) grated cheese
salt, pepper
pinch of oregano or tarragon
3 tbs. olive oil

Preheat the oven to gas mark 4 (350°F). Cut the stalk off the aubergine and slice into thin slices. Salt liberally and leave to stand for 1 hour. Rinse and pat dry. Grease a very shallow pie dish with a little olive oil. Cover with a layer of aubergine. Trickle olive oil over the aubergine. Drain the tomato, roughly chop it up and spread it over the aubergine. Scatter with finely chopped onion rings. Season with salt, pepper and herbs. Cover with a layer of cheese and either criss cross with anchovies or scatter with salami. Trickle with the rest of the olive oil and bake for 40 minutes.

VEGETABLE STEWS

There are lots of delicious ways of cooking vegetable stews. The basic method for cooking is to sauté the harder vegetables, such as root vegetables, and onions first in butter or oil and then add liquid — tomatoes, wine, stock, soup — put the whole lot in a casserole in a fairly slow oven or on top of the stove on a low heat and cook for 45 minutes to 1 hour. Obviously vegetable stews take far less time to cook than meat stews.

Chilli sans carne

8 oz. (225 g.) dry red kidney beans/tin of beans
2 onions
3 peppers, green or red
1 x 14 oz. (400 g.) tin of tomatoes
3 tbs. olive oil
salt, pepper
¼ tsp. of chilli powder or more if you like hot food
2 cloves garlic

142

If using dried beans, soak them overnight. Cook the beans in 2 pints of water for 1 hour without salt. Peel and slice the onions and garlic. Cut the stalks from the peppers and discard any white pith or seeds from inside. Slice the peppers. Heat the olive oil in a deep frying pan and sauté the sliced onions and garlic. When the onions are soft, add the sliced peppers and tomatoes, with the juice from the tin. Season with salt, pepper and chilli. Stir in the beans and a little of the water from cooking the beans, if you cooked your own. If using tinned beans, drain them and add a cup of water. Bring to the boil and turn down to simmer for 30 minutes. Add more water from cooking the beans if the sauce dries up. Cook until the beans are soft. Serve with rice and butter.

Ratatouille

Probably the best-known of the tomato vegetable stews.

1 large aubergine
1 red pepper
1 green pepper
4 courgettes
1 large Spanish onion
2/3 cloves garlic
salt and pepper
pinch of basil/dried basil leaves
4 tbs. olive oil
1 x 14 oz. (400 g.) tin of tomatoes
4 tbs. chopped parsley

Wipe the aubergine and cut off the spiny stalk. Cut in slices, liberally sprinkle with salt and lay on a plate. Stand for 1 hour. The salt will help to draw the bitter juices from the aubergine. Rinse and pat dry. Cut into quarters. Peel the onion and slice into rings. Peel and chop the garlic very finely or crush. Wipe the courgettes and cut off the ends, slice into rings. Cut the stalks from the peppers and slice in long thin slices. Cut away any seeds or white pith inside. Heat the olive oil in a large deep saucepan. Sauté the onions and garlic until they become limp and transparent. Stir in the aubergines. Aubergines tend to soak up vast quantities of oil so raise the temperature a little to help seal the outsides. As the aubergines begin to colour and soften, stir in the peppers and courgettes. Sauté for 4 or 5 minutes and then pour in the tinned tomatoes. Fill the tomato tin with water and add a little to the pan. Roughly break up the tomatoes in the pan. Season with salt, pepper and basil and bring to the boil. Cover with a tightly fitting lid and simmer gently for 45 minutes to 1 hour. This dish improves the longer it is cooked. Stir from time to time to prevent the tomatoes sticking to the bottom of the pan. Serve sprinkled with chopped parsley, hot or cold.

143

Add 4 oz. (115 g.) chopped mushrooms for the last 10 minutes' cooking if you wish.

Broad beans, bacon & tomato stew

1 lb. (450 g.) broad beans
8 oz. (225 g.) streaky bacon (optional)
half a head of finely chopped cabbage — white or green
¼ tsp. caraway seeds
small tin of tomatoes
1 clove garlic
few chopped leaves of mint
salt and pepper
2 tbs. olive oil/cooking oil
1 small sliced onion

Peel the onion. Finely slice the cabbage and onion. Peel and crush the garlic. Shell the beans. If the shells are pale green and tender, they can be cooked with the beans. In this case, slice as runner beans. Chop the bacon into chunks. Heat the olive oil in a large saucepan and sauté the onion and garlic with the pieces of bacon. When the bacon begins to crisp and the onions are limp and transparent, add the caraway seeds, cabbage and beans. Sauté for a few minutes and then turn the heat down and cover. Let the vegetables stew in their juices for 15 minutes and then pour in the tin of tomatoes and roughly break up the tomatoes. Season and bring to the boil. Turn down to a gentle simmer and cover. Cook for 35 to 40 minutes until all the vegetables are soft.

Serve with rice sprinkled with mint leaves.

Use dry cider or white wine instead of tomatoes.

Creamy onions & carrots

1 lb. (450 g.) carrots
1 large onion
1 clove garlic
a handful of chopped parsley
2 oz. (55 g.) butter
1 oz. (25 g.) wholemeal flour
¾ pint (430 ml.) milk

Scrub the carrots and cut off the tops and tails. Cut in circles. Peel the onion and slice in circles. Peel and chop or crush the garlic. In a large saucepan, melt the butter and sauté the carrots, onion and garlic. Keep turning until the onion softens, cover the pan, turn the heat down to a minimum and let the onion and carrots stew in the butter for 30 minutes. Stir in the flour and, when the mixture thickens, add the milk. Keep stirring until all the flour is blended in and then bring to the boil. Simmer covered for 10 minutes and serve with a generous handful of chopped

144

parsley stirred in. Correct seasoning before serving.

Runner beans, fennel & spring onions in white wine

1 lb. (450 g.) green beans
1 bulb of fennel
bunch of spring onions
salt, pepper and knob of butter/tbs. of oil
½ pint (290 ml.) chicken stock/white wine

Preheat the oven to gas mark 5 (375°F). String the beans (i.e. take off the stringy bits running down the back) and slice diagonally. Wash the fennel and cut in long thin strips, including the leaves. Rinse the spring onions and cut off the hairy root ends. Slice with the green leaves in long thin lengthways strips. Grease a deep ovenproof dish. Mix the vegetables together and turn into the greased dish. Pour the stock or wine into the vegetables until it is halfway up the dish. Season with salt and pepper. Cover and cook in the oven for 25 minutes or until the vegetables are tender.

Cheese, ham & vegetables

Use the same vegetables as above but sauté until soft in 1 oz. (25 g.) butter and then wrap in rolls of cooked ham, cover with a thin cheese sauce (see p. 83) and bake for 30 minutes.

Cauliflower cooked in tomato

1 head of cauliflower
1 large onion
1 small tin of tomatoes
2 cloves garlic
salt, pepper
chopped mint
1 oz. (25 g.) butter/3 tbs. of olive oil

Break the cauliflower into flowerets. Slice the onion and garlic finely. Heat the butter or olive oil in a large, deep frying pan and fry the onions and garlic until soft. Stir in the cauliflower and continue sautéing. As the cauliflower gradually softens, pour in the tin of tomatoes. Season with salt and pepper, cover with a tight lid and allow to stew at a very low heat until the cauliflower is cooked but fairly crisp (about 10 minutes). Sprinkle with a pinch of dried basil, oregano or chopped mint if you have it. This is a fairly dry dish when cooked so be careful not to allow it to burn on the bottom of the pan.

145

White bean stew

8 oz. (225 g.) white haricot beans/tinned beans
2 large onions
2 large carrots
2 cloves garlic
1 bay leaf
salt and pepper
1 x 14 oz. (400 g.) tin of tomatoes
2 pints (a generous litre) stock or water
1 oz. (25 g.) butter/3 tbs. olive oil

If you are using dried beans, soak them overnight. Cook for 1 hour in 2 pints (a generous litre) of water or stock. While the beans are cooking, peel and slice the onions, scrub and slice the carrots and peel and finely chop the cloves of garlic. Heat the oil in a large saucepan and sauté the onions and garlic until they are soft and golden brown. Add the tomatoes with their juice to the onions, bring to the boil and cover. Turn down to a low simmer for 10 minutes. Season. Stir in the beans with the stock or water; if you cooked them, add the water in which they were cooked. Cook at a low heat for 1 hour or until the beans are tender.

You can add lightly sautéd sausages or bacon to this stew with the tomatoes.

Aduki bean stew

The wonderful thing about aduki beans is that, unlike any of the other beans, they do not have to be soaked before cooking and they only take 45 minutes to cook. They also have one of the sweetest flavours and can be used for any of the dishes in the book where beans are called for — just omit the soaking time. Buy them in health-food stores or Chinese supermarkets.

8 oz. (225 g.) aduki beans
1 pint (575 ml.) water
10 spring onions/3 leeks
1 large parsnip
1 large carrot
small tin of tomatoes
salt and pepper
pinch of dried thyme
3 tbs. cooking oil
¼ tsp. chilli powder
mustard seed/cumin seed

Scrub the carrot and the parsnip and top and tail. Slice into chunks. Rinse the spring onions and cut off the top inch of the leaves and the hairy root end. Rinse the aduki beans in cold water and pick them over to be sure there are no stones or bits of twig that have escaped the sorter. Heat the oil in a large saucepan and sauté the

146

whole spring onions, parsnip and carrot. Keep turning them until they are beginning to soften and then add the tin of tomatoes, aduki beans and thyme. Do not put any salt in until the end of the cooking but season with pepper, spices and a little chilli powder. Add an extra helping of water so that the vegetables and beans move freely in the pan. Don't add the whole pint (575 ml.) at once or the stew will be watery. Check the pan from time to time during the cooking and add more liquid when necessary. The beans will absorb quite a lot of liquid. Bring to the boil and then turn down to simmer with a lid on for 1 hour.

Cauliflower cheese

The essence of good cauliflower cheese is to use strong cheese and plenty of it. It is also vital that the cauliflower is only cooked till just tender and is very well drained of water. Otherwise you suddenly find your beautiful, creamy sauce being invaded by cooking water.

1 head of cauliflower
1 oz. (25 g.) butter
1 oz. (25 g.) flour
¾ pint (430 ml.) milk
8 oz. (225 g.) at least of strong grated cheese
salt, pepper and dry English mustard

Cut away only the coarsest leaves around the head of the cauliflower. Then drop the whole thing into boiling salted water. The water need not cover the head; as long as you have a lid on, the tender flower part will cook in the steam. Drain when the point of a knife slips easily into the base of the cauliflower. Leave standing for a couple of minutes in a colander or sieve to drain away cooking water. While the cauliflower is cooking, melt the butter in a small saucepan and stir in the flour. Keep stirring until the two are thoroughly blended together. Add the milk very slowly beating into the butter and flour as you go. Bring to the boil. Season with salt, pepper and dry mustard. Allow to simmer for 10 to 15 minutes and then stir in the cheese. Pour the sauce over the cauliflower, sprinkle with grated cheese and toast under the grill until golden brown.

Variations
— Leeks, potatoes and onions are all delectable served this way, or make a mixture of them all.
— Grate garlic or onion over the cauliflower with the top layer of cheese.
— Lay strips of anchovy or streaky bacon over the cauliflower and sauce and grill.

Stir frying

You will need a broad, rounded flattish spoon or spatula or large cooking chopsticks to toss the vegetables. The idea is to cook everything very fast, so the oil must be very hot and what has to be cooked should be thin (use deep frying pan).

(i)   Chop vegetables (and meat/fish) into small, even slices.
(ii) Heat 1 - 2 tablespoons of vegetable oil. Do not use olive oil for Chinese-style recipes.
(iii) At this stage throw in any seeds or spices that you are using — coriander, fennel, yellow or black mustard seed, chopped green chilli, chopped garlic, ginger, sesame seeds — and let them pop in the hot oil and permeate it with their flavours. Cover the pan or they'll shoot all over the kitchen.
(iv) When they stop popping, throw in the vegetables. Onions and root vegetables first, followed 5 minutes later by any softer vegetables — peppers, cabbage, etc.

If you are using tomatoes, use only the hard fleshy part and not the seeds and juice which will make the other vegetables stew. Put them in last with any mushrooms and fresh herbs. Fresh coriander leaves are particularly good. It should all take 20 - 25 minutes to cook, depending a little on the amount you are cooking and which vegetables you choose. They are cooked when they are still firm to bite, but not raw. A word of warning: the cold food may lower the temperature of the oil so turn the heat up for a couple of minutes after adding the vegetables to the pan.

Adapt this method by turning the heat as low as it will go after the first five minutes of cooking and covering the pan with a tight lid. The steam from the cooking vegetables will condense into water on the lid and drop back into the pan to slowly stew them in their own juices. Give the pan a shake every time you pass and the occasional stir to stop things sticking on the bottom; 30 - 35 minutes cooking time.

GRAINS

Rissottos

The most tasty way of cooking risotto or rice dishes with meat and vegetables is to sauté all the ingredients together until soft and then add the rice and stock. You will have to watch the pan more carefully than you would if you were cooking the ingredients and rice separately and then mixing them together, because it is difficult to judge exactly how much liquid you will need to cook the rice or grains without ending up with a watery pallid dish of washed-out rice and veg. So it is best to add the liquid throughout the cooking as the rice becomes dry. If you add too much water when the rice is perfectly cooked, don't go on cooking or you will end up with gruel; either strain off the extra liquid and use it to make a sauce or add more vegetables that will cook in the hot rice like mushrooms chopped finely or spring onions, or add an ingredient like tinned tuna, chopped red or green pepper or

148

shredded lettuce that will bulk out the rice but needs no cooking.

To make a miso gravy: blend 2 teaspoons of miso into the extra stock, heat to just below boiling and serve.
Creamy sauce: beat yogurt, sour cream or single cream into the extra stock and serve as a dressing.
Tomato sauce: strain off the extra liquid. Melt ½ oz. (15 g.) butter in a frying pan and fry a few chopped tomatoes and a crushed clove of garlic. Add the extra stock and simmer for 15 minutes and serve with the rice.

You will eventually become adept at judging the amount of liquid that you need for a moist risotto. Sauté the vegetables in butter for preference; this flavours the rice wonderfully. To help decide how much liquid you will need, remember 1 cup of brown rice will cook to perfection in 2 cups of water and 1 cup of white rice needs 1½ cups of water. For both of these amounts bring the rice and water to the boil together and then turn down as low as possible, cover and allow to cook. White rice needs 15 to 20 minutes. Brown rice needs 40 minutes. Sort through brown rice before cooking for stones, dirt and twigs, and then rinse in a fine sieve under running water. Allow extra liquid to cook the vegetables and meat.

    ½ tsp. turmeric is used to colour rice yellow.

    A few strands of saffron will colour the rice and give a sweet honeyed, nutty flavour.

    Use long or short grain brown rice, Italian risotto rice or Indian Basmati.

Chicken, peas & new carrots

6 oz. (170 g.) cooked chicken or other poultry
4 spring onions
½ head finely shredded green cabbage
4 new carrots
¼ lb. (115 g.) frozen peas
1 cup of brown or white rice
1 tsp. of mustard seeds
salt, pepper
1 oz. (25 g.) of butter/3 tbs. cooking oil
fresh chopped parsley
pinch of tarragon
2 - 3 cups of chicken stock/water

Cut the chicken into small cubes. Peel the onions, scrub the carrots and wash cabbage; chop them all into small pieces. Heat the butter or oil in a large, deep frying pan. Throw in the mustard seeds and cover while they pop. Sauté the onions and carrots until they begin to brown a little around the edges. Stir in the chicken and rice and let them turn pale gold in the butter. Some of the grains will probably pop. Add 2 cups of stock or water and bring to the boil. Season with salt, pepper and herbs. Turn down to a gentle simmer. If you are using white rice, stir in the shredded cabbage and frozen peas straight away. If you are using brown rice, let the rice simmer for 30 minutes and then add the peas and cabbage. Check the pan approximately every 10 minutes and add more liquid if necessary. Serve with a handful of fresh chopped parsley stirred in and knobs of butter. If using white rice, cooking time will be about 20 minutes; if using brown rice, cooking time will be about 40 minutes.

Mixed vegetable rice

1 large onion
1 large carrot
4 tomatoes/small tin of tomatoes
3 - 4 cups water/stock
¼ lb. (115 g.) of sliced green beans (frozen will do)
1 red pepper
1 cup of brown or white rice
salt, pepper
4 oz. (115 g.) sweet corn (tinned or frozen will do)
1 clove garlic
2 oz. (55 g.) mushrooms
1 oz. (25 g.) butter

Peel the onion and chop finely. Scrub the carrot, cut off the top and tail, and dice. Cut away the stalk from the pepper, remove seeds and white pith from the inside and dice. String the beans and slice diagonally. Crush the garlic and slice the mushrooms. If using fresh corn on the cob run a sharp knife down underneath the kernels and cut away from the cob; tinned corn should simply be drained. Chop the tomatoes if using fresh.

Melt the butter in a large deep frying pan and sauté the carrot, onion and garlic until golden. Add the rice, tomatoes, beans, fresh corn, red pepper, salt and pepper. Sauté for 5 minutes and then add 2 cupfuls of water or stock. Bring to the boil and turn down to simmer with a tightly fitting lid: total cooking time for white rice will be about 20 minutes; if brown rice, about 40 minutes. Check the liquid from time to time during the cooking. If you are using frozen beans or corn or tinned corn add them with the chopped mushrooms 5 minutes before serving. Serve with chopped fresh herbs and butter.

Tomato rice

1 x 14 oz. (400 g.) tin of tomatoes
1 large onion
1 clove of garlic
pinch of dried basil/chopped fresh basil leaves
1 oz. (25 g.) butter
1 cup of rice
salt and pepper

Peel and finely slice the onion. Peel and chop the garlic. Chop the basil leaves, if they are fresh. Heat the butter in a large, deep frying pan. Sauté the onion and garlic until soft. Add the rice and the tin of tomatoes and half the tomato tin full of water. Roughly break up the tomatoes in the pan. Season with salt, pepper and dried basil. Fresh basil should be stirred in 5 minutes before serving. Bring to the boil and then turn down to a low simmer until cooked. Check during cooking in case more liquid is needed. Cooking time for white rice is about 20 minutes, 40 minutes for brown rice.

Pilau rice

1 cup rice, Basmati preferably
2 cups water/chicken stock
pinch of turmeric — vary according to how yellow you want the rice
2 tbs. of frozen peas
leftover meat or chicken scraps/2 oz. (55 g.) peeled prawns
chopped hard-boiled egg
1 tsp. mixed mustard seed, cumin seed, coriander, ajvain
half chopped green chilli (optional)
1 oz. (25 g.) butter/ghee
1 cardamom pod, salt
fresh coriander (optional)

Heat the butter or *ghee* in a large, deep frying pan. Throw in the chopped chilli and the spices (except turmeric) and cover. Wait until they have all finished popping and then stir in the rice and turmeric. Salt and add the stock. Bring to the boil and then turn down to the lowest possible heat. Simmer for 5 minutes and then add the frozen peas, chopped meat scraps or prawns. Cover and continue simmering until all the rice is cooked, adding more liquid if necessary. This will take about 20 minutes. Serve scattered with chopped hard-boiled egg and fresh green coriander leaves if you can get them.

Miso rice

1 cup brown rice
2 cups water
1 tbs. of miso

1 tsp. sesame seeds
2 tbs. sesame oil if you have it, otherwise olive or vegetable oil

Heat the sesame oil in a large deep frying pan and throw in the sesame seeds. Cover and wait for the seeds to pop. Stir in the rice and gently brown in the oil. Add the water and bring to the boil. Turn down to simmer. Spoon out enough water to dissolve the miso and then stir back into the rice. Cook covered until all the water has been absorbed — about 40 minutes.

Millet

Is a buttery, golden grain with a pleasant nutty flavour.

1 cup of millet (grain not flakes)
3 cups water
½ oz. (15 g.) butter or cooking oil
salt

Sauté the millet in the hot oil or butter until it turns golden brown. Pour in the water, bring to the boil and salt. Simmer covered for 25 to 30 minutes until all the water is absorbed. Serve in place of rice or pasta.
    You can finely chop vegetables and sauté in the oil with the millet and cook as above.

Buckwheat

Is a brown, nutty, sweet protein-rich grain. It is very warming in the winter and goes well with gamey foods or as a vegetable pilau. Use ready-roasted buckwheat.

2 cups of water
1 cup of buckwheat
pinch of salt

Add the buckwheat to boiling salted water. Bring back to the boil and then turn down to simmer for 20 minutes. Take care, it sticks very easily to the bottom of the pan. Serve with sautéd vegetables. Onions are particularly good.

3-grain cereal

6 oz. (170 g.) brown rice
6 oz. (170 g.) wheat
6 oz. (170 g.) rye
Soak the wheat overnight. Cook for 1 hour in 1 pint of water. Add the rice and rye and another pint of water. Season with a pinch of salt. Bring to the boil and then simmer until all the grains are cooked (about 45 minutes).

PASTA

Macaroni cheese

8 oz. (225 g.) uncooked macaroni
*8 oz. (225 g.) grated mature Cheddar cheese. Use mild if you pre-
fer or a mixture of leftover cheeses*
1 oz. (25 g.) butter
1 oz. (25 g.) plain white/wholemeal flour
¾ pint (430 ml.) of milk
salt and pepper
¼ tsp. dry mustard

Cook the macaroni in boiling salted water until soft (about 12 minutes). It should not be completely limp but offer a slight resistance to the teeth. While the macaroni is cooking, grate the cheese. Melt the butter slowly over a low heat in a saucepan. Stir in the flour with a wooden spoon. Keep stirring until the flour and butter are completely mixed together with no lumps or pockets of flour. This should take about 2 minutes. The mixture should be golden not brown. Remove from the heat and add about 1/3 of the milk, hot or cold but not boiling. Whisk together with the butter and flour with a balloon whisk or wooden spoon. You can use an electric beater. When the mixture is smooth return to the heat and keep stirring until it comes to the boil. Slowly stir in the rest of the milk. Keep stirring over the heat until the sauce thickens. Season with salt, pepper and mustard and stir in the cheese, keeping back 1 oz. (25 g.). Allow the sauce to simmer gently for 10 minutes while the macaroni is cooking. Drain the macaroni in a colander and tip into a greased, shallow ovenproof dish. Pour in the cheese sauce and mix well together; sprinkle cheese on top and brown under the grill until the cheese goes a rich golden brown. If the grill isn't high enough to take the dish, brown briefly in the oven at gas mark 5 (375°F).

You can also include chopped tomato in the macaroni or grate onion on top.

Easy macaroni cheese

8 oz. (225 g.) dry macaroni
4 oz. (115 g.) grated strong cheese
1 oz. (25 g.) butter
2 chopped tomatoes
2 chopped spring onions

Cook the macaroni in boiling salted water for about 12 minutes. Grate the cheese, peel and chop the onions; chop the tomatoes. Toss the cooked macaroni, onions, cheese and tomatoes together in a deep ovenproof dish, season with salt and pepper. Dot with butter and either serve as it is or brown under the grill for a couple of minutes. The heat of the macaroni will melt the cheese.

Lasagne

Is traditionally made with at least 3 different sauces between the layers of pasta — usually meat, cheese and tomato — but you can also add mushrooms, Italian sausage, olives, anchovies or whatever you like. It's simpler to make with just tomato sauce and cheese and very delicious.

Lasagne is possibly the only sort of pasta that is a little tricky to cook. The wide thick sheets can stick together while cooking if you are not careful and then taste raw and hard. Have a large pan of boiling water on the stove and add to it 1 teaspoon of salt and 2 tablespoons of oil — olive for preference. This will help to prevent the pasta sticking together. Drop in only 4 or 5 sheets at a time, placing them in the water one by one. Let them cook for 15 minutes, checking from time to time that they have not stuck together. Fish out with a perforated spoon — easier said than done, since the lasagne is now very slippery — and lay to dry on a clean tea-towel. Continue cooking in batches until you have enough (allowing a layer on the bottom of your dish, one in the middle at least, and one on the top). Make sure the top layer of lasagne is covered when cooked, otherwise it will go hard.

Cheese & tomato lasagne

8 oz. (225 g.) lasagne
8 oz. (225 g.) mozzarella cheese
8 oz. (225 g.) ricotta/cream cheese
2 oz. (55 g.) butter

Tomato sauce
1 large Spanish onion
14 oz. (400 g.) tin of tomatoes
3 tbs. olive oil/1 oz. (25 g.) butter
1 - 2 chopped cloves garlic
salt and pepper
1 pinch of dried oregano/basil/fresh basil leaves

Peel and slice the onion in rings. Peel and chop or crush the garlic. Heat the oil or butter in a saucepan. Slowly melt the onion and garlic in the oil or butter, until they are soft and transparent. Add the herbs, salt, pepper and tomatoes to the onions. Bring to the boil and then turn down to a medium heat, cover and simmer gently. This sauce needs about 20 minutes to cook but longer will only improve the flavour. If it seems to be sticking to the bottom of the pan, add a little water or wine.

While the tomato sauce is cooking, cook the lasagne; preheat the oven to gas mark 5 (375°F). Slice the mozzarella into thin slices and crumble the ricotta. Lightly grease a shallow, oven-proof dish, line with a layer of lasagne and pour in a layer of tomato sauce. Lay 2 or 3 strips of pasta over the tomato sauce. Cover with a layer of mozzarella and ricotta or cream cheese. Top with another layer of lasagne, tomato sauce and lasagne, ending up with the 2 cheeses. Dot with butter and bake for 30 minutes.

Variations

(i) Use another 4 - 8 oz. (115 g. - 225 g.) of pasta and add another layer of meat sauce (see p. 98). Cook for 40 minutes.

(ii) Boil 8 oz. (225 g.) Italian sausages in plenty of water for 15 minutes. Chop in slices and add to the tomato sauce. Cook for 40 minutes.

(iii) Use layers of the cheese sauce in the macaroni cheese recipe instead of ricotta and mozzarella.

(iv) Make layers of lasagne, cheese sauce and thick slices of ham. Ham off the bone has the best flavour. Cook for 30 minutes.

(v) Cook half a head of cauliflower broken into flowerets in the tomato sauce. Fill the tomato tin with water and add to the sauce.

(vi) Grate Parmesan cheese over the top layer.

Gnocchi can be made with semolina, mashed potato or a mixture of semolina and cornmeal.

Semolina gnocchi

12 oz. (340 g.) semolina
1½ pints (860 ml.) milk
½ oz. (15 g.) butter
10 oz. (285 g.) grated cheese
grated nutmeg/1 clove chopped garlic
salt, pepper
½ tsp. dry mustard

Chop the garlic very finely. Bring the milk to the boil in a large saucepan. Turn down to a low heat and gradually add the semolina. Stir with a wooden spoon until the mixture thickens. It is ready when it begins to leave the sides of the pan and great fat slow bubbles are bursting on the surface. Stir in the garlic, salt, pepper, mustard and 2 oz. (55 g.) of cheese. Run the cold tap over a flat plate and spread the semolina mix over the plate 1″ (2 cm.) thick. You will find it easiest to spread with a wet palette knife. Allow to cool for at least 1 hour in the fridge. Cut into 1″ (2 cm.) squares. Butter a shallow baking dish and lay the squares of gnocchi like little tiles over the dish. Sprinkle with the rest of the cheese and brown under the grill.

Variations
(i)   Use half semolina and half cornmeal.
(ii)   Bake in the oven at gas mark 5 (375°F) for 20 minutes covered with a thick layer of tomato sauce.
(iii)   Lay the gnocchi on a thick layer of cooked spinach and bake for 20 minutes at gas mark 5 (375°F).
(iv)   Lay on a bed of ratatouille, cover with cheese and bake at gas mark 5 (375°F) for 20 minutes.

Pasta with fennel & ham

1 large bulb of fennel
Parmesan cheese
4 - 6 oz. (115 - 170 g.) of ham
2 cloves garlic
4 oz. (115 g.) of mushrooms
1 oz. (25 g.) butter/2 tbs. olive oil
salt and pepper
a little dry white wine
8 oz. (225 g.) spaghetti or other pasta shapes

Cook the pasta in boiling salted water until *al dente* (offers slight resistance to the teeth). Slice the ham into strips. While the pasta is cooking, boil the whole bulb of fennel in salted water until a knife point slips easily into the base (about 10 minutes). Drain, but keep the water if you are thinking of making vegetable soup within the next couple of days. Chop. Peel and chop the garlic and cut the mushrooms into slices. Heat the butter or oil in a large deep frying pan. Sauté the garlic until it is soft and then add the wine and chopped fennel. Cook for 10 minutes over a gentle heat stirring occasionally. Season with salt and pepper. Add the mushrooms and cook for another 5 minutes. Stir in the drained pasta and serve with Parmesan cheese.

Aubergine & bacon sauce for pasta

1 large aubergine
1 large onion
6 oz. (170 g.) streaky bacon
1 small tin of tomatoes
2 cloves garlic
salt and pepper
4 or 5 capers (optional)
½ oz. (15 g.) butter/1 tbs. olive oil
pinch of dried basil/fresh basil
Parmesan cheese
8 oz. (225 g.) shell pasta

Slice the aubergine across and sprinkle heavily with salt. Leave to stand for at least 1 hour. Rinse and pat dry. Cut into bite-size chunks. Peel and slice the onion. Peel and chop the garlic. Cut the bacon into 2″ (5 cm.) strips. Put the pasta on to cook. Heat the oil slowly in the frying pan with the bacon. The fat in the bacon will gradually supplement the oil in the pan. When the bacon starts to fizzle and crisp around the edges add the onion and garlic. Turn the heat up until the onion is frying quite briskly. As it softens, add the aubergines. Sauté until the aubergine softens and then add the tinned tomatoes, roughly break them up in the pan and cover. Cook for 30 minutes and then add the capers and serve with pasta.

Tuna & artichoke hearts

1 tin of tuna
1 tin of artichoke hearts
1 clove of garlic
juice of half a lemon
1 oz. (25 g.) butter/2 tbs. of olive oil
salt and pepper
pinch of dried oregano
8 oz. (225 g.) pasta

Cook the pasta in boiling salted water. Slice the artichoke hearts into quarters. Heat the butter or oil with the peeled and chopped or crushed garlic and then add the artichoke hearts. Sauté them lightly until they begin to acquire a golden brown tinge. Gently flake in the fish and keep turning until it is heated through. Season with salt, pepper and herbs. Mix in a large bowl with the hot drained pasta and the juice of half a lemon.

Cannelloni

Cannelloni are the fat tubes of pasta that can be stuffed with a meat or vegetable filling and baked under a blanket of cheese or cheese sauce. They must be cooked before being stuffed.

To cook the cannelloni
With cannelloni you might encounter some of the same problems in cooking as with lasagne, i.e. they tend to stick together. The answer is to use the same method of cooking. Salt a large saucepan of water with a teaspoon of salt and pour in 2 tablespoons of olive oil. Cook 6 or 7 pieces of cannelloni at each go and then remove from the boiling water when soft and drain while the next batch is cooking. Cooking time is about 15 to 20 minutes.

Stuffings

Meat filling

For 8 oz. (225 g.) cannelloni

8 oz. (225 g.) minced beef
1 green pepper
1 large onion
8 stoned black olives
2 cloves garlic
salt and pepper
pinch of basil
pinch of oregano
1 egg
2 tbs. Parmesan cheese
2 tbs. of olive oil

Peel and chop the onion and garlic as finely as you can. Chop the green pepper and olives (removing the stones if there are any — a bore). Heat the olive oil in a frying pan. Fry the onions and garlic until they are soft and then add the meat and green pepper. Continue frying until the meat is completely browned (about 10 minutes) and no raw lumps remain, tip the pan towards you and spoon out excess fat. Add the chopped olives and season with salt, pepper and herbs. Take off the heat and allow to cool. Beat together the egg and the cheese. When the meat is fairly cool, fold in the cheese and egg mix. If the meat is too hot it will cook the egg instead of binding the mixture together. Stuff the filling into the cooked tubes of cannelloni and place in a buttered ovenproof dish. Cover with a layer of cheese sauce or slices of mozzarella, dot liberally with butter and bake at gas mark 5 (375°F) for 45 minutes. The pasta *must* be completely covered with cheese or it will dry up unappetizingly around the edges when cooking. If using cheese sauce, the recipe on p. 153 for macaroni cheese will be good.

Cheese & spinach filling

1 egg
1 lb. (450 g.) spinach (½ lb.; 225 g. frozen)
4 oz. (115 g.) ricotta/cream cheese
2 teaspoons grated Parmesan

salt, pepper
nutmeg (optional)
1 oz. (25 g.) butter/2 tbs. olive oil

Wash the spinach thoroughly and cook in a large saucepan with
½ oz. (15 g.) butter or a tablespoon of olive oil. The water from
washing the spinach will be enough to keep it from burning (see
p. 28). If using frozen, thaw it. When the spinach is cooked or
thawed, chop and drain thoroughly, turn it into a large bowl with
the cheeses and beat them together with the egg. Season with salt,
pepper and a grate of nutmeg, or a pinch of ground nutmeg. Fill
the cannelloni with the mixture, cover with cheese sauce and bake
at gas mark 4 (350°F) for 20 minutes.

Use the same recipe for cheese sauce as in macaroni cheese (see
p. 153).

Buckwheat spaghetti

Is one of the nicest wholemeal pastas. It is usually made in Japan
and you can buy it in health-food stores and Chinese and Japanese
grocers. Cook it as ordinary pasta. It is particularly good served
with:
(i)   Sauted spring onions, streaky bacon and diced parsnips.
(ii)   Mushrooms and shrimps sautéd in butter.
(iii) Sautéd mixed vegetables with tamari soy sauce.

PASTRY

My most agonized memories of domestic science classes at school
concern the dreadful struggles I had with reluctant pastry, chasing
crumbly bits around the mixing bowl, fingers glued up with sticky
dough, and, worst of all, patching together the rolled out and
increasingly grubby fragments in an effort to make one complete
piece. In the end I found the perfect strategy – I got my best
friend to make it for me. For years I eschewed any dish that
required pastry or bought a packet of the wonderfully compliant
frozen stuff. I would gape with astonishment at friends who
seemed able to perform this miraculous act. And then one day I
went home, got out the mixing bowl and, with only the
vaguest memory of the correct proportions, produced a passable
apple pie. Maybe it worked because my hands weren't shaking at
the thought of getting nought out of ten, but really I began to
think that it wasn't quite so difficult after all. A modicum of self
confidence and the observance of a few golden rules and you should
be OK.
  (i) Keep all utensils and ingredients cold. Put everything, mixing
       bowl included, in the fridge for half an hour before you begin.
 (ii) Wash hands in very cold water before touching the ingredients.
(iii) Handle the pastry as little and as gently as possible.

(iv) Use as little liquid as possible.

(v) Remember that it is the amount of air you incorporate into the pastry that will expand and make it light and flaky.

Shortcrust pastry

The 'short' is the shortening or fat content of the pastry. The more fat there is in the pastry the more crumbly it will be. It can be all butter, all margarine, a mixture of the two or half of either and half lard. Surprisingly, you can also use cooking oil for making pastry and it is much easier to rub in. For every 2 oz. (55 g.) of flour use 1 tablespoon of oil. Beware though, a strongly flavoured oil will swamp other flavours.

Flour

Wholemeal flour is much more nutritious than white flour, but it needs a little practice in handling or the pastry can be very heavy. It can help to increase the fat content by 1 - 2 oz. (25 - 55 g.) and to keep water to a minimum. Experiment with using half wholemeal flour and half plain flour. You can use plain or self-raising flour.

Moisture

Use water with a squeeze of lemon juice, or milk or a combination of the two. You can substitute part of an egg mixed with the other liquids — this makes a richer pastry, and avoids the problems of too much water, which makes pastry hard. If you are using tinned fruit to fill the pastry, add the syrup instead of water to the pastry.

Proportions

The approximate proportion for flour and fat for shortcrust pastry is half as much fat as flour. So for 6 oz. (170 g.) of pastry, which is enough to line an 8″ (20 cm.) dish, you would use 4 oz. (115 g.) of flour and 2 oz. (55 g.) of fat; if adding egg, 2 tbs. of beaten egg. With amounts over half a pound it is wise to increase the amount of fat to about two thirds of the weight of the flour. For 1 lb. (450 g.) of flour you could use 10 - 11 oz. (285 - 310 g.) of fat. Use 1 teaspoon of salt per lb. of flour even in sweet pastry. Use as little liquid as possible.

Sweet pastry

For sweet pastry, add 1 tablespoon of caster or soft brown sugar per 2 oz. (55 g.) of fat to the pastry mix. Rub into the fat and flour before adding water.

Method

(i) Sift the flour through a fine sieve into the mixing bowl.

This not only sorts out any lumps which are in the flour but starts the process of adding air to the pastry. It is not absolutely necessary, however, if you can't face it.

(ii) Cut the fat into the tiniest possible pieces with a knife and scatter in the flour. It will be easier to 'rub' into the flour if you don't drop all the fat in a heap in the middle. Try and sprinkle them so that they are dusted with a fine coating of flour.

(iii) Wash hands in very cold water.

(iv) With the fingertips gently lift up handfuls of the flour and butter and rub the butter lightly into the flour. The movement is a bit like the Hollywood cliched sign for a foreign beggar wanting cash. Do this well above the mixing bowl so that it traps more air as it drops. Always try to pick up more flour than butter, too much butter will melt between your fingers and make everything greasy.

(v) When the flour and fat are blended together, the texture should be like fine breadcrumbs. Take a little cold water, 2 tablespoons would be enough for 6 oz. (170 g.) of pastry, and sprinkle a tablespoon at a time over the flour and fat. Mix each spoonful in as you go with a table knife, cutting the liquid into the mixture. Stop adding water when the crumbs start sticking together. They should not feel damp or sticky to the touch, but if you push them together into a large ball it should stick together. This is a really crucial stage: if you use too much water and handle the pastry too much, it will be tough when it is cooked.

(vi) If you have time, it is a good idea to put the pastry back in the fridge for half an hour at this stage.

(vii) Flour your hands, the rolling pin and the surface on which you are going to roll the pastry. Place the pastry in the centre of the surface. If you are making a top and bottom cover for a pie, cut the mixture in half and roll the two pieces separately. Roll the rolling pin away from you, picking it up at the end of each roll. Never roll backwards and forwards — it will squash all the air right out of the pastry. Keep turning the pastry round and over to make sure it is not sticking. If it is sticking sprinkle on a little more flour. If the pastry falls apart as you roll it out, return to the bowl and add a bit more water. But if you're filling a pastrycase, it doesn't matter if it breaks.

(viii) When you have rolled it out to the size you need — check by holding the dish over the top, there should be an inch or two sticking out all the way round — slide a palette knife under the edge and slowly roll the pastry on to the rolling pin. This is the easiest way to handle fragile pastry. Roll it from the

rolling pin onto the pie dish. You should previously have greased the pie dish.

Cooking
Pastry is usually baked in a fairly hot oven; the richer it is, the hotter the oven. The starch swells up with the moisture and mingles with the fat.

Cook pastry according to instructions in individual recipes.

Frozen pastry
If your pastry consistently fails, go out and buy frozen. It's pretty good — and safe. Make sure it's thawed before you roll it out, and follow cooking instructions on the packet.

Neatening the edges of pastry
When you have to join two layers of pastry together, slice around the pie rim with a knife — this is a most satisfying feeling. Then either frill by pressing down with the back of a knife or pinch together with the fingers.

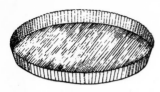

Open pies & flans
You can make an open pie or flan either on an ovenproof plate or shallow dish or in a crinkle edged porcelain flan dish. A simple and cheap way of producing an impressive free standing flan is to invest in a metal flan case with removable bottom. These cases are much cheaper than the lovely porcelain ones and are easy to use; simply stand the cooked flan on a small upturned dish and the circular side to the flan case will come away.

For an 8″ (20 cm.) flan case use:

4 oz. (115 g.) flour, plain, wholemeal or white
2 oz. (55 g.) fat — butter/margarine/lard
a little water
for sweet pastry add 1 tbs. of brown or caster sugar

Baking blind
If you are making a quiche or open pie whose filling needs less cooking time than the pastry, it is essential to cook the pastry case before adding the filling or the pastry on the base of the pie will go soggy. But if you just put the case in the oven by itself the pastry will bubble up from the baking dish and shrink around the edges. After lining the dish with pastry, prick the base with a fork so that air can escape; then line the pastry case with a sheet of aluminium foil or greaseproof paper and scatter dry beans inside. The pastry case will hold its shape as you bake it with this weight inside. Bake at gas mark 6 (400°F) for 8 minutes. Remove the foil and beans and bake for another 3 minutes if it is going to be filled and cooked again. If it is going to be filled with a raw or pre-cooked filling, finish off the cooking until the case is a pale golden brown. This will take about 20 - 25 minutes.

FLAN FILLINGS

Use partially cooked cases (as above) for all these fillings.

Bacon, egg & onion

4 rashers streaky bacon
2 eggs
2 tbs. milk
1 small onion
1 oz. (25 g.) butter
4 oz. (115 g.) grated cheese
salt, pepper, dry English mustard
1 chopped clove garlic (optional)
1 tbs. chopped chives or parsley

Peel and chop the onion finely and peel and crush the garlic. Cut the bacon into chunks. Heat the butter in a frying pan and fry the bacon, onion and garlic together until the onions are soft and transparent. Set aside to cool. Beat together the eggs, milk and cheese. Season with salt, pepper, mustard, herbs, and add bacon mixture. Fill the partially cooked flan case and sprinkle with grated cheese or Parmesan. Bake until golden brown at gas mark 5 (375°F). This usually takes about 35 minutes. Give the dish a shake to see if it's done: if it wobbles, it needs more cooking.

Asparagus

½ lb. (225 g.) asparagus
2 eggs
2 tbs. milk
½ oz. (15 g.) butter/a little oil to grease the dish
salt, pepper and dry English mustard

Cut off all the woody ends of the asparagus. Cook in boiling water for 5 minutes and then drain. Mix together the eggs, milk, salt, pepper and half the cheese. Pour a layer of egg mixture into the partially cooked pastry case (see above), and then make a 'wheel' of asparagus spears with the points to the centre. Pour over another thin layer of eggs and milk and sprinkle with the remaining cheese. Bake at gas mark 5 (375°) until the top is golden brown. About 35 - 40 minutes.

Sliced potato filling

2 large potatoes
1 onion
2 oz. (55 g.) grated cheese
1 egg
4 tbs. milk
salt and pepper
½ oz. (15 g.) butter

Scrub the potatoes, cut in half and bring to the boil in salted water and cook for 10 minutes. Cool and slice finely. Peel the onion and slice in fine rings. Beat together the milk and egg. Season with salt and pepper. Build up layers of potato and onion slices in a partially cooked flan case (see above), finishing with a layer of potatoes. Pour in the milk and egg mix and sprinkle with grated cheese. Dot with knobs of butter. Cook in a medium oven, gas mark 5 (375°F) for 40 - 45 minutes.

Spinach flan filling

1 lb. (450 g.) spinach/½ lb. (225 g.) frozen leaf spinach
1 small onion
2 eggs
6 oz. (170 g.) cheese
½ oz. (15 g.) butter
salt and pepper

Wash the spinach thoroughly. Place the wet leaves in a large saucepan with the butter and cover. Cook on the lowest possible heat until the spinach is soft. If using frozen, thaw it in a sieve or colander to drain off liquid. Peel and chop the onion finely and mix with the spinach. Beat the egg and fold into the spinach. Season with salt and pepper. Turn the filling into the partially cooked pastry case (see p.163) and bake at gas mark 5 (375°F) for 35 - 40 minutes.

Leek & anchovy filling

1 lb. (450 g.) leeks
2 eggs
4 or 5 fillets of anchovy
6 oz. (170 g.) grated cheese
½ oz. (15 g.) butter

Wash the leeks and chop into rings. Heat the butter in a frying pan and sauté the leeks until they are soft and floppy. Allow to cool. Beat the eggs and cheese together, retaining 1 oz. (25 g.) of cheese to scatter on the top of the flan. Cut the anchovies into 2 or 3 pieces each. Stir the leeks and anchovies into the egg mixture. Season with salt and pepper. Pour into the flan case which has been partially cooked (see p. 163), scatter with cheese and bake for 35 - 40 minutes until the top is golden brown at gas mark 5 (375°F).

SWEET FLANS

Open apple tart

8" (20 cm.) uncooked sweet or plain shortcrust pastry case (p.163)
4 cooking/eating apples
2 tsp. brown sugar (if using cooking apples)
3 tbs. apricot jam
2 tbs. water

Bake blind an 8" (20 cm.) pastry case. Cook at gas mark 6 (400°) for 8 minutes; remove the foil and beans and bake for another 3 minutes.
   While the pastry is baking, peel and core 4 cooking or eating apples. If you use eating apples, you do not need to sweeten them with sugar but cooking apples have a tarter flavour. Cut the apples into even half-moon slices.
When the pastry is ready, lay the apple slices in concentric circles. Dot with butter and shake 2 teaspoons of brown sugar over them (unless using eating apples) and bake at gas mark 6 (400°F) for 35 minutes. While the tart is cooking, melt 3 tablespoons of apricot jam in a saucepan with 2 tbs. water and pour evenly over the apples when they are cooked. Serve hot or cold with cream.

Strawberry flan

Bake an 8" (20 cm.) flan case with sweet or plain shortcrust pastry (see p. 163) for 8 minutes at gas mark 6 (400°F) and then remove the foil and beans. Cook for another 20 - 25 minutes until golden brown. While the case is cooking, wash and hull 1 lb. (450 g.) strawberries and cut in half. When the flan case is cooked arrange on top the halved strawberries in neat circles, cut side down. Sprinkle with sugar or not according to taste.

You could beat ½ pint (290 ml.) of double cream until it was stiff and coat the cold flan case with it before adding the straw-berries.

Apricot flan

8" (20 cm.) uncooked sweet or plain shortcrust pastry case (see p. 163)
2 lb. (1 kilo) apricots
½ oz. (15 g.) butter, cut in little squares
2 tsp. brown sugar (optional)

Cut the apricots in half and remove the stones. Chop half of them and spread them over the base of the pastry case. Dot with a few squares of butter. Cover with circles of the remaining apricot halves. Dot with butter and bake as gas mark 6 (400°F) for 35 minutes. Shake with a little brown sugar when cooked.

Use the same recipe for plums.

Treacle tart

Make an 8" (20 cm.) partially cooked pastry case (see p. 163) Sprinkle with 2 oz. (55 g.) wholemeal breadcrumbs and cover to just ¼" below the rim of the case with golden syrup. Squeeze with lemon juice and bake at gas mark 4 (350°F) for 20 minutes.

CLOSED PIES

Steak & kidney pie

1 lb. (450 g.) of stewing steak) lots of butchers sell this ready
6 oz. (170 g.) kidneys   ) mixed together
1 large onion
1 large carrot
2 tbs. cooking oil or dripping
1 bay leaf
1 egg
salt, pepper and dry English mustard
2 oz. (55 g.) wholemeal flour
6 oz. (170 g.) shortcrust pastry (see p. 163)
1 pint (575 ml.) beef stock

Cut the stewing steak into chunks. Cut the white gristly core out of the kidneys and cut into chunks. Peel and slice the onion. Scrub the carrot, top and tail and chop into chunks. Heat the oil or dripping in a large heavy saucepan. Dip the meat first into the flour and then into the hot fat. Keep sautéing the meat until it is brown on all sides and then add the onion and carrot. Keep tossing until the vegetables begin to soften and then cover the meat and vegetables with stock. Season with salt, pepper and ½ teaspoon of mustard and add the bay leaf. Turn the heat up until bubbles begin to appear around the edges of the pan and then turn down to a gentle simmer. Cook, covered, for 1½ hours, stirring from time to time.

While the steak and kidney are cooking, make the pastry. Grease a deep pie dish and preheat the oven to gas mark 6 (400°F). Cut a thin strip of pastry and, damping your fingers with a little milk, wet the rim of the pie dish and smooth on the strip of pastry. When the meat is cooked, spoon it with a perforated spoon into the pie dish; you will need a pie funnel or an upturned egg cup in the centre, otherwise the pastry descends into the gravy and goes soggy. Pour in the stock from the cooking after the meat to about halfway up the dish. Cover the pie with pastry, seal the edges, make a steam hole over the opening of the funnel and decorate with any scraps of pastry cut into leaves. Beat the egg and paint (with a pastry brush) over the pastry for a glossy top. Cook for 35 - 40 minutes or until the pastry is cooked. Serve the extra stock as gravy.

Chicken pie

For a chicken pie use the recipe for chicken casserole (see p. 90); strain off the stock, cut the chicken and spoon the chicken and vegetables into a deep dish. Fill halfway up the dish with stock and add ¼ lb. (115 g.) of peas (they can be frozen). Roll out 6 oz. (170 g.) shortcrust pastry (see p. 163). Cut a long thin strip

167

and, with a little milk on your fingers, smooth it on to the rim of the pie dish. Place a pie funnel or egg cup upside down in the centre of the dish and cover the whole thing with pastry. Brush with beaten egg and cook at gas mark 6 (400°F) for 35 minutes.

Blackberry & apple pie

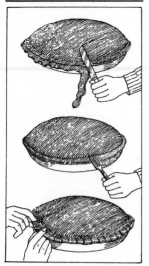

1 lb. (450 g.) blackberries
1 lb. (450 g.) cooking apples
10 oz. (285 g.) sweet or plain shortcrust pastry (see p. 163)
2 tbs. brown sugar
knob of butter to grease the pie dish/drop of oil

Preheat the oven to gas mark 6 (400°F). Wash the blackberries and shake dry. Peel, core and chop the apples. Grease a 1½ pint (860 ml.) pie dish. Make the pastry and cut into two. Roll out one half to cover the inside of the dish but let it overflow the rim, do not trim off. Roll out the other half to cover the top. Fill the pie with the mixed apples and blackberries and place a pie funnel or upturned egg cup in the centre; sprinkle with sugar. Cover the top with pastry and make a steam hole over the funnel or egg cup. Trim and neaten the edges. Cook for 40 minutes at gas mark 6 (400°F) and then reduce the heat to gas mark 4 (350°F) for 10 minutes. Serve with cream.

Redcurrant & raspberry pie

Follow the directions for blackberry and apple pie, but instead use 1½ lb. (675 g.) redcurrants and 1 lb. (450 g.) raspberries. Rinse the raspberries and pull the stalks off the redcurrants before adding to the pie with a shake of brown sugar. Cook for 45 minutes at gas mark 6 (400°F).

Gougère

This is a simple way of making choux pastry. (Choux pastry is the kind éclairs are made of.)

Choux pastry

2 oz. (55 g.) butter
4 oz. (115 g.) plain flour
4 oz. (115 g.) grated cheese
¼ pint (145 ml.) water
3 eggs

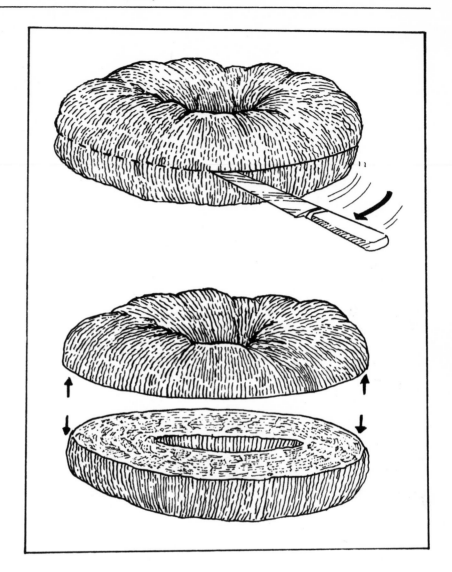

Filling
1 lb. (450 g.) leeks
½ lb. (225 g.) potatoes
3 oz. (85 g.) grated cheese
¼ tsp. cumin seeds
salt and pepper
½ oz. (15 g.) butter

Preheat the oven to gas mark 6 (400°F). Heat the butter and water together in a saucepan to boiling. Take off the heat and stir in the flour. With a wooden spoon beat the flour, water and butter together until the mixture leaves the sides of the pan and forms a ball. Let stand until cool and then slowly beat in the beaten eggs

169

until the mixture is completely smooth. Grease a baking tray with a little butter and form a ring with the pastry mix. Sprinkle with the cheese and bake for 50 minutes. The pastry will puff up and expand enormously — it is really quite exciting and looks very impressive. Split open and fill.

Filling
Scrub the potatoes and cut into quarters, put into cold salted water and bring to the boil. Turn down to simmer. Cut the leeks into rings and wash thoroughly. Add to the potatoes as they are cooking for the last 10 minutes. Drain and mash together in a basin with the butter, cheese, cumin seeds, salt and pepper. Fill the inside of the pastry ring and serve.

Variations
Use any of the fillings for pancakes (see p. 126)

Eclairs

The same choux pastry mix is used for eclairs. Use the same amounts, but spoon on to a greased baking sheet in long sausage éclair shapes. Cook at gas mark 6 (400°F) for 45 minutes.

Chocolate topping
1 x 8 oz. (225 g.) of plain chocolate

Fill a small saucepan a quarter full with water. Break the chocolate into squares and place in a small heatproof bowl inside the saucepan. Heat the water to a gentle boil and stir the chocolate until it melts. Do not fill the saucepan so full that water leaks over the edge of the bowl into the chocolate. Spoon the melted chocolate onto the tops of the cooked eclairs. Split them open and fill with whipped cream.

SALLY'S FAST CHEESE TREATS

Cheese roll

You don't even have to make the pastry.

4 oz. (115 g.) grated cheese
2 oz. (55 g.) butter
2 eggs
salt and pepper
8 oz. (225 g.) frozen puff pastry
chopped parsley/chives (optional)

Melt the butter in a saucepan. Add the grated cheese and eggs beaten with chopped herbs and salt and pepper. Set aside to cool. Roll out the pastry quite thinly into a large square. Spread the cheese mix in the middle and fold the pastry over and over to make an oblong parcel. Pinch together the three sides. Brush the

top with beaten egg or milk. Bake at the top of the oven at gas
mark 7 (425°F) for 15 minutes until golden brown.

Greek *filo* & spinach pie

1 packet of filo *pastry (available from Greek shops)*
1 lb. (450 g.) spinach/½ lb. (225 g.) frozen spinach
½ lb. (225 g.) Greek feta cheese
olive oil
small chopped onion
½ oz. (15 g.) butter

Wash the spinach carefully. Sauté the chopped onion in a little
butter and add the spinach with the rest of the butter. Cover
tightly and place on a very low heat. Cook until soft. If using
frozen spinach, thaw in a sieve or colander before adding to the
onion. *Filo* comes in large flat sheets which have to be painted
with oil as they are stacked up. Oil a long, oblong baking tray.
The pastry should spread out over the edges of the tray. Paint
6 sheets one by one on one side and place on top of one another.
Spread with the spinach and onion mix. The spinach should be
well drained, not runny. Crumble feta over the spinach. Place
six more oiled sheets of *filo* over the top of the spinach. Pinch
together the top and bottom layers of pastry so you have a neat
package. Bake for half to three quarters of an hour at gas mark 6
(400°F), until the pastry is golden brown and very crisp on top.

Baklava

1 packet of Greek filo *pastry*
½ lb. (225 g.) butter
10 tbs. clear honey
1 lb. (450 g.) shelled nuts — almonds, hazelnuts, walnuts,
  pistachios only

Preheat the oven to gas mark 6 (400°F). Grind the nuts in a coffee
grinder or chop finely with a knife. Melt the butter in a bowl over
a saucepan of water. It should be melted but not at all brown.
Paint a large square baking tin with melted butter. You really do
need a pastry brush for *filo* pastry. The bottom layer of baklava
is nine sheets of *filo* pastry built up one on top of the other each
painted with melted butter. After the bottom nine sheets, pile
all the nuts into a thick layer and then cover with nine more sheets,
painting with melted butter as you go. Make diagonal cuts at 3″
(7 cm.) intervals crisscrossing the top of the pastry and pour the
honey over the whole lot. Bake for 30 - 40 minutes until the pastry
turns a rich golden brown.

CRUMBLE

Is like pastry before any liquid is added and it is rolled out. It is a biscuity topping for fruit pies and, omitting any sugar, for vegetable dishes. Add finely chopped dates, figs or sultanas if you like.

Basic crumble

3 oz. (85 g.) butter or margarine
6 oz. (170 g.) plain/wholemeal flour
¼ tsp. salt

Rub the fat into the flour until it is the consistency of fine breadcrumbs.

Sweet crumble
For cheese crumble mix in 3 oz. (85 g.) finely grated cheese. sugar into the crumble mix.

Cheese crumble
For cheese crumble mix in 3oz (85 g.) finely grated cheese.

Garlic crumble
Mix a finely chopped clove of garlic into the crumble.

Onion crumble
Grate a small onion and mix into the crumble.

Nut crumble
Add 2 tbs. mixed, chopped nuts or sprinkle with 1 tsp. of sesame seeds.

Apple crumble

1½ lb. (675 g.) of cooking apples
2 tbs. of brown sugar or honey
    (If you prefer not to use sugar in cooking the fruit, use eating
        apples instead of cooking apples. They don't need sweetening)
grated lemon rind (optional)
½ pint (287 ml.) water
3 oz. (85 g.) butter or margarine
6 oz. (170 g.) plain flour
3 oz. (85 g.) caster or soft brown sugar
sprinkle of ground ginger (optional)

Peel the apples or not as you please. Core and slice thinly. In a heavy bottomed saucepan heat the apples, water, sugar and lemon rind. Cook slowly covered until the apples are soft (about 15 minutes). Pour into a 2 pint pie dish. Rub the fat into the flour as you would with pastry, until it is the consistency of fine breadcrumbs. Rub in the sugar and ginger. Sprinkle the crumble over the apples. Bake at gas mark 4 (350°F) for 30 - 40 minutes until the top is golden brown.

(handwritten: 1 10/04 TRY AGAIN SERVES 6)

Rhubarb crumble

1½ lb. (675 g.) rhubarb
3 tbs. brown sugar or honey
3 tbs. water
2 tbs. raisins or sultanas
crumble topping (see p. 172)

Cut all the leaves off the rhubarb and wash. Peel off the thick outer skin. You will need to peel away more skin at the base of the stalk, since it thins out towards the leaves. Chop into 2″ (5 cm.) chunks. Put the rhubarb in a thick bottomed large saucepan with the water and honey or sugar and cook over a very low heat, covered, for 10 minutes until the rhubarb is falling into a purée. The length of cooking time depends on the age and thickness of the rhubarb. Make a thick layer of rhubarb in a deep buttered dish and cover with crumble. Cook as above.

Apricot crumble

Soak 8 oz. (225 g.) of dried or wild apricots overnight in 1 pint (575 ml.) water or fruit juice. Cook between two layers of sweet crumble for 30 - 40 minutes.

Pear crumble

Use pears instead of apples or mix the two together. Proceed as above.

Blackberry & apple crumble

Use half blackberries and half apples. Cook the apples first but just rinse the blackberries and stir into the hot apple. Proceed as above.

Gooseberry crumble

Top and tail 1 lb. (450 g.) gooseberries and cook in ¼ pint of water (145 ml.) and 4 tablespoons of honey or raw brown sugar until soft. Proceed as above.

VEGETABLE CRUMBLES

Leek & potato crumble

2 large potatoes
1 lb. (450 g.) leeks
6 oz. (170 g.) grated cheese
½ tsp. cumin seeds
salt, pepper, dry English mustard
1 egg
¼ pint (145 ml.) milk
crumble topping (see p. 172)

Scrub the potatoes, quarter and bring to the boil in salted water. Cook at a bubbling simmer for 10 mins. While the potatoes are cooking, wash and chop the leeks. Add the leeks to the potatoes and continue simmering until they are both cooked. Drain, but keep the cooking water for stock. Set aside to cool. Mix together the milk, egg and grated cheese and season with salt and pepper. Mash together the potatoes and leeks and fold in to the eggs, milk and cheese. Pile into a deep buttered pie dish and cover with a layer of crumble (see p. 172). Shake a few cummin seeds over the crumble. Cook at gas mark 4 (350°F) for 30 - 40 minutes until the top is golden brown.

Tomato, bacon & aubergine crumble

6 oz (170 g.) streaky bacon
1 x 14 oz. (400 g.) tin of tomatoes
1 large onion
2 cloves of garlic
salt and pepper
1 large aubergine
3 tbs. olive oil
crumble topping (see p. 172)

Wipe the aubergines, cut off the stalk and cut into thick slices. Scatter with salt and leave to stand for 1 hour. Rinse and pat dry. Cut into chunks. Peel the onion and slice. Peel and chop the garlic. Cut the bacon into chunks and place in a large frying pan with the olive oil. Heat slowly until the bacon begins to crisp and then add the onions and garlic. Sauté until golden brown and then add the aubergine. When the aubergine begins to colour, pour in the tin of tomatoes and roughly break up the tomatoes in the pan. Bring to the boil and then turn down to a gentle simmer. Cook with a tightly fitting lid until the aubergine is soft. Season with salt and pepper. Stir from time to time and add more water if it gets too dry. Butter a deep pie dish and pour in the tomato and aubergine sauce. Top with a layer of crumble and bake at gas mark 4 (350°F) for 30 - 40 minutes or until the top is brown.

Parsnip, carrots & cauliflower in cheese sauce

1 head of cauliflower
1 large parsnip
2 large carrots
1 large onion
½ oz. (15 g.) wholemeal flour
1 oz. (25 g.) butter
½ pint (290 ml.) milk
salt, pepper and dry English mustard
8 oz. (225 g.) grated cheese

Scrub the parsnip and carrots and cut into chunks. Peel the onion and quarter. Put all three into cold salted water and bring to the boil. Simmer until tender (about 15 minutes). Cut off the stalk and coarser leaves from the cauliflower. Cut into chunks. Cook with the other vegetables for the last 10 minutes. Drain the vegetables, keeping the water for stock or soup. While the vegetables are cooking, melt the butter in a thick bottomed saucepan; when it bubbles, beat in the flour with a wooden spoon. Heat the milk until little bubbles appear around the edge of the pan and then beat into the flour and butter, or use cold milk. Keep stirring until the sauce thickens and then season with salt, pepper and mustard. Simmer for 10 minutes and then stir in the grated cheese. Butter a deep pie dish and mix together the vegetables and cheese sauce. Cover with a layer of crumble and bake at gas mark 4 (350°F) for 30 - 40 minutes.

PUDDINGS

You will also find recipes for puddings in other sections of the book. In eggs: lemon soufflé omelette (p. 120), fritters (p. 124), pancakes (p. 126), apple batter (p. 130), meringues (p. 131), custard (p. 132). In pastry: sweet flans (p. 165), sweet pies (p. 168), eclairs (p. 170), baklava (p. 171), crumbles (p. 172).

Rum & chocolate cake

8 oz. (225 g.) crumbled digestive biscuits
6 oz. (170 g.) finely grated plain chocolate
4/5 tbs. rum or a miniature bottle of rum
3 oz. (85 g.) butter
3 oz. (85 g.) caster sugar
1 egg

Crumble the digestive biscuits (this is easier to do if you put them in a plastic bag and crush with a rolling pin) and sprinkle with the rum. Grate the chocolate with the rough side of a cheese grater. It is much easier to do if you have chilled it in the fridge first. With the back of a wooden spoon, cream together the butter and sugar and beat in the egg. Sprinkle a 7″ (18 cm.) round sponge sandwich tin with a thick layer of grated chocolate and then a thick layer of crumbled digestive biscuit. Spread with the butter, sugar and egg mix and then another layer of biscuit. Top with the remaining chocolate and with clean, dry hands press down hard. Cover tightly with aluminium foil and chill for at least 8 hours, overnight is best. Before serving, run a knife around the edge of the tin and then place the serving plate on top. Turn the whole thing upside down and the cake should fall out of the tin. Tap the tin with your knuckles if it seems reluctant.

Chocolate mousse

4 oz. (115 g.) plain chocolate
1 oz. (25 g.) butter
juice of 1 small tart orange
4 eggs

Break the chocolate into small squares and melt in a bowl sitting in the top of a saucepan of boiling water. Beat with a wooden spoon. Remove from the heat. Separate the egg whites and yolks. Stir the butter thoroughly into the chocolate and then briskly beat in the egg yolks. Stir in the orange juice. Beat the egg whites until they form glossy stiff peaks when the whisk is lifted out. Fold the chocolate into the egg whites gently but thoroughly. Pour into individual serving dishes and chill in the fridge for at least 1 hour before serving. On the other hand, don't leave it too long or it 'separates' and goes liquid at the bottom. Serve with shortbread.

Disgustingly sickly ginger pud

I've tried to keep this out of the book but everybody except me loves it.

1 packet ginger biscuits
1 wine glass full of dry sherry/brandy
½ pint (290 ml.) of single cream

You will need a pretty serving dish for this recipe. Immerse the biscuits in the sherry but do not let them soak or break up. Beat the cream until it thickens slightly. Make layers of the sherry flavoured biscuits and cream, topping with cream. Chill for 1 hour before serving. The longer you leave this pud the more the biscuits disintegrate so if you like mushy puds leave it longer. If you serve it immediately there is a pleasant contrast between the crunchy biscuits and the creamy cream.

Grilled bananas

6 bananas
2 oz. (55 g.) butter
2 tbs. brown sugar
pinch of cinnamon
a very small pinch of nutmeg

Grease an ovenproof dish. Peel the bananas and slice in two lengthways. Line the dish with bananas. Dot with butter and sprinkle with the sugar, cinnamon and nutmeg. Grill for 20 minutes until all the butter and sugar have melted and the bananas are soft (or put in the oven). You can also bake bananas in the oven; leave them in their skins and peel when cooked (about ½ hour).

Lynn's fruit pudding

Peel and chop together about 1½ lb. (675 g.) of mixed fruit. Include apples, pears, bananas, grapes, soft red fruits, pineapple, cherries and any other seasonal fruits. Fill an ovenproof casserole and pour cider over the fruit to just below the surface. Bake, covered, at gas mark 5 (375°F) for 30 minutes until the fruit is soft. Serve with cream or yogurt.

Hasty pudding

2 pints (a generous litre) of milk
2 tbs. butter
5 eggs
1 cup sugar
¾ cup plain flour
pinch of salt
2 drops vanilla essence/pinch of nutmeg

Bring the milk to the boil with the butter. Take off the heat and allow to cool in a pie dish, stirring now and then. While the milk is cooling, beat together in a blender or hand whisk the eggs, sugar, flour and salt. When the milk is cool but not cold, beat the two mixtures together. Pour into a deep ovenproof pie dish and bake at gas mark 5 (375°) for 35 to 40 minutes until it has a pale golden sheen.

Oranges & yogurt

Peel 1 orange for each person and slice through the flesh into fine slivers. Stir into plain yogurt — a small pot for each person — and chill for 1 hour before serving. Other fruits are also good served this way.

Yogurt & honey

This is my favourite way to eat yogurt. Pour plain yogurt into individual small glasses, leaving a space of about 1" (2 cm.) at the top. Chill until set in the fridge. Pour ¼" - ½" (½ - 1 cm.) of clear honey on top of the yogurt and serve. The cold tart yogurt is delicious with the sweet runny honey. You could toast a few chopped hazelnuts and beat them into the yogurt. Simply chop the hazelnuts and toss gently under the grill until they are pale golden brown.

Ice cream with chocolate sauce & almonds

3 oz. (85 g.) vanilla ice cream per person
1 oz. (25 g.) plain chocolate per person
1 tbs. sliced toasted almonds per person

Toss the almonds under the grill to toast. Break the chocolate into squares and melt in a bowl over a pan of boiling water. Place a scoop of ice cream on each plate, pour over a dribble of chocolate and sprinkle with almonds. If you can't be bothered to melt the chocolate, grate it instead, it makes lovely fine curls when grated with a cheese grater. Even simpler, buy a squeezy pack of ready-made chocolate sauce (but don't bother to invite me to dinner).

Summer pudding

2 lb. (1 kilo) mixed soft fruits: raspberries, strawberries redcurrants, blackcurrants, blackberries, loganberries, goose-berries, chopped peaches or apricots
2 oz. (55 g.) sugar
a little water
6 - 10 slices of white, thinly sliced (and preferably stale) bread

You should use at least half red fruits. Clean all the fruit and pick off any stems. Place them in a large saucepan with the sugar and about ¼ pint (145 ml.) or less of water. Stew over a low flame for 5 minutes. If you use gooseberries, start them off first for an extra 5 minutes. While the fruit is cooking, cut the crusts from the bread and line a deep pudding basin so that the bread completely covers the sides and the bottom. Fill with the fruit (which should completely fill the dish) and cover with slices of bread. Place a plate and a heavy weight on the top and chill for 24 hours. Put a plate on top of the basin, and turn upside down. Cut into slices like a cake and serve with cream. All the juice will have been absorbed by the bread, forming a delicious, red pudding.

Bread & butter pudding

10 slices stale brown or white bread
butter
2 oz. (55 g.) granulated sugar
3/4 tbs. raisins

Grease a shallow ovenproof dish. Preheat the oven to gas mark 4 (350°F). Cut the bread, and butter the slices generously. Layer the bread and butter in the dish and sprinkle with raisins. Bake for 20 minutes until pale golden brown.

Apple charlotte

2 Bramley cooking apples
3 oz. (85 g.) granulated sugar
3 oz. (85 g.) butter
6 oz. (170 g.) brown or white breadcrumbs

Preheat the oven to gas mark 6 (400°F). Lightly grease a shallow ovenproof dish. Peel the apples and core. Cut into fine slices. Place a thin layer of apples in the dish and sprinkle heavily with breadcrumbs and sugar. Dot with butter. Repeat until the dish is full, top with breadcrumbs, sugar and knobs of butter. Bake for 30 minutes on the middle shelf of the oven, until the breadcrumbs are brown and crispy.

Steamed sponge pud

Don't be put off, this bears no resemblance to school food. You do need a double boiler to cook it though.

2 oz. (55 g.) butter
2 oz. (55 g.) sugar
2 oz. (55 g.) plain flour
2 tbs. golden syrup
2 tbs. washed sultanas
1 egg

Cream together the butter and sugar and then beat in the egg. Beat in the flour. Stir in the sultanas. Lightly butter a pudding basin and pour in the golden syrup. Pour the sponge mix on top and cover with foil or a plate. Place in the top half of a double boiler and steam gently with the cover on for 1½ hours. To turn it out, put a plate on top of the basin and turn upside down.

For chocolate pudding, add 2 tbs. of drinking chocolate to the mix and omit the sultanas and syrup. Grate a layer of plain chocolate into the pudding basin before the sponge mix.

Lychees & cream

Chill a tin of lychees or 1 lb. (450 g.) of peeled, stoned, fresh lychees for at least 1 hour, before serving with single cream. Chilling lychees really improves their flavour.

Lemon pudding

3 eggs
¾ pint (430 ml.) milk
8 oz. (225 g.) breadcrumbs
1 large lemon
2 oz. (55 g.) sugar

Grate the rind from the lemon and squeeze the juice. Preheat the oven to gas mark 3 (325°F). Separate the whites and egg yolks. Beat the yolks and the milk together — in a blender if you have one. Mix with the breadcrumbs, lemon rind and juice and the sugar. Whip the whites until they form stiff peaks. Fold the whites into the milk mix. Turn into a 2 pint (1 litre) pie dish and bake for 50 minutes.

Trifle

½ pint (290 ml.) double cream
½ pint (290 ml.) custard — made from a packet (you'll need to
  add hot milk)
10 bought Boudoir biscuits/sponge cakes
generous wine glass of dry sherry
1 banana
1 chopped eating apple
4/5 heaped tbs. of tinned raspberries or strawberries
any other fruit that you like chopped into chunks
strawberry jam/or any other

179

Cut the biscuits in half lengthways, spread jam in between the halves, rejoin and then cut into 2" (5 cm.) chunks. Fill the bottom of a serving bowl with the chunks of biscuit. Scatter evenly with the sherry. Layer the fruit on top of the biscuits and pour in 3 tablespoons of the liquid from the tinned fruit. Pour the custard over the fruit. Leave in the fridge for 2 hours until the custard is set. Whip the cream until it is thick and spread in a layer over the custard. Decorate with flaked almonds.

This is a very basic trifle recipe, you can vary it as you wish with different fruits; more, less or no alcohol; real custard, etc., etc. It is ideal for using up leftover sponge cake.

Lemon cheese

You must have a liquidizer for this.

small pot cottage cheese
1 - 2 tbs. caster sugar
2 tbs. yogurt (optional)
1 oz. butter
1 egg yolk
juice and rind of 1 lemon

Grate the rind of the lemon and squeeze out the fruit. Melt the butter. Put all ingredients into a liquidizer and blend; chill until set firm. Serve with nuts or fruit and sweet biscuits. You can vary this recipe by adding cream instead of yogurt, substituting cream cheese, and adding honey.

Petit pot au chocolate

Again, you must have a liquidizer.

½ pint (290 ml.) single cream
1 egg
7 oz. plain chocolate
pinch of salt and a few drops vanilla essence

Heat the cream in a saucepan (do not boil); break up the chocolate and put in liquidizer, add hot cream and blend. Add egg and blend again. Put in the fridge for at least an hour. This is very rich, so serve in tiny pots with sweet biscuits.

Chapter 4

Vegetables

and How to Prepare Them

Artichoke: cut off the stem. Cut off also any dry leaf points (if the artichoke is a bit old. No need to wash since any bugs will be washed out in the boiling water in which you cook them. Cook in boiling water with a squeezed wedge of lemon, a whole split garlic clove, a tablespoon of cooking oil and a generous pinch of salt. Or steam. They are done when you can easily slide the sharp point of a knife into the place where the stem was and the leaves can be pulled off easily. Drain and serve hot or cold. Length of time for cooking depends on the age and size of the artichoke: twenty minutes for a tender young one and about an hour for an older one.

If you are eating them hot, serve with butter: melt 1 oz. (25g.) of butter per artichoke slowly in a heavy bottomed saucepan with a crushed clove of garlic. The way to eat an artichoke, by the way, is to start pulling off the leaves from the outside, working your way into the middle. Dip the bottom of the leaf into the butter, and bite off the fleshy bit. The best part is to come: at the end you find a crown with spikes sticking up all over it; pull all the spikes off, and underneath is the 'heart'.

You can also eat artichokes cold with vinaigrette; if you want to put them in salads, etc., you can use the Italian bottled artichoke hearts.

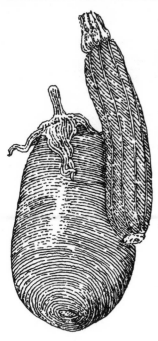

Asparagus: cut off only the bottom inch of the stalk if it is hard and woody. Finely pare away the bottom 2″ - 3″ of outer dry skin on the fatter white asparagus. The asparagus season is so short that it is a shame to waste this exquisite vegetable by eating it as a starter before a main course that will swamp the subtle memory of its flavour. A 1 lb. bunch of asparagus makes a sensual and very adequate meal for 2 served with fresh, warm bread and butter.

Aubergine: cut off the stem. Wipe with a damp cloth. Cut in slices crosswise. For all aubergine recipes except Sugar Daddy salt the aubergine and leave to stand for an hour before rinsing and drying with a paper towel. This makes aubergines less bitter.

Avocado pear: choose a good avocado pear, and there's only one thing that you can do to ruin it and that's swamp it with other flavours. Choosing a good one is another matter altogether. Tell the greengrocer which day you want to eat it and he should be able to pick one that is ripe enough. Check it first before you leave the shop. Hold it gently between your hands. When ripe the flesh should give very slightly under a little even pressure, the black stub of the stalk at the pointed end should be loose and wobbly and the flesh around it really quite soft. Any soft black marks on the skin will probably mean that it is overripe but you may find that these avocados have a better flavour than ones in apparently pristine condition. They are also suitable for mixing chopped into salads but be careful to sprinkle the flesh with a little lemon juice or it will blacken if exposed to the air for even a short time. Cut avocados lengthwise and gently pull the two halves apart, flip out the stone with the point of a knife. They can be served with a variety of fillings in the centre — vinaigrette, mayonnaise, shrimps or tuna, taramasalata, sour cream and chopped herbs, cream cheese; or in long thin slices alternating with cheese or ham or fruit, or chopped and mashed in salads.

Beans: both the green varieties of beans and cooked dried beans are good in salads. Beanshoots are delicious too — but take care when buying that they are crisp and white and pale green. They go brown and slimy very quickly when stored. It is often best to buy them at a Chinese supermarket where the turnover is fairly rapid. They need very little cooking or can be eaten raw.

Bobby beans, or *French beans*: break off ends and leave whole.

Runner beans: top and tail. Run a potato peeler or sharp knife down the edge to remove 'string'. Cut in diagonal slices.

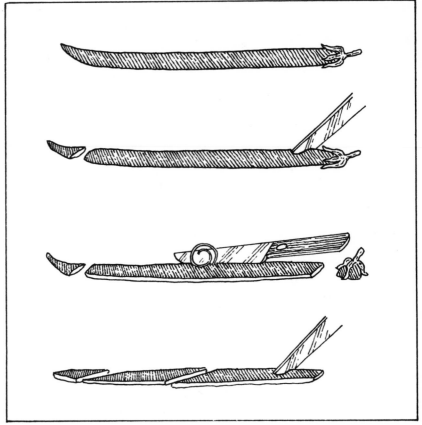

Broad beans: remove beans from pods. If the pods seem very tender and pale green, top and tail and cut as runner beans and cook them with the beans.

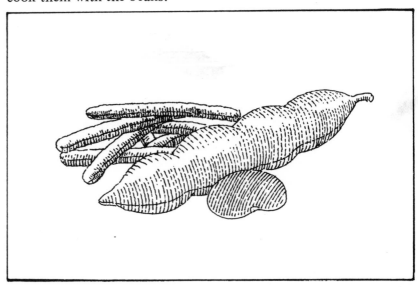

Beet leaves: the green leaves from the tops of fresh beetroot can be washed and served in a mixed green salad.

Beetroot: you can either buy beetroot ready cooked or cook it at home yourself. For ready cooked beetroot remove the skin by gently pushing with the fingertips; it should slide off easily if the beet has been freshly cooked. Pare away the knobbly top with a sharp knife. To cook fresh beetroot first wash away all of the mud from the surface and then cook in lots of boiling salted water. Depending on their size and age they can take from 20 minutes to 2 hours to cook. Do not pierce the skin or the juices will bleed out into the cooking water, leaving a grey and tasteless tuber.

Beetroot in salad tends to turn everything red so it is sometimes better to serve it by itself with a little vinegar or lemon juice and grated onion, or mix it into the salad just before serving. Beetroot is delicious served with a strongly flavoured olive oil, sea salt,

Broccoli: cut off tough ends. Separate into individual stems.

Brussels sprouts: peel off any discoloured outer leaves. Slice off the end. Sprouts are very tightly packed and the inside will cook much slower than the outside unless you cut a cross into the end.

Cabbage: hard white cabbage and red cabbage make good winter salads. They are crisp and tightly packed, unlike the ordinary cabbage. They don't need washing, just peel off the outer leaves until you reach the hard shiny tightly packed ones. Cut in half and chop finely or grate. White and red cabbage do not need to be washed. Serve with apple, onion, pear, dried fruit, beanshoots, cress, tomatoes. A yogurt dressing with caraway seeds would be good. Spring greens, green cabbage: rinse, cut off tough stalk. Slice in ribbons; steam/boil 5 - 10 mins.

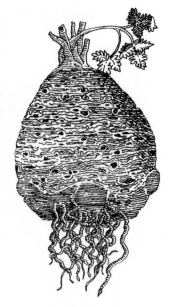

Chinese cabbage: use chopped Chinese cabbage in a salad exactly as you would lettuce. It can also be steamed or stir fried.

Carrot: carrots are an excellent source of Vitamin A. Grate into salads or cut into matchsticks for crudités (see p. 33) or celeriac salad (see p. 20). Carrots can be used as a sweetener to balance bitter vegetables like endive.

Cauliflower: break cauliflower flowerets into salads. Rinse with cold water. Cook whole with head above boiling water.

Celeriac: peel away knobbly skin and cut into matchsticks (see p. 28). Serve with carrots, apples or alone in lemon or vinaigrette dressing, or with mayonnaise.

Celery: separate into sticks. Scrub off any dirt. Leave whole in sticks or cut into smaller pieces. Store in jar or jug full of cold water. Chop across for mixed salads. Dry the leaves in a moderate oven until crisp and store in a screw-top jar to use as seasoning.

Chicory: a slim white tightly packed salad vegetable much resembling an elongated tulip. Each leaf is frilled with pale green. Chicory has a slightly bitter taste in salad so it should be balanced with something sweet like tomatoes, nuts, beetroot or fruit. A cream dressing will have the same effect. It doesn't need washing, simply break off the leaves one by one or cut across.

Corn: strip off the green outside leaves and cook whole in boiling salted water for 7 - 10 minutes. Serve with melted butter or pull off the stem for salads.
   The sweetest corn is usually frozen corn, because the sugary sap that collects in the individual kernels whilst it is still attached to the plant turns to a bland flavoured starch immediately the ear is harvested. Frozen corn is shucked and frozen in the field within half an hour of picking and so less of the flavour has disappeared.

Courgette: cut off the stem and cut in slices crosswise or into matchsticks. Courgettes can be a little bitter if used raw in salad. So first chop in fine slices and dunk in boiling water for 2 - 3 minutes before cooling and adding to salad. (This is called 'blanching'.) Good in combination with chick peas and tomatoes.

Cucumber: some recipes seem to suit unpeeled cucumber better, particularly if you are cutting it into matchsticks to use with a dip; others, like cucumber salad made the French way (see p. 21), are more tasty with the peel removed. To pare away the finest layer use a swivel-bladed potato peeler.

Dandelion leaf: very occasionally available in greengrocers but really something to gather in spring. Stick to those growing in fields and not from roadsides where they are in danger of being polluted by dogs and the fumes from passing cars. Pick only the very young tender leaves. Mix with sorrel leaves if you can find them. Dress with a well flavoured vinaigrette to mask any bitterness. Dandelion is a diuretic and is not called *Pis en Lit* for nothing — so beware. It is also a good source of iron.

Fennel: a fat bulbous version of celery, with a strong flavour of aniseed. The stems are so tightly packed together that it rarely needs more than a wipe over with a damp cloth to clean. Cut in sticks or across. Save the ferny leaves to scatter over the salad, for flavouring dressings or to serve with fish. It will need other equally

185

robust flavours if it is not to overwhelm a salad. Spicy tomatoes, radishes or red and green peppers in a lemon juice and mint dressing would be suitable. Delicious cooked.

Green and red pepper: wipe with a damp cloth. Cut away stem and white pithy ribs inside. Shake out seeds. Any pith left in will taint the flavour of the peppers with a hint of bitterness. Cut in ring or long strips.

Jerusalem artichoke: scrub roughly, cut off any discoloured knobs but do not attempt to peel unless you have hours to spare.

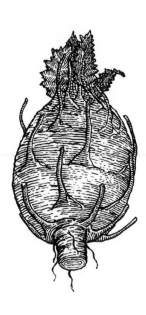

Kohl-rabi: a cabbage flavoured turnip. Wash in cold running water. Dry and cut in strips. Use in small quantities in green salads. Do not peel. Serve cooked and chilled with vinaigrette or mayonnaise.

Leek: If you want to eat the hairy root of the leek it will do you no harm and it tastes good too *but* you will have to scrub it well to remove all the muck. Peel off any slimy or papery outside leaves (it's best to avoid buying leeks like this as they're a bit past it). At the other end the tougher dark green leaves shroud tender paler inner ones so don't just cut off the top and chuck it out. 'Sharpen' it like a pencil point so that only the outside is cut away. Unblemished outer leaves can be kept for stews and soups. There are two ways of cutting leeks:
(i)   Across in circles. This is the easiest for washing. Cut the leeks and put them in a bowl of cold water. Push the circles apart

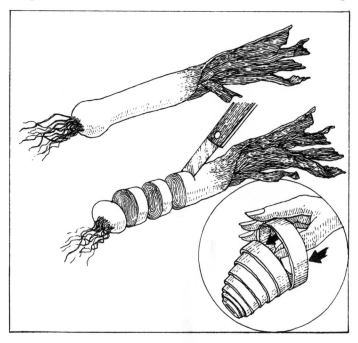

with your thumb so that the water can wash away any fine particles of sand between the leaves. Swish about in the water and leave to stand for a few minutes so that the sand can settle to the bottom of the bowl. Scoop the leeks out into a colander and throw away the water. Don't pour the water through the colander — all the dirt then ends up again on the leeks. Repeat until the water is clear.

(ii) Lengthways. Cut off the root ends and trim back the coarse green tops. Slice lengthways either in halves or in quarters. Cut them in halves crosswise if you are going to lay them in a short dish. Wash by running the cold tap down in between the leaves. Shake off the excess water.

Only cook young, tightly packed leeks whole. Roll them between the fingers like a cigar; if the leaves don't move around loosely they should be fairly clean inside but try running the cold tap down among the leaves and then shaking them hard to dislodge any muck.

You can use leeks either raw or cooked in salad. Raw they should be used with discretion as they can be very hot. Use them where you might use onion or chives. For a cooked leek salad choose only the young, tightly packed, slim leeks. Wash in cold running water and cut off most of the green tops. Cook in boiling water for 15 minutes at most. Allow to cool and serve with a vinaigrette dressing or mixed in a potato salad.

Lettuce: there are lots of different types of lettuce. They all have distinctly different flavours but they're pretty much the same when it comes to cleaning. Only wash lettuce if it looks as if it needs it; it is a pity to drench the inner leaves with water when they have been so carefully protected under layers of outer leaves. Iceberg or Webb's wonder lettuces hardly ever need washing beyond the first few outer leaves. For lettuce that does need washing, break off individual leaves and wash under a gently tunning cold water tap. Dry by shaking in a salad shaker or gathering up in a dry tea-towel unless you are lucky enough to possess a salad spin dryer. These absurd machines seem the epitome of decadence, but are in fact wonderfully efficient. They dry the lettuce by spinning it in a perforated basket inside a closed bowl and they *do* dry it perfectly without breaking of bruising the leaves. Never cut lettuce with a knife, tear it with your fingers.

Types
Leaf lettuce: the most common lettuce in our shops, often the cheapest and frequently the most tasteless. What little flavour there is can be drowned in too much washing water. So, wash sparingly and dry well. Crisp in the fridge before serving. Flavour much enhanced by a a garlicky vinaigrette.

Cos lettuce: long, fleshy, resilient leaves with a strong sweetish flavour. Keeps fresh longer than most. Good for serving whole leaves to scoop up mushy dips like taramasalata or houmous.
Webb's wonder and Iceberg: hard, crisp, crunchy lettuces. Very pale green in colour and a little watery in texture. Can sometimes be rather bland but at best are sweet and delicious. Chill before serving.
Cabbage lettuce: large, firm, round, hearty, apple green lettuce. Mild flavour, soft leaves.
Curly endive: exquisite to look at and rather bitter to taste. A feathery, wiry, sharp green plant. Use in moderation in a mixed salad with a sweetish or mustardy dressing.
Broad leaved endive or escarole/batavia: similar in flavour to the curly version but with small broad flat leaves.
Red lettuce: a sweet crispy broad leaved lettuce with red fringes to the leaves; it is not seen a great deal in this country which is a pity because it is very good.
Radiccio: not a true lettuce, a broad leaved red and white head of slightly bitter-sweet leaves with a long root.

Mangetout peas: top and tail and leave whole.

Marrow: cut off stem. Peel or not according to recipe. If unpeeled, rinse before cooking. Remove seeds. Don't overcook.

Mushrooms: wipe with a damp cloth. Cut off hard base of stem. Use sliced in mixed salads or in a yogurt dressing, whole in crudités.

Mustard greens: are hot and peppery. Wash under running water, pat dry and use in small quantities.

Nasturtium leaf: peppery taste, use in moderation in salads.

Okra: has a tendency to go unpleasantly slimy when it is cooked alone; if you don't fancy that, it is best used in stews, soups and curries, in the same way as any other vegetable — its gelatinous qualities help to thicken the liquid.

If you want to use it as a vegetable on its own, you can try boiling or steaming it first and then tossing for 10-15 minutes under a high grill. This gives a slightly barbecued flavour which is rather pleasant. Alternatively bake it in a shallow dish with lots of butter for about 20 minutes, at gas mark 5 (375°F).

Onion: an invaluable addition to salads both for its taste and as a protection against colds and heart disease. Unless you have a strong and imperturbable digestion it is probably best to serve the milder varieties raw in salads — spring onions, sweet red onions, Spanish onions and chives. Spring onions: cut off the hairy root end and, unless it is unblemished, peel off the top layer of skin. Cut off the very coarse green tips although they can be used in cooking or finely chopped as a substitute for chives. Cut in rings or serve whole. Sweet red onions and Spanish onions should be peeled whole and cut in fine circles. Soak in yogurt or vinaigrette for a milder flavour. Shallots are the small onions with dark red skins, much prized by those who like French cooking. With their sharp, sweet flavour, they are suitable for sauces and dishes where you need an onion flavour without bulk. Spring onions are mostly used in salads; buy carefully, they should be clean, crisp and firm. Kept too long, like all onions, they go soft and slimy and the flavour changes for the worse.

How to chop an onion (or clove of garlic): cut the onion in half and peel back the skin. Do not cut off the roots, they're the bit that makes your eyes water. Place the cut side flat on a chopping board and cut long slices through the onion (not through the root but from the root to the tip). Cut across the other way in slices.

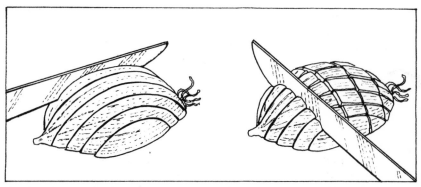

Garlic: the method is the same. Peel the papery skin off the garlic. With a very sharp knife cut through from root to tip leaving the segments joined at the root. Finely chop across.

Parsley: rinse very thoroughly under cold running water; it can be full of sand. Cut off stem and chop or cut into sprigs.

Parsnip: a root vegetable with a sweet flavour. Peel or not as you wish and cut lengthways. The core is tough in large old ones, and is best removed.

Peas: as with corn, frozen peas are usually better than those you buy in shops.

Potato: can be boiled, baked, fried, roasted or steamed; eaten hot or cold peeled or unpeeled, but never raw.

Radish: cut off leaves and wispy roots. Wash in cold water. Cut a cross deep into each one and chill in a bowl of cold water in the fridge for an hour before serving. Serve in salads or with salami, French bread and unsalted butter as a starter.

Salsify: the young green leaves can be used in salad. Scrape and boil for 20 minutes in lightly salted boiling water with a squeeze of lemon juice. Slice, chill and serve with vinaigrette dressing. Or serve hot.

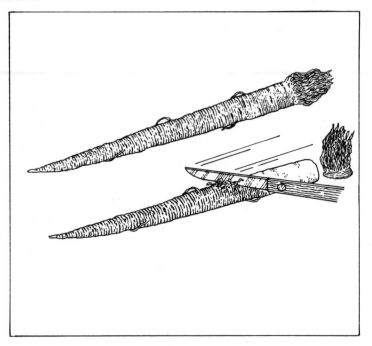

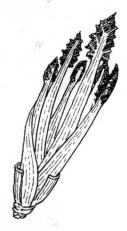

Seakale: wash under cold running water. Cut off tough stems. Tear into large chunks.

Spinach: to wash, fill a washing-up bowl with cold water. Throw in the spinach. Shake the leaves around in the water and, this is the tedious bit, take out each leaf one by one and break off the last couple of inches of stem, rip away any discoloured or slimy bits, chuck out the odd weed. When you've done all of this you'll see a lot of mud and sand and bits of rubbish have sunk to the bottom of the bowl; throw this lot out, rinse the bowl and repeat the whole process at least twice more until the water is completely clear. It's boring, but it's worth it — fresh spinach is wonderful. Half the battle is in buying clean, fresh-looking spinach from the green-grocers. If it look exhausted and full of scraps and yellow leaves don't bother with it. Leave whole for cooking — chop or puree afterwards. Frozen spinach is a poor substitute for fresh. The leaf variety is best.

190